J. Mendes (Jacob Mendes) De Solla

The Jewish Student's Companion

First Part: Post Biblical History. Second Part: Explanation of Mosaic Commands

J. Mendes (Jacob Mendes) De Solla

The Jewish Student's Companion
First Part: Post Biblical History. Second Part: Explanation of Mosaic Commands

ISBN/EAN: 9783337030926

Printed in Europe, USA, Canada, Australia, Japan

Cover: Foto ©ninafisch / pixelio.de

More available books at **www.hansebooks.com**

Student's Companion.

FIRST PART:

Post Biblical History.

SECOND PART:

Explanation of Mosaic Commands.

BY

J. MENDES DE SOLLA, DR. TH.

NEW YORK:
HEBREW BOOK UNION.
1880.

[ALL RIGHTS RESERVED.]

PREFACE.

The author of Ecclesiastes, already in his time, when no printing and little writing was known, observed that "there is no end to the making of many books." It is no wonder, therefore, that in our days, when book-making has become so universal, any new production issued from the press is apt to be received with the remark that we have already too many books. But though the Preacher was gifted with wisdom, more than all his contemporaries, knowledge was very limited then, and no intelligent person will deny that with the general spread of learning the demand for new books must keep pace. The method of imparting knowledge is from time to time changed, and we believe improved, and new mediums of instruction to correspond with the new methods are naturally required. The author of this volume, therefore, deems it unnecessary to say anything further by way of apology for the appearance of this new production of his labors, feeling as he does the earnest conviction that a book such as he now ventures to lay before the public is much needed to aid our scholars in the study of History and Theology.

As to the first part, it is certainly desirable that every Jew should have at least a superficial knowledge of the history of his nation; that he should have vividly before him at least the principal links in the long chain of events since the exodus from Egypt, down to our own days. As not every one can devote sufficient time to the regular study of history, this SYNOPSIS may prove both instructive and pleasant to the earnest inquirer who desires to refresh his memory, or acquire some new information.

Our national history is a subject of honest pride to us; the study of it is calculated to inspire us with courage and fortitude in persevering in our efforts to uphold the proud name of our ancestral nobility; a nobility not resting on vain aristocracy or empty titles, but on the sterling qualities of endurance for the sake of principle; of sacrificing worldly interest to the conviction of doing right; of struggling and persevering on the path of duty, when deviating from the same would bring honor, fame, and wealth. And it is our post-biblical history especially—I might say exclusively—which tends to inspire us with these exalted sentiments; it is the history of our martyrdom through many ages, not of the time "when Israel dwelt safely every man under his vine and under his fig-tree," which teaches us what man is capable of enduring and accomplishing, if he has the will and the firmness to walk steadily on the right course. That great lesson our rising generation stands much in need of learning, and that this humble production may serve as a step towards promoting this end is the writer's earnest desire.

The second part of this book is of still greater importance, inasmuch as it concerns the practical part of our religion. History is a great teacher of morals, but we may learn ethics likewise from various other sources. A direct and positive information, however, of what we ought to do or abstain from doing, and the reasons why we should do this and avoid doing that, is of far more urgent necessity, particularly to the young. In the present enlightened age, we cannot satisfy ourselves with the specious reasoning that we do such or so because we were told to do so by those wiser and better than ourselves; that we saw our fathers do so before us, and that we cannot be wrong in following in their steps. (We want a reason, and a valid reason, for what we are required to do;) and unless our religious performances are based on the consciousness that we are doing what is right and useful, such performances are vain and valueless. The second part of this book, then, is intended to give an insight, at least, into the general intention and tendency of the Mosaic Laws, in accordance with the views of the great Maimonides, as laid down in his Moreh Nebuchim, (and to explain such laws especially as appear to us incomprehensible because not reconcilable with our present mode of thinking.) In order, therefore, that those who continue, as far as practicable, the strict observance of the Mosáic laws, may be better informed as to the origin of these institutions; (and that those who do not adhere to them as a whole may know the reasons why some are retained and others discarded,) it is important for both to be enlightened in regard to that which constitutes the basis of their faith and their acts of devotion. This information the second part of the book is intended, in a measure, to supply.

That, in the compilation of this book, I have made use of various works in English and other languages need not be said, for no writer of history can give his readers but what he finds in the works of his predecessors; but I here candidly state that I have not hesitated, in many instances, to copy, *nearly verbatim*, or to translate from other works even to the extent of whole paragraphs. My reason for not always crediting the author I copied or translated is, that I have in most cases abbreviated, added, or changed, and to particularize each line or phrase, mixed up as it is with my own words, would produce such a confusion of inverted commas, spaces, and dottings, as to disfigure the typographical appearance of the book, and be a source of annoyance to the reader. I have done as Molière said: "Je prends mon bien où je le trouve." I make this general statement to exculpate myself of the crime of plagiarism.

J. M. DE SOLLA, DR.TH.

CURACAO, W. I., August, 1879.

FIRST PART.

A SYNOPSIS OF
Post-Biblical Jewish History.

TABLE OF CONTENTS.

FIRST PERIOD.

	PAGE
The nation divided into two kingdoms,	1
Termination of the kingdoms of Israel and of Judah,	2
Jews in Babylon. Rebuilding of the Temple. Ezra and Nehemiah,	3
The Samaritan and the Egyptian Temples. Jews at Alexandria,	5
Jews under Persian and Grecian Rule. The Maccabees,	7
The Sadducees, Essenes, Pharisees, and Karaites,	8
The Asmonean dynasty,	10
Pompey's attack on the Temple. Jews in contact with Romans and Idumeans,	11
Herod as Governor. The last of the Asmoneans,	12
Herod's reign,	13
Herod's reign, continued. His end,	16
Archelaus,	18
Judea a Roman Province. The Sanhedrin,	19
Agrippa I. Queen Helena,	20
Caligula's reign. Massacre at Alexandria,	21
Troubles in Babylon. Assinai and Anilai,	23
Agrippa II. The Zealots. Internal disturbances,	25
Revolt of the Jews against Rome. Cestius defeated,	27
Vespasian sent to subdue the Judeans. Galilee conquered,	28
Titus' advance on Jerusalem. Description of the city and Temple,	30
The attack on Jerusalem. Horrible scenes in the city. Final destruction,	33
Biography of Philo and Josephus,	36

SECOND PERIOD.

	PAGE
Revival of the Jews under rabbinical authority. They revolt again, and are subdued by Hadrian,	39
Barcochab's Messiahship,	41
The Patriarchate. The Mishnah,	42
Constantine adopts Christianity,	43
Origin of the Talmud,	44
The reign of Justinian. Taking of Jerusalem by Chosroes. Jews controlling the slave-trade,	45
The rule of Mohammed. Influence of Islamism upon the Jews,	47
The kingdom of Khozar,	49
Dominion of the Patriarch of the West, and the Prince of the Captivity,	50
The Jews in Spain. Moses in sackcloth,	52
Spanish Jewish scholars and statesmen,	54
Aben Ezra and Maimonides,	59
Jews in Arabia, India, and China,	63
Jews in Africa,	65
Jews in Italy,	70
Jews in France,	72
Jews in Germany,	77
The Crusades,	84
Jews in England. Jewish wealth and usury,	89
The Inquisition,	96
New settlements of the Spanish Exiles.	103

THIRD PERIOD.

The Reformation,	106
Jews in the Sclavonian Countries,	110
Shabbetai Zebi and Joseph Frank,	115
Jews in the Netherlands,	118
Eminent scholars of Holland,	126
Re-establishment of Jews in England,	133
Jews in France and Italy, after the middle-ages,	137
Jews in the East. The Damascus blood-accusations,	146
Jews in Germany, Austria, and the Sclavonian countries in the latter ages,	150
Moses Mendelssohn and his cotemporaries. Modern Jewish Reform,	156
Jews in America,	165

SYNOPSIS

OF

POST-BIBLICAL JEWISH HISTORY.

FIRST PERIOD.

FROM THE TERMINATION OF THE KINGDOM OF ISRAEL TO THE DESTRUCTION OF THE SECOND TEMPLE.

THE NATION DIVIDED INTO TWO KINGDOMS.

The object of this book being to teach the post-biblical history of our nation, it might be thought unnecessary to repeat anything stated in the Bible. But as some of my young readers may not have the later events recounted in the sacred book clearly before their mind, I shall begin by holding up before them a few of the principal points of our biblical history, and by so doing form a link between the biblical and post-biblical.

They will remember perhaps that, after the death of Solomon, the Jewish nation was divided into two separate kingdoms, under different rulers; one part being called the kingdom of Judah, under Rehoboam, and the other the kingdom of Israel, under Jeroboam. The kingdom of Rehoboam consisted of the two tribes of Judah and Benjamin, and they held Jerusalem as their capital; while Jeroboam ruled over the remaining ten tribes, whose capital was first at Shechem, but finally and permanently Samaria.

Counting from the revolt of the ten tribes against Rehoboam, there had been nineteen kings over the people of Judah, besides queen Athalia; and nineteen kings over the people of Israel. Most of the rulers of both kingdoms were bad, and some extremely wicked; yet among the kings of Judah there were more God-fearing men than among the others, and therefore the kingdom of Judah lasted longer than that of Israel.

Termination of the Kingdoms of Israel and Judah.

Now the termination of the kingdom of Israel happened in this way. When Hosea, who was the last king of that portion of Israel, had ruled about six years, Shalmaneser, king of Assyria, declared war against him, and made him his tributary. They then remained in peace for some time; but Hosea would not quietly submit to the rule of another king over him, and formed a conspiracy against his superior; whereupon Shalmaneser rose against Samaria, and held it in siege for three years, and in the ninth year of Hosea's reign took possession of the country, made Hosea a prisoner, and carried the Israelites as captives to a distant part of his dominions; and this put an end to the kingdom of Israel which had lasted 215 years. This portion of the descendants of Abraham are known by the name of the Lost Ten Tribes.

The kingdom of Judah still continued for about one hundred and thirty years after the independence of the ten tribes had ceased, but they were frequently harassed by the surrounding powers. Jehoahaz, one of their kings, was defeated by an Egyptian king, and carried captive to Babylon, where he died. Then his brother Jehoiakim was appointed in his stead, but held tributary to the king of Egypt. Shortly afterwards, Nebuchadnezzar sent an army to invade Judea, took Jerusalem, put Jehoiakim in chains, and led a great many Israelites to Babylon, and from that time we begin to count the Babylonian captivity. A small portion of the Jews remained yet in Palestine and held possession of the Temple, and Jehoiachin, son of Jehoiakim, was appointed to rule instead of his father. Scarcely, however, had he reigned three months when Nebuchadezzar himself, at the head of his army, took possession of Jerusalem, plundered the Temple of all the golden vessels which Solomon had made, and led the king Jehoiachin to Babylon, where he remained in prison for thirty-seven years.

The final doom of Judah was now fast approaching. Zedekiah, who was its last king, had made a treaty with Nebuchadnezzar to be subject to his rule, but in the ninth year of his reign he entered into a league with the king of Egypt and revolted against his superior. Now came a third invasion of Jerusalem by the Chaldeans, who held it in siege for eighteen months; and in the eleventh year of Zedekiah, on the 10th of Tebet 3338 A.M., Nebuchadnezzar took Jerusalem by storm, and on the ninth of Ab of the same year, the first Temple, which had stood about four hundred years, was totally destroyed, and Zedekiah brought in chains to Babylonia, where he remained in prison till he died. Thus Judah was driven away out of their land, 860 years after they had been put in possession of it by Joshua.

JEWS IN BABYLON. REBUILDING OF THE TEMPLE. EZRA AND NEHEMIAH.

The Jews in Babylonia were not ill-treated, however; they were treated with kindness, were allowed to hold property, and some were even appointed to posts of honor and responsibility; but they were not contented; their greatest longing was to return to their native land. They were, after all, but captives, and often they sat by the river-side to weep and mourn the loss of their beloved country, of their cherished freedom. In this condition they continued some fifty years. It was then that Cyrus, king of Persia and

Media, conquered Babylonia, and the Jews became tributary to the Persian kingdom. We must bear in mind that the Jews here spoken of were those only who had constituted the kingdom of Judah, and which still formed an integer, to the exclusion of those of the kingdom of Israel, which had been dispersed by Shalmaneser. The former now assumed the name of Jews (Jehudim) after their patriarch Judah, and were thenceforth so designated.

Cyrus, the new king, was friendly to the Jews. Daniel, the exemplary youth who so nobly maintained his religious principles, even in opposition to the decrees of his mighty master Nebuchadnezzar, and refused to bow to the idol the latter had erected, had grown old under the reign of the Persian kings and risen to great dignity and power; and it is quite probable that through his influence the welcome edict was issued by Cyrus that the Hebrews might return to their own land. He not only gave them permission to go back and rebuild the Temple, he gave them back all the gold and silver vessels, 5400 in number, which Nebuchadnezzar had carried away; and under the leadership of their chieftain Zerubbabel, some 42,000 Jews, with their families and servants—only a portion of those that inhabited Babylonia—went forth joyful and hopeful, returning to their dear native land. They at once set about erecting an altar for the regular sacrifices, and the families went each to look after their landed property, the inheritance from which they had been driven.

But the Jews did not succeed in rebuilding their Temple without delay. The Samaritans, being jealous of the prosperity of the Jews, spoke evil against them, and the rebuilding of the Temple was interrupted. These Samaritans were a people of mixed races, being partly of Jewish and partly of heathen descent; and so was their religion a mixture of Jewish and heathen practices. They had adopted the books of Moses as the guide of religion, and now desired to join the genuine Jews in the erection of their new Temple; but the latter rejected them disdainfully and would have nothing to do with them. Hereupon the Samaritans did all in their power to oppose the Jews; they sent a letter to the king who had succeeded Cyrus, stating that it was dangerous to the Persian kingdom to let the Jews rise to power again; and thereupon the Jews were ordered to discontinue their building. Fifteen years later, however, under the reign of Darius II., the new Temple was finished and dedicated.

During the long reign of Darius, the Jews enjoyed peace and prosperity. He was succeeded by Xerxes I., and it is supposed that this was the Ahasuerus mentioned in the Bible, with whom happened the memorable event in the history of Mordecai and Esther with which I suppose you are all acquainted. In the reign of the succeeding monarch happened the immigration to Jerusalem of many more Jews under Ezra, the great scribe, who afterwards gathered up and wrote down the various books of the Bible; subsequently Nehemiah exerted himself to re-establish the observance of the law among his people, and to rebuild and fortify the city of Jerusalem; and both of these men were zealous workers and faithful leaders; the history of whose life and action you find fully described in the Scriptures.

THE SAMARITAN AND THE EGYPTIAN TEMPLES. JEWS AT ALEXANDRIA.

Now you must know that, besides two temples which the Jews built at Jerusalem, there were two others dedicated to the worship of Jehovah. Manasseh, the son of a high-priest, having married the daughter of Samballat, a leader of the Samaritans, was expelled from among his people. Thereupon Samballat assembled his people and induced them to build a rival temple on mount Gerizim, not far from Jerusalem, which still deepened the hatred already existing between the two parties. This temple stood two hundred years, and was destroyed by Hyrcanus I., a priest of the Asmonean family, of which we will speak more fully hereafter. Another temple was established in Alexandria, where a great many Jews (some 30,000 families) had settled under the Ptolemies. Onias, a genuine Jewish priest, having been much in favor with Ptolemy Philometer and queen Cleopatra, obtained from the king an abandoned and half-ruined Egyptian temple which he transformed into a Jewish place of worship, and where divine service was performed as at Jerusalem. This temple remained till the time of Vespasian, the Roman conqueror (66 C.E.).

Alexandria being then the retreat of Grecian learning, the Jews turned their attention to general literature and philosophy. It is said that the celebrated Greek translation of the Scriptures, called the Septuagint, was made or at least begun at that period; that seventy-two Jewish translators were, for that purpose, shut up in separate rooms by order of Ptolemy Philadelphus, where each of them completed the new version; and that, by way of a miracle, the translations were all found to agree word for word. There is, however, no good authority for this statement, and it may be regarded as a groundless tradition, a mere matter of fiction. The Alexandrian Jews, though frequently annoyed by both the native Egyptians and the Greeks, and rebuked even by their own brethren for adopting the Greek language and literature, mingled nevertheless in all national transactions, and obtained the highest honors of the state. Onias, who built the temple, filled the most eminent offices in the state and in the army; and at a later period we find Chelcias and Ananias, two Jews, commanding the armies of Cleopatra.

Jews under Persian and Grecian Rule. The Maccabees.

Returning to Palestine, we find that the Jews for a long time enjoyed perfect peace under the administration of their high-priests and local governors, until the time of Alexander the Great. When this monarch became the conqueror and ruler of Persia, he brought Judea' also under the rule of his sceptre, but it does not appear that the Jews suffered materially from this change of government. After the death of Alexander, the eastern world was frequently agitated by cruel wars, and Judea, in its turn, was more than once attacked and conquered, again released, and again subjected by Egyptian and by Syro-Grecian rulers, while at the same time internal strife and division among the Jews themselves increased the misfortunes brought on them by foreign tyranny, and eventually led to the plunder and ruin of the holy city and almost to the complete extermination of the Jewish people. The different sects denominated Pharisees, Sadducees, and Essenes had sprung into existence by that time, and constituted the different factions of the nation. It was now about two hundred years since the erection of the second Temple. Antiochos Epiphanes had ascended the throne, and the Jews were his subjects. He determined to exterminate the Jewish religion and substitute instead that of the Greeks. He made a violent attempt to execute his purpose; marched against Jerusalem, took possession of the Temple, slaughtered many Jews and sold many more as slaves. At that time arose the heroic family of the Asmoneans who, with the small forces under their command, repelled the mighty Antiochos, and regained their independence and the possession of their city and Temple. This is the history of the Maccabees which gave rise to the feast of Hannucah, the same which you hear recited every year and is therefore unnecessary to be repeated here at length.

THE SADDUCEES, ESSENES, PHARISEES, AND KARAITES.

We have spoken in the preceding paragraph of the different sects among the Jews. Now, before proceeding with the narrative of our history, I will inform you of the origin and opinions of these respective sects. Three classes chiefly are to be distinguished; the Sadducees, the Essenes, and the Pharisees; and likewise the sect of Karaites may be mentioned here, which, though it made no figure in history till a later period, is to be considered as a branch of the Sadducean school. The Sadducean sect is generally believed to have originated with Zadok, one of the disciples of Antigonos of Socho, president of the Sanhedrin, who lived about 250 years before the common era. The principles of that sect were, a firm belief in the divine origin of the Bible, but a total rejection of the Oral law and rabbinical tradiions. They denied the immortality of the soul, a future recompense, the resurrection of the body, and the existtence of angels. This sect was never very numerous, but its adherents were of the highest and most literary classes. The origin of the Essenes is still more doubtful. Some suppose it to have begun at the time of Samuel the prophet; others, with more probability of correctness, believe that this sect originated among the Hellenists, that is, Jews who long dwelt among the Greeks, adopted the Greek language, and having studied the philosophy of Pythagoras and Plato, amalgamated the same with the doctrines of the Mosaic books. The Essenes were much given to a secluded mode of life, to study and contemplation; and their doctrines were much involved in secrecy. This much, however, is known, they held adoration of God and benevolence to mankind to constitute the essence of religion. They believed in the validity of the Mosaic laws, not so as to be bound to a literal observance, but adopting the spirit of them. One of their principles was that God can be worshiped only in spirit, through inward virtue; they therefore rejected sacrifices and all ceremonies, even those of the Mosaic code. They believed in immortality, in hell and paradise. They despised riches, and lived in a state of communism. We find accounts of them down to the time of Justinian and no further. The Pharisees were the strict adherents to the rabbinical laws and traditions, believing that these oral laws were of divine origin, having been verbally imparted by God to Moses, and transmitted to posterity. They believed in the immortality of the soul, in future reward and punishment, and the resurrection of the body, which latter doctrine they seem to have mixed up with ideas of the transmigration of souls, that is, that after man's death the soul passes into another body, which was the doctrine of Pythagoras. The Pharisees appear to have at all times constituted the majority of the nation. The sect of Karaites appears to have assumed its distinct form about the time of Hyrcanus I., or shortly before it. They agree with the Sadducees on the point of rejecting the authority of the oral laws, and on that account the Rabbinists have placed them on an equality and under the same denomination with the Sadducees; but the Karaites emphatically disclaim the similarity, as they firmly believe in immortality, in future retribution, in resurrection and restoration of the Jews under the Messiah. About the beginning of the eighth century, Karaism revived under the leadership of R. Anan and his son Saul, who are considered the founders of modern Karaism, and since that time down to the present it has been a confirmed sect in many parts of the world. Karaite congregations are yet existing in many towns in the East, in Austrian Galicia, and in the Crimea. They are especially noted for their frugality, industry, and integrity, and the sect has produced many men of profound scholarship.

The Asmonean Dynasty.

Resuming now the thread of our history, we begin with the condition of the Jews during the reign of the Asmoneans. Since the time of the first Temple, when Zedekiah, the last king of Judah, was dethroned and imprisoned, the Jews had had no king. They were since governed by their high-priests, who did not assume the royal title or dignity. Jonathan, son of Mattathias and brother of the valiant Judas the Maccabee, appears to have been the first who united in himself not only the functions, but also the titles of king and high-priest, and with him commenced the reign of the Asmonean princes. His brother and successor Simon re-established the independence of his nation from the Syrian sceptre; negotiated for a cessation of the taxes to which they had been subject, and peace and tranquillity reigned for a few years among the nation. It was in the reign of Simon also that the first Jewish coin, the shekel and its smaller denominations, were struck. Judas, in his time, had already made a treaty of alliance with the Romans, and this treaty was ratified or renewed by Simon, and thus the Jews began to intermix with the Romans. Simon was assassinated by his son-in-law Ptolemy. (None of these noble Asmonean brothers had been allowed a peaceful end; they all died as martyrs for the independence and glory of their people.) After the death of Simon, his son John Hyrcanus, then Aristobulus, then Alexander Janneus, then the latter's widow Salome Alexandra, and after her the rival brothers Hyrcanus II. and Aristobulus, were the successive rulers of the nation. These two brothers were for some time contending for the occupancy of the throne which rightfully belonged to Hyrcanus, the elder of the two. But the younger was of a bold and restless disposition, and having by his daring enterprises gained the affections of the people, the milder Hyrcanus at length yielded the sovereignty to his ambitious brother, retaining for himself but the high-priesthood.

POMPEY'S ATTACK ON THE TEMPLE. JEWS IN CONTACT WITH ROMANS AND IDUMEANS.

Hyrcanus I. had subjected Idumea, a country bordering on the south of Palestine, and forced its inhabitants to embrace Judaism. These Idumeans became afterwards a source of great misfortune to the Israelites; one of them, Antipater, whose father had held the position of governor of Idumea, acquired great influence over the feeble minded Hyrcanus, who was instigated by his crafty advisers to renew the strife with his brother for possessing the throne. Both gathered a number of followers and an animated struggle ensued. At this juncture an outsider interfered to settle the difference. This arbitrator was the Roman warrior Pompey. At first he put on the appearance of impartiality, listened to the complaints of the parties, and put off his decision for a next meeting. In the mean time Pompey attended to his more important business, namely, that of conquering Arabia; and after having subjected many of the Asiatic powers, marched upon Judea for the purpose of subjugating it to the Roman rule. The weak Hyrcanus and his party yielded at once, but Aristobulus resisted. The troops of the latter posted themselves in the Temple and held it against the enemy for three months. The Temple being on a hill, was an almost impregnable stronghold, and was lost only through an over-scrupulous observance of the Sabbath, the Jews believing it to be a desecration of the day to carry on war, except it be absolute self-defense; and the enemy, taking advantage of this circumstance, found an opportunity of storming the Temple on that day without meeting with any resistance.

Pompey showed himself a generous enemy. On entering the Temple, he was exceedingly surprised to find that it was not like other temples, filled with statues or symbols of the Deity. The numerous golden vessels, and the large amount of treasure he found, next excited his wonder; but he left it all untouched, and ordered his soldiers to vacate the Temple.

He appointed Hyrcanus as high-priest, but without the royal title, and exacted no more than an annual tax from the country, while Aristobulus with his sons and daughters were carried to Rome as prisoners. Hyrcanus being deprived of royal power, the Idumean Antipater was appointed governor, and Judea virtually, though not nominally, became a Roman dependency. The Jews now became gradually more and more intermixed with the Roman people. Besides those who had been carried thither as captives, others voluntarily settled there, and these really formed a community of their own, and were recognized as Roman citizens. Antipater, though a Jew by name, had not the interests of the nation at heart, and sought to gain power by ingratiating himself with Cæsar, whom he rendered material service, supplying him with troops and taking up the sword in his defense. He was consequently rewarded by receiving from Cæsar the right of Roman citizenship and the appointment of procurator over the whole of Judea. The cunning Idumean governor found his influence and power daily increasing, and the object he now aimed at was to overthrow the Asmonean dynasty, and substitute that of his own family. For this purpose he appointed his eldest son Phasael to the government of Jerusalem, and his younger, Herod, to that of Galilee, the northern province of Palestine.

Herod as Governor. The last of the Asmoneans.

This appointment of Herod as governor of Galilee was the first step which led him to that high, though not enviable position which he afterwards attained. The sceptre had now virtually departed from the Asmonean house. The Israelites had been governed by them for more than a hundred years, and become attached to them, though their government never was very prosperous; Antigonus the son, and Aristobulus the grandson of Hyrcanus were the only surviving branches of the family, and, like the rest of them, were doomed to an untimely and unnatural death. Antigonus, it is true, had by an unexpected circumstance—the rising of the Parthians—gained the ascendency, and held both the sceptre and the office of high-priest for a short period of three years and a half, but he was rather an instrument in the hands of a political party than a self-dependent monarch; his power was soon wrested from him; and being defeated in battle, he was sent to Rome, where at the urgent solicitations of Herod he was ignominiously put to death. Thus perished the eighth and last of the Asmonean princes who wielded the sceptre. Young Aristobulus, the son of the latter, was yet alive, and his presence seemed an obstacle in the way of the usurper Herod. He was tall and handsome, and the eyes of the people rested upon him as the relic of past grandeur and glory. Some unforeseen events might concur to bestow upon this last scion the crown which his ancestors had so honorably worn. But the crafty Herod lacked no means for accomplishing his purpose, and despatching any object adverse to his interests. Under the pretences of friendship, he invited the youth to Jericho, to one of his mansions; gave orders to his servants to drown him while bathing, as if by accident; and thus the last male survivor of the Asmonean family was put out of the way.

HEROD'S REIGN.

We have in the above paragraph spoken briefly of Herod, so undeservedly called *the great;* but his career was too important, too full of intrigues and atrocious crimes, and of too great an influence on the fate of the nation to require no more than a passing notice. This wicked adventurer so worked himself into the favor of the emperor Augustus and Mark Antony that they united in conferring on him the crown of Judea. His character was bold, fiercely passionate, and most barbarously cruel, yet his talents as a statesman and a warrior were eminent. One of his first acts after assuming the rein of government was the murder of all the members of the Sanhedrin who had opposed his rule, excepting only two of them who had shown themselves favorable to his cause. As proofs of his relentless cruelty we may cite the following instances which constitute but a small part of the long list of his atrocities. Herod married successively ten wives, the second of whom was Mariamne, an Asmonean princess of exceeding beauty; indeed, she was considered the most beautiful of the whole nation. The love he bore her was exceeded only by his extreme jealousy. Being obliged to leave Jerusalem in order to meet Mark Antony on a hazardous mission concerning his government, he intrusted the cares of the realm, as well as his beautiful wife, to his uncle Joseph, with the strict but secret charge, that if he should fail in his mission and perish, Mariamne was to be immediately put to death. Joseph betrayed this secret to Mariamne, and on Herod's return she asked him if it could be that he truly loved her when he had given that fatal order for her death. This roused his suspicions about her fidelity and he would have slain her on the spot, were it not that the charm of her beauty restrained him; and his whole vengeance fell on Joseph, whom he ordered to be executed. A second time he had occasion to leave the capital, and again he committed Mariamne to the care of two friends, with the same injunctions that she was to be slain if he failed to return. Mariamne and her mother were imprisoned in a castle, and knowing her husband's sentiments towards her, she succeeded in extorting from her jailer the secret charge he had received concerning her fate. Herod returned and was received by his queen with disdain; she reproached him with his inhumanity, for having murdered her brother, her grandfather, and other relations; and scorned to receive his caresses. To make matters worse, Herod's sister, Salome, caused a false accusation to be brought against the queen, of intentions to poison the king. Herod summoned the queen before a tribunal, accused her of infidelity and murderous intentions, and the sentence of death was pronounced over her. The most violent passions now raged in Herod's breast. Love and indignation strove for the mastery. The latter prevailed, however, and he issued the fatal order for her execution. The loss of Mariamne left an indelible gloom upon Herod's mind. Day and night he was haunted by the image of his beloved murdered queen. He often called her name and endeavored to soothe himself in a measure by ordering the death of her executioner. Another instance of this man's unbounded cruelty we find in one of his last orders, issued about the close of his life. Feeling his end approaching, he commanded that some members of all the principal families in Judea be seized and imprisoned in a hippodrome; he then ordered his sister Salome and her husband that, as soon as he should have expired, the whole number of persons in the hippodrome should be unsparingly massacred, in order that, with the news of his death, a general mourning should spread over all the land. This sanguinary order, however, was never carried into effect. To enumerate all the wicked acts of this cruel monster would require several more pages, and take up more space than we can here devote to their recital. Even his own sons, Alexander and Aristobulus, whom Mariamne had borne to him, he accused of treason and had them executed, and we hesitate not to assert that, among all wicked rulers that swayed a sceptre, wore a crown, or mounted a throne, the detestable Herod I. deserves to be placed at the head of the list.

HEROD'S REIGN CONTINUED. HIS END.

The history of Herod's reign would, however, be quite incomplete should we neglect to give an account of some other acts of his life which do not partake of that monstrosity we have just depicted. It is but too often the case that we see the wicked live in prosperity, even in glory; but the outward appearance of their good fortune does not generally correspond with their inward tranquillity and happiness. Solomon says, "The prosperity of fools (that is, of the impious) shall destroy them." And so it really was with Herod. His repeated successes served only to feed the flame of his violent passions which burned in his breast, and destroyed his peace; but outwardly his magnificence was great indeed, and under his reign the Jewish nation rose to great temporary splendor; though he never succeeded in gaining the attachment of his subjects, who ever looked upon him as an intruder, the murderer of the faithful Asmoneans, and the robber of their national rights. The costly and magnificent palaces and other structures erected by Herod surpassed all that had ever been seen in Palestine and were too numerous to be all mentioned here. We will describe only a few of them. He rebuilt and considerably enlarged the city of Samaria, the former capital of the kingdom of Israel, and peopled it with his Greek and Syrian soldiers, and descendants of the Samaritans (ever the eyesore of the Jews) and called it Sebaste (the August*), in honor of his mighty Roman protector. A small town, called the Tower of Straton, situated on the sea-coast, was changed into a fine, large city and its harbor made safe by the sinking of immense stones which formed a pier, and thereon were placed two colossal statues,

---

* The student should bear in mind that this first Roman emperor here alluded to bore the multifarious name of Caius Julius Cæsar Octavianus Augustus, and is often designated by one or other of these names.

one representing Rome, the other Cæsar, and it was adorned with a splendid theatre and a spacious amphitheatre after the Grecian style. This city was called Cæsarea, in honor of the imperial family, and twelve years were required to rebuild it. In order to flatter still more the pride of Augustus, Herod introduced the Olympic exhibitions, where all sorts of games, such as wrestling, racing, fighting of wild beasts and men, were performed. These ferocious amusements of the Greeks and Romans were quite distasteful to the Jews, and confirmed their dislike to Herod who, it was evident, endeavored to replace the religious idea of the Jews by that of the heathen. He also built Gaba, Heshbon, Antipatris, Cypron, Phasaelis, and other towns, most of which were named after his Roman friends and members of his family, and in this way he unnecessarily exhausted the wealth of Judea. Seeing that he was sinking more and more in the estimation of his subjects, he at length determined on a measure to reconcile and appease them. He announced his intentions to rebuild the Temple at Jerusalem and make it more magnificent than it ever had been. Consequently the old building was pulled down, and on its site was erected one of greater extent and surpassing splendor. White marble blocks of incredible size and finest quality, costly woods and precious metals, were used unsparingly; many thousands of men and years of labor were employed in its erection; and the nation saw with the utmost pride the new fabric of stately architecture with its glittering towers and pinnacles of gold crowning anew the brow of Moriah. Herod I. was born seventy-one years before the beginning of the common era, and attained nearly to the age of seventy years. In the thirty-third year of his reign took place the birth of Jesus of Nazareth, upon whose reputed sayings and opinions the Christian religion has been founded, some two or three hundred years after his death. After long mental and bodily suffering, Herod died of a loathsome disease, and was buried with great pomp in one of his palaces called Herodium.

Archelaus.

Herod's testament divided the kingdom of Judea among his three sons Archelaus, Herod Antipater, and Olympias; but it was made subject to the approval of Augustus. While this was pending, Archelaus assumed the direction of affairs at Jerusalem. The populace was turbulent, divided in opinion, and Jerusalem was torn asunder by the differences of religious and political parties. The people demanded that the severity under which they had been should be mitigated, their taxes be lightened, political prisoners released, and justice be done to those who had suffered by the cruelty of the late king, whereupon the new ruler addressed the multitude in a conciliatory speech, promising to satisfy them as far as lay in his power. The people, however, were not satisfied with promises; riots occurred daily; strangers entered to take advantage of the occasion and make themselves master both of the royal power and of the treasures; and strife and bloodshed were the almost immediate results. Archelaus had inherited much of the cruelty and rapacity of his father, but not his abilities. He was not able to hold the people in subjection as his father had done. The decision of Augustus confirmed him in the possession of his power, but without the royal title, which was reserved in case he should prove himself worthy of wearing the crown, but to this dignity he never attained. Complaints of his unjust and tyrannical government were repeatedly brought before the emperor, with petitions from the Judeans that they might be freed from the oppression of the unworthy king; until at last he was summoned to Rome to defend himself. The complaints against him were investigated, he was convicted of misgovernment, and after a rule of nine years was dethroned and banished to Vienna, in Gaul, whence he never returned.

JUDEA A ROMAN PROVINCE. THE SANHEDRIN.

After the removal of Archelaus, Judea was declared as part of a Roman province under the viceregency of Syria, and all the internal affairs of the country were under direction of Roman officers. Only the administration of the Jewish laws, when they came not in contact with matters touching on politics, were left to the Sanhedrin; while even the execution of capital punishment, the appointment or removal of a high-priest, and other important matters properly belonging to the judicial power of the Sanhedrin, were controlled by a Roman officer. Now it is necessary that you should know something about the body called Sanhedrin, its origin and its functions. The word Sanhedrin means council or assembly, and is applied particularly to an assembly of judges among the Jews, whose province it was to debate upon and decide ecclesiastical and civil points of law. There was one *great Sanhedrin* consisting of seventy-one members, usually presided over by the high-priest, whose authority extended over the whole nation; and there was besides a smaller Sanhedrin, consisting of twenty-three members, in every large town of the country. The great Sanhedrin was properly no more than an ecclesiastical court; its functions were chiefly to interpret and determine the laws of the Mosaic code, not losing sight of the oral or traditional interpretations connected with the same and adopted as authoritative. It was further in the province of that body to decide upon the opening of war with foreign powers, upon the extension of the temple and city limits, and to watch over and preserve the family records so as to prevent any admixture of foreign blood among the Jewish race; while doubtful or difficult cases of any kind were also brought before them for adjustment All civil and criminal proceedings were adjusted by the smaller Sanhedrin of twenty-three, and some of the minor points were treated even by a council of three. The great

Sanhedrin held their sittings in a semicircular form in one of the chambers of the Temple; their discussions were public, and strangers were even permitted occasionally to enter into their debates. The origin of the institution is doubtful. Its source may be traced as far back as the time of Moses, who gathered seventy elders to deliberate with himself the affairs of the nation. A similar gathering in the time of Ezra was called the great synagogue, and later, when Grecian manners and Grecian names became more prevalent among the Jews, the institution was entitled Sanhedrin.

Agrippa I. Queen Helena.

Some time elapsed between the deposition of Archelaus and the appointment of his successor, who was Agrippa I., grandson of Herod. He was in Rome during the serious disturbances between the senate and the army, and having acted with great moderation, and rendered very valuable services to the empire, was rewarded by having the crown of Judea bestowed on him, and by the investiture of all the dominions which had belonged to his grandfather. On assuming the reins of government, he showed the greatest respect for the national religion, and to a great extent gained the affections of his subject; and after a reign of seven years, died in the fifty-fourth year of his age. Agrippa left a son of the same name, who at his father's death was only seventeen years old. He was thought not sufficiently advanced in years to hold the reins of government, and Judea was again placed under the administration of a Roman governor. A singular event took place at this time, which was that Helena, queen of Adiabene, a district beyond the Tigris, adopted the Jewish faith; and what is still more singular, her son Izates, who had been sent by his father, King Monobazus, to a far-off country on the Persian gulf, also embraced Judaism, without the mother and son knowing of each other's conversion.

During a grievous famine which then raged in Judea, both Helena and her son sent large quantities of grain, dried figs, and money to be distributed among the poor inhabitants of Judea. This Jewish convert Izates succeeded his father on the throne, reigned very successfully for twenty-four years (a converted Jewish king over a heathen nation), and his remains as well as those of Helena were transported to Jerusalem and there placed in a splendid tomb.

Caligula's Reign. Massacre at Alexandria.

Before speaking of the successor of Agrippa, we must turn our attention for a while to the state of the Jews at Alexandria, and the vicissitudes which befell them when Agrippa began to reign. I have told you already that a large number of Jews had taken up their abode in Alexandria, and that they had even established a temple there, with the same form of worship as was conducted at Jerusalem; in fact, the Alexandrian community had become a kind of rival to that of Jerusalem, and was looked upon as such by their brethren in Palestine. It is supposed there were at that time not less than a million of Jews in Egypt. During the reign of Augustus and Tiberius, the first two emperors of Rome, the Jews, though not quite independent, enjoyed considerable freedom in the exercise of their religion and in their civil rights; now that Caligula had ascended the throne, matters assumed a different aspect. This silly monarch was not satisfied to be looked upon as the sole and absolute master of a mighty empire, he wished to be adored as a god,* and ordered temples and statues representing his person to be placed all over his dominions, that the people might worship him; and the Temple at Jerusalem was also to have a statue of the

---

* Not unlike Clothaire I. (560), who, astonished to find himself dying, exclaimed, "Quel est ce roi des cieux qui tue ainsi les grands rois de la terre?"

emperor. To this the Israelites could not submit, as it would have been a violation of the first principle of their religion. The Jews opposed themselves with all their might against this mandate, and a bloody war might have been the result, but fortunately for them, before the command was enforced, the glad tidings came that Caligula had been assassinated, and thus they escaped this imminent danger. But Alexandria became the scene of terrible strife and massacre. This great metropolis was inhabited chiefly by Egyptians, Jews, and Greeks, each of whom was detested by the other two, and hated the others in return. Now, when Agrippa left Rome for Palestine to take possession of his throne, he stopped on his way at Alexandria, and the Greeks, exasperated at seeing a Jew in regal splendor, with a large retinue in glittering armor, offered him the grossest insults, and the ire of the populace being once aroused, they found an easy pretense for a general attack on the Jews They insisted that the image of the emperor should be placed in all the Jewish places of worship, and not contented with carrying out this design, they set about demolishing or burning some of their oratories. Their dwellings and storehouses were next plundered, and the goods openly shared in the market-place. The Jews, being driven to one narrow quarter of the city, suffered fearfully from the heat and foul air, and famine and pestilence were the result; those who ventured to come out were slain and often put to the most cruel tortures and their dead bodies dragged about the streets to fully satisfy the brutal vengeance of their enemies. It was the morning spectacle of the theatre to see the Jews scourged and tortured in different ways before being led to execution; and this horrible tragedy was succeeded by dances and farces and other theatrical amusement. I might tell you much more about the inhuman acts of these ferocious Greeks—acts which make the blood run cold and make one wonder how beings in human form could be so degenerate, and so deprived of all humanity; but the scene is too horrible to dwell upon longer than necessary. We will only add that these barbarities might have been prevented if Flaccus Aquilius, the Roman prefect at Alexandria, had used his influence and power to that end, but he also was a Jew-hater, and instead of opposing these rioters, rather encouraged them in their bloody deeds. But we find many examples, especially in the history of the Jews, of the wicked receiving their reward even in this world, and Flaccus may be named as one of them. He fell into disfavor with the emperor, was seized and his property confiscated, then banished, and ultimately put to death by order of Caligula.

Troubles in Babylonia. Assinai and Anilai.

But not only in Egypt were the Jews subjected to much suffering, also in Babylonia, where a great many of them resided, a cloud of ruin and desolation burst over their heads. You have read before, that, when the Jews left Babylon to return to Jerusalem under Zerubbabel, a number of families remained behind. These had now become very numerous. The great cities of Nehardea and Nisibis were inhabited chiefly by them, and it was in the former that their celebrated theological school was established, from which proceeded so many great men of learning. The Babylonian Jews did not, like those of Alexandria, build themselves a temple and secede from the Palestine community; they were, notwithstanding their attachment to their homes, strict adherents to the ancient law and to the Jerusalem Temple, to the support of which they largely contributed; nor did they, like the Alexandrians and Palestinians, intermix with the Gentiles around them; they preserved their nationality distinct and pure, and thus for a long series of years they lived in peace and in affluence. But, as is often the case, an occurrence, insignificant in itself, led to important and fatal results. Two orphan brothers, Assinai and Anilai, both high-spirited youths, were apprenticed to learn the weaver's trade, and one day, thinking themselves ill-treated by their master, ran away. Not knowing where to go, or what to do for their support, they joined a band of bold robbers which infested the eastern shores of the Euphrates, and became their captains. They even built a fortress and became so formidable that the King of Parthia sent troops to subdue them, but these were defeated with great slaughter. The King rather admired their extraordinary valor, made terms of peace with them, and thinking it best to enlist them in his service, appointed Assinai, the elder brother, as governor of an independent state in Mesopotamia. Though robbers, they still remained Jews, and the state they governed was Jewish, and flourished during sixteen years; but the younger brother married a heathen woman, and being upbraided for this by his brother the governor, the woman, fearing that she might be obliged to leave her husband, administered poison to her brother-in-law, and consequently the government passed into the hands of Anilai the younger. The new governor was quite as brave, but not so prudent as his deceased brother. He attacked some of the surrounding territories, was first victorious and then was defeated, and fled to his native city Nehardea. The Babylonians pursued and captured Anilai, and he and his whole band were routed and slain. But, not satisfied with this, the populace, exasperated against the Jews because of Anilai and the depredations formerly committed by the brothers, began a general attack on the peaceful Jews all over the country, and many thousands of them suffered persecution and death, attended with the usual cruelties practised by the heathen upon their conquered enemies, of which we had an example in the preceding paragraph.

Agrippa II. The Zealots. Internal Disturbances.

We now return to Judea to learn of Agrippa's successor, and the general state of affairs in that country. We said before that, when Agrippa I. died, he left a son too young to succeed him, and that consequently the administration of affairs was left to a Roman governor. This state of things continued for a number of years under the magistracy of three successive governors. In the mean time Agrippa's brother, Herod II., was appointed by Claudius over the temple and the treasury, and with power to appoint high-priests. As he was not invested with any political or royal authority, he cannot properly be ranked among the kings of the Herodian dynasty. After his death, Agrippa II., son of Agrippa I., was made king of Judea. But this last king of the Jews had not much of a Jewish heart, did not share the sentiments of his subjects, and was indifferent to their interests. He had long resided at Rome, was educated and had formed connections there, and was consequently more of a Roman than a Jew. In his time the condition of the Jews in Jerusalem and in all Judea grew worse and worse. Sanguinary conflicts between the Jews on one side, and the Roman and Syro-Greek soldiers on the other, became the order of the day, and the final ruin of Judea was fast approaching. What was still worse, the Jews among themselves were not united in purpose. A political faction, who assumed the appellation of Zealots, and whose deep hatred of the Romans would not allow them to submit in the least to the foreign yoke, endeavored to their utmost to disseminate the opinion that Jews ought not to submit to any rule but the divine, and ought to oppose the enemy at all hazards and at all sacrifice of property, family, and life; while others of more moderate temperament advised submission to the inevitable, and others again were anxious to purchase peace at any cost. Thus the spirit of discontentment spread, and the utmost agitation prevailed in Jerusalem. While such was the state of the city, the country was not much more secure. Robbers multiplied and grew bolder, and no man's life or property was secure. Among those who were set to regulate public affairs, there was no patriotism, no national sentiment, each of them endeavored only to dominate, and enrich himself, regardless of all probity and justice. The Judeans had to submit even to the administration of an unprincipled tyrannical man, by name Felix, who was born a slave, associated with robbers and assassins, and exercised the authority of a king by consequence of his appointment. Also in the provinces adjoining Judea, a war of extermination raged, and the horrid retaliation which the Jews inflicted on their enemies whenever they proved the stronger party, tended only to fan the flame of discord and anarchy which prevailed. I might devote many pages to a description of the events which took place during the short reign of Agrippa II., which, though in many instances heart-rending, would yet be interesting and instructive, but they are too numerous and too complicated to find a place in this concise narrative. I will, therefore, hasten to the close of this first epoch of our history, giving you in but a few short items the succession of events which led to the destruction of Jerusalem. You will know from the history of Rome, which I suppose you are studying, that after the death of Claudius there were yet four more emperors of Rome before Vespasian ascended the throne. These men were all so extremely wicked and foolish that it is not worth while here to mention their names; and yet to the rule of such men, "tyrants, madmen, fools, and monsters, the most detestable the world has ever seen" (as Dr. Raphall justly calls them), to the arbitrary will of these the Jewish nation and the whole Roman empire were subject.

REVOLT OF THE JEWS AGAINST ROME. CESTIUS DEFEATED.

The Jews, driven to despair by the unendurable oppression they had suffered for so many years, at last determined to unite their forces and to risk everything for the sake of gaining their independence. It certainly was a desperate conclusion they had come to, for to declare war against Rome was to defy the whole force of the civilized world. But what will man not do when driven to mad despair by such grinding tyranny! And we must not forget that it was not so much political independence they were striving for; but their religion, which was to them dearer than life, was at stake, and that had been most wantonly trampled upon by their enemies. The Jews, therefore, manfully resolved to conquer or die. They refused henceforth to pay tribute to Rome, declared themselves openly against their governor, and demanded his immediate withdrawal. Agrippa addressed the multitude and made some efforts to calm their rage, showing them the rashness of defying the power of Rome, and was enabled for awhile to arrest their fury; but, when he attempted to persuade the people to render the usual allegiance to the present governor until another should be sent by the emperor, their indignation was aroused to its highest pitch, they denounced also their king as treacherous to their cause, assailed him first with insulting language, then with stones, and he was obliged to flee from the city. While the people of Jerusalem were thus preparing themselves for defensive and offensive warfare, Cestius Gallus, governor of Syria, hearing of the revolutionary proceedings going on in Jerusalem, gathered his troops to bring the turbulent Jews to subjection. The Zealots, whose numbers had now increased to immense proportions, prepared to meet the invader, and disregarding the sanctity of the Sabbath, armed themselves with undaunted energy as well as weapons. Cestius halted at about a mile off the city, expecting that the very appearance of his army of 30,000 strong would overawe the Jews into quiet submission. But the Zealots attacked the adversary with such vigor that they slew five hundred of them, losing but twenty-three, and returned home laden with rich booty. Three days later, Cestius made another advance on Jerusalem and burned some of the suburbs. For five days the Romans made various assaults, while the Jews defended themselves with the most resolute valor, till at length the enemy were forced to retreat. After a few more similar combats, Cestius withdrew his troops. The insurgents had been all the while in dreadful consternation and were almost ready to surrender, but when they saw the enemy continue to retire, they gained new courage, sallied forth from the city, and boldly pursued the enemy with the utmost rapidity, and did not cease until they had routed the whole army of the Romans. With hymns of victory, they re-entered the capital, having suffered hardly any loss and having slain of the Romans 5,300 foot and 380 horse, while many instruments of war and an immense spoil fell into their hands. The Romans had since long not suffered so disgraceful a defeat; and the sting was more keenly felt since it was inflicted, not by a powerful adversary looked upon as an equal, but by a people who had long and patiently endured the Roman yoke and humbly submitted to the imperial will.

Vespasian Sent to Subdue the Judeans. Galilee Conquered.

The stubborn defence of the Jews against the attacks of Cestius and the subsequent defeat of the latter's army was tantamount to a declaration of war, and Judea was now in open rebellion against Rome. This was in the year 66 of the common era. Nero was then the emperor, and, learning with astonishment the shameful defeat of his troops under Cestius, began to make preparations for the entire subjection of the insurgents. He appointed Vespasian, the ablest general in the empire, as commander-in-chief of the army that was to subdue Judea, and Titus, Vespasian's eldest son, who was then with his father at Athens, was made his lieutenant. Vespasian sent his son to Alexandria to bring two legions to his aid, while he himself went to Syria to collect all the Roman troops from the neighboring tributary kings. When the two generals, father and son, had collected an army of nearly 100,000, they marched toward Galilee, there to commence operations. Joseph, son Mathias, better known as Josephus, and of whom you will hear more hereafter, was intrusted by the Jews with the defense of Galilee. This was a very fertile country, and its inhabitants, a bold, hardy, and warlike race, were very numerous: Its fortifications also were many and of immense strength, and Josephus, who had also about 100,000 under his command, and being possessed of very eminent military talents, might have successfully defended the province intrusted to his charge, but he seemed to be little inclined to wage war with so powerful an opponent, and more in favor of an amicable settlement between his people and the Romans. At all events, Vespasian made fearful inroads into Galilee, took city after city, all of which, however, were defended by the besieged with most resolute courage, but had to yield to superior forces and numbers. Josephus himself, finding further defense impossible, was base enough to renounce his party, forsake his people and his faith, and enter into a bond of friendship with Vespasian. Having conquered the whole of Galilee, Vespasian allowed his troops to recover from the fatigues and hard struggles they had undergone; and towards the end of February, 68, entered on his second campaign. In the mean time the Judeans were very active in preparing their defense of Jerusalem, but unfortunately they were devoured by intestine strife to such an alarming extent that the enemy thought it advisable to let them alone, as they among themselves were doing a good deal of the work of destruction for him. About the middle of June, 68, Vespasian found himself at Cæsarea, about fifteen miles north of Jerusalem, superintending the construction of powerful battering rams and other engines of war for an attack on the capital, when the death of Nero was announced to him. The conflagration of Rome, Nero's suicide, and the assassination of two other emperors are events which do not properly belong to our history, and were of no material influence thereon. Passing over, therefore, the transient reigns of Galba, Otho, and Vitellius, we find Vespasian in possession of the throne of the Roman empire and Titus in command of the army in Judea.

Titus' Advance on Jerusalem. Description of the City and Temple.

Political troubles at the seat of government and in other parts of the Roman empire had delayed the march on Jerusalem for nearly twelve months, and it was not resumed until the year 70. In the spring of that year, Titus, with an army of 80,000, undertook in good earnest the long projected plan of demolishing the Jewish capital and Temple, at once the pride and the stronghold of the nation. But he found it by no means an easy task. That you may have an idea of the difficulties the enemy had to overcome, let me give you a short, and of course but a superficial description of Jerusalem and its proud Temple. Jerusalem was built on three hills; it was some five miles in circumference; its inhabitants may have been half a million or more. It was fortified with three walls, all of immense strength and thickness; but these walls were not exactly one inside the other all around the city, each one defended a separate quarter of the town and required a separate siege and attack before the whole could be taken. The first or outer wall was built of solid stones thirty-five feet long and the wall was seventeen and a half feet thick; on its top were battlements three and a half feet and pinnacles five and three quarters, making together a height of nearly forty-five feet. The inner walls were nearly similar to the one just described. These walls were mounted respectively with sixty, fourteen, and eighty towers of the same solid masonry, from which the besieged could defend themselves against their assailants. The most magnificent of all these towers was called Psephina, opposite to which Titus encamped. It was octagon, $122\frac{1}{2}$ feet high, commanding a noble view of the country and of the sea around it. Each tower had a different name, after some one beloved or esteemed by the monarch who built it. They were differently constructed, some defended by breastworks and bulwarks, divided in lofty chambers luxuriously fitted up, provided with baths and large tanks above to receive rainwater. These lofty towers appeared still higher from their situation on a steep hill. In addition to these regular defenses, there were several detached castles or fortresses of great strength, of which the Antonia was the most considerable. On one of the hills, Mt. Zion, stood the king's palace or one of the palaces, surrounded by a wall thirty-five feet high, adorned by towers at equal distances, and by spacious barrack-rooms with a hundred beds in each. It was paved with every variety of rare marble; timbers of unequalled strength and workmanship supported the roofs. The chambers were countless, adorned with all kinds of figures, the richest furniture, and vessels of gold and silver. There were numerous cloisters with columns of different orders, the squares within of beautiful verdure; around were groves and avenues with fountains and tanks, and bronze statues pouring out the water. The fortress Antonia stood alone on a high and precipitous rock near ninety feet high, at the northwest corner of the Temple. The whole face of the rock was fronted with smooth stone for ornament, and so slippery as to make an ascent impracticable. The fortress was seventy feet high, and had every luxury and convenience of a sumptuous palace, or even of a city; spacious halls, courts, and baths. It appeared like a vast square tower, with four other towers at the corners, three of them between eighty and ninety feet high. Towering above the whole city was the Temple, a fortress in itself, and equal in strength to any at that time known. It covered a square of a furlong (one-eighth mile) each side. The hill on which it stood had been built up on the sides with perpendicular walls in no part lower than 525 feet; some of these stones were seventy feet square. Thus Jerusalem was a mass of fortifications, an accumulation of strength and beauty, and might have remained inaccessible to the enemy, had its possessors been of one mind, and unanimously defended it. The supply of water from natural springs was abundant, and stores of provisions there were sufficient to last for years, but these were mostly destroyed by the inhabitants while they quarreled and fought among themselves. I cannot begin to describe the magnificence of the interior of the Temple, its divisions, its courts, its gates, and its furniture. It would be injustice to say a few words about it, you must read that in a larger book than this. Even the roof of the Temple was set all over with sharp golden spikes to prevent the birds from nestling and defiling it. At a distance, the whole structure looked literally like "a mount of snow fretted with golden pinnacles," and when the sun arose above the Mount of Olives, which it directly faced, it was impossible, even for a Roman, not to be struck with wonder, or even for Titus not to betray emotion. Yet this was the city which in a few months was to lie a heap of undistinguishable ruins, and the Temple itself, which seemed built for eternity, not "to have one stone left upon another."*

THE ATTACK ON JERUSALEM. HORRIBLE SCENES IN THE CITY. FINAL DETRUCTION.

The Roman legions made their approach on Jerusalem from the North, where the resistance was least formidable, and before making an assault, Titus himself, with an escort of 600 horse, came close to the city to reconnoitre. Finding the gates closed and not a man on the wall, not even a sentinel, he apprehended no immediate danger, and the squadron proceeded more closely, turning towards the high tower of Psephina; when all of a sudden the gates flew open, and a multitude of soldiers rushed upon the astonished cavalry, effectually cutting off Titus with a few followers from the rest of his escort. This was a critical moment. The general could not proceed, nor turn back without facing the enemy, and almost had the chief of the Roman army fallen a prize into the hands of the beleaguered Jews. But it seems they were so intoxicated with their momentary success as to be incapable of taking advantage of their good fortune; and Titus, with redoubled vigor and by the assistance of his followers, cut his way through and escaped. So trifling a circumstance could not in the least deter the Roman chief, though it taught him a lesson of caution. The next day the work on the embankments was begun and soon the enormous battering rams appeared which were to play on the wall; but no sooner were they within bow-shot than the besieged harassed the men with all sorts of missiles, sometimes sallying out in considerable numbers and damaging in a few hours what the Romans had labored days to accomplish. Night and day the Romans toiled; night and day, by stratagem and force, the

---

* Much of this description is taken verbatim from Milman's History.

Jews impeded their progress. At last one tower came down. The terrible engines continued their destructive work and the first wall began to totter. The Jews retired to the second, and after the most reckless defence and considerable damage to the assailants, this also had to yield. It was re-taken from the Romans, but again lost. The Jews still kept up their courage, persevered resolutely, and fought desperately; but, alas! the destruction from within was worse than that from without. Provisions were short, and the horrible famine began its ravages; there was nothing more to eat; men ate chopped straw, gnawed their belts, their shoes. The most delicate females, accustomed to abundance and luxury, prowled about the streets, mad with hunger. The famine had steeled every heart, extinguished even parental and filial affection. Brothers and sisters, parents and children, snatched from one another the most miserable morsel; and, most horrible to relate, one woman, Miriam, daughter of Eleazar, possessed of wealth which availed her nothing, and finding no one merciful enough to put an end to her misery, wildly resolved to slay her own infant, cook it, and consume part of it. The story reached the Roman camp and touched the stoutest heart. Titus then used every means to induce the people to surrender, and employed Josephus to address his countrymen and convince them of the impossibility of holding out, but he had forfeited all influence upon them by his base desertion. Exhausted with the toil of so many weeks and months of constant battle, Titus withdrew his troops to allow them a little rest, and give the besieged time to consider a capitulation, but they remained obstinate and unyielding. In the meanwhile the famine increased, and pestilence set in. The houses were full of dying women and children, the streets with men gasping out their last breath. The corpses remained unburied, and the stench of the putrid bodies affected even the Romans outside; yet the most horrible sufferings, the most appalling scenes could not move the cruel and stubborn Zealots to yield their point. The stately Temple still stood defiantly before the enemy; the Jews said it *could* not be taken, for it was the Temple of God. But Providence had otherwise decreed. Wall after wall, and fortress after fortress fell into the hands of the enemy. The fighting had been carried on most desperately for more than five months, day and night, and every inch of ground the Romans gained cost streams of blood. It is generally conceded that the Jews fought with as much bravery and skill as was ever displayed by any nation in any battle. Nearly a million and a half of human lives had been sacrificed. At last, on the fatal 10th of Ab, also the 10th of August, of the year 70, the Romans entered the precincts of the Temple, which Titus endeavored to spare from destruction; but a soldier, without orders, threw a fire-brand into one of the side chambers, and soon the flames spread all over the edifice. The Romans were struck with wonder at the splendor they beheld; everything around them was radiant with gold, and the excited soldiers began to plunder with insatiable vengeance. The treasures found in Jerusalem were so great that gold fell in Syria to one-half its value. The fertile lands of Judea were disposed of, and many thousands of the captives were sold into slavery to fill the treasury of the Roman emperor. Thus fell the metropolis of Palestine, and with that event ceased the nationality of the Jewish people. But the consuming fire which destroyed the Temple became the fire of a new inspiration for the Jewish people, and the storms which scattered them to all parts of the earth became the forerunners of a new creation, the speedy development of which became a blessing to all the world.

Biography of Philo and Josephus.

The young student may ask perhaps whence we derive all this historical information; how we know all these particulars, of which they find nothing in their books or general history. The answer to these questions is, that the works of several historians who lived at the time those events took place, or shortly afterwards, have been preserved to us. Such are Dion Cassius, Strabo, and Tacitus; but our information is derived chiefly from the writings of two Jewish historians, Philo and Josephus, of whom we will here give a short biographical description. Philo Judæus was an Alexandrian by birth, of priestly descent, born of wealthy parents, and connected with the most influential of his countrymen; his brother being one of the chief officers or ministers of Egypt. He was thoroughly acquainted with Grecian literature and philosophy, as well as with the tenets of his religion, and his character was that of deep moral earnestness, with a strong desire to seek and know the truth, and for this purpose he often retired to the wilderness to lead a more contemplative life. The partiality which he felt for the teachings of Plato seems to have caused much confusion in his mind, through his attempts to amalgamate the Platonic philosophy with the Mosaic laws, giving to the latter a mystical interpretation and thus reconcile the two systems. To retain the truths of Platonism in Judaism, to vindicate them and elicit them from the Mosaic books, was the principal task which Philo set himself, and seems to be the object of most of his writings, which were numerous. We know Philo more as a philosopher, a speculator in mysticism, than as an historian; but as the things which he recorded were the events of his own time, and as, moreover, his reputation is not tarnished by the spot of double-dealing, treachery, and self-aggrandizement, such as attach to the character of Josephus, whose statements often differ materially from those Philo, the historical information we have from him is of great importance. Cotemporary with Philo and in the same city lived Apion, also a man of great learning, and author of a history of Egypt, but a great enemy of the Jews. Philo endeavored to defend his brethren against the attacks of this enemy; and when the citizens of Alexandria lodged a complaint with the emperor Caligula against the Jews residing there, charging them with disaffection to the Roman sovereignty, they sent Apion to Rome as their envoy, and Philo was selected on the part of the accused to defend their cause. This mission was attended with considerable danger, and Philo narrowly escaped with his life, not being permitted even to speak on the subject before the prejudiced imbecile monarch. Various editions of Philo's works are extant, and esteemed on account of their antiquity and intrinsic worth.

Josephus, son of Mathias, was descended paternally from a priestly family, and by his mother's side from the Asmoneans, and was born at Jerusalem A.C. 37, when Caligula was emperor. At the age of sixteen he attached himself to the sect of the Essenes, and for three years led a studious and ascetic life, and then became a zealous member of the sect of Pharisees. At the age of twenty-six he visited Rome, gained admission and influence with the empress, and on his return to Judea was made governor of upper and lower Galilee, in which capacity he bravely defended Jotapata against Vespasian. He was taken prisoner, however; but his life was spared at the intercession of Titus, to whom he predicted that he would become Roman emperor, and who became his friend and patron. Josephus was possessed of eminent abilities, and bears a high reputation as an orator, a soldier, and a statesman, but especially as an historian he is famous and of some authority. During the conquest of Palestine by the Romans, Josephus acted a very important part. Having at first defended his country with all the ability of an accomplished general, afterwards, seeing the impossibility of holding out against so powerful an enemy, he joined the peace faction and used all his influence and oratorical powers to induce the Jews to make terms with the Romans, rather than sacrifice their country and Temple, but the Jews would never listen to such propositions. Finding at last that all his efforts at reconciliation were of no avail, Josephus forsook his own people, and with many others who shared his views went over to the Romans, for which base act he is justly denounced as a traitor. He lived afterwards in Rome in high favor with the emperor, who conferred on him a very considerable portion of land and great honors, and permission to assume the imperial name "Flavius" Josephus. At Rome he first wrote the "History of the Jewish Wars" in the Syro-Chaldaic language, which was the vernacular of Palestine, and afterwards translated the work into Greek, for the benefit of the western Jews and of the Romans. Many years afterwards he wrote his great work "The Jewish Antiquities," two books against Apion in defense of his own people, besides other works, all written in elegant pure Greek. The time of his death is uncertain. History loses sight of him in his 56th or 57th year.

SECOND PERIOD.

FROM THE DESTRUCTION OF THE SECOND TEMPLE TO THE TIME OF THE SPANISH INQUISITION.

Revival of the Jews under Rabbinical Authority. They Revolt again, and are Subdued by Hadrian.

After the destruction of Jerusalem and the dispersion of the Jews, it might be supposed that their national integrity was entirely dissolved. This, however, was far from being the case. From what appears on the records of general history, and in the opinion of eminent literary men, the Jews seem to be an inexhaustible race, which, notwithstanding the mighty efforts to exterminate them, can never be destroyed. Thus we find that the Jews ever maintained their unity in character, in customs, in language, and above all in religion. Deprived of their Temple, they established more firmly their Synagogue, which was at once a place for worship and for the study of the law, and the Rabbis, or the learned in the law, were invested with supreme authority; and it is the unwavering attachment of the Jews to their law and their religion which has ever enabled them to hold together as one body. Milman, the historian, justly observes, "Perpetually plundered, yet always wealthy, massacred by thousands, yet springing up again from their undying stock, the Jews appear at all times and in all regions; their perpetuity, their national immortality, is at once the most curious problem to the political inquirer, to the religious man a subject of profound and awful admiration."

Though the political existence of the Jews was now annihilated, and themselves dispersed all over Asia, Africa, and Europe, they soon revived again under the form of two separate communities, presided over by their spiritual leaders. The one on the West of the Euphrates, who still inhabited Palestine, was under the leadership of the " Patriarch of the West," and included all Jews dwelling in the Roman Empire; the other in Mesopotamia, under the "Prince of the Captivity," to whom all eastern Jews paid allegiance; and from that time dates Rabbinism as an acknowledged authority, although the introduction of traditional laws and interpretations appears to have begun in the time of Simon the Maccabee, and gradually attained its growth during the whole period of the Second Temple. Of the offices and powers of these rabbinical leaders we will speak more fully hereafter. For a short period, during the reigns of the emperors Domitian and Nerva, the Jews remained tranquil and enjoyed the blessings of peace under the guidance of their spiritual leaders; but under the reign of Trajan, the united communites of Babylon, Egypt, Cyrene, and Judea rose again in open rebellion, at first with considerable success, but after an obstinate struggle and an enormous loss of life, estimated at 600,000, they were finally subdued and afterwards most cruelly oppressed by the emperor Hadrian. In order to remove forever all hopes of a restoration of the Jewish kingdom, Hadrian founded a new city and a colony of Romans on the site of Jerusalem, and a temple dedicated to Jupiter on the spot where the Jewish Temple had stood. The city was called Ælia Capitolina. The Jews were forbidden to approach the city, and in order to keep them away, the image of a swine was placed over the gate leading to Bethlehem. The study of the law, to which the Jews now clung as their greatest treasure, their only hope, was interdicted; the observance of the Sabbath and, in short, every religious observance was strictly forbidden them, and

the Jewish race seemed, indeed, in danger of becoming
extinct; and in that dark period they had no other hope
but that the expected Messiah would make his appearance
to deliver them.

BARCOCHAB'S MESSIAHSHIP.

The prophecy that the glory of the Second Temple should
surpass that of the first (Hag. ii. 9) had not been verified,
except as to its external grandeur. Some very important
parts were wanting. The high-priest wore no breast-plate,
the oracle was there no more, the priests were not consecrated as heretofore, the nation had lost its independence,
and the hope that Israel would at some time or other be
restored to its former greatness became, and has been to
this day, one of our principal points of faith. The belief
that the Messiah, a descendant of the house of David, would
again redeem them, had now become deeply rooted in the
hearts of all Israel,* and no wonder that in such time of
tribulation any one bold enough to declare himself to be
that deliverer would soon find a number of adherents
among the weak-minded who had nothing else to hope for.
Such a bold impostor indeed appeared now under the
assumed name of Barcochab (Son of the Star), who pretended to be the new redeemer of his people. Gradually
he succeeded in gaining multitudes of people on his side,
and they rose in open hostility against Hadrian. They succeeded to some extent, made themselves masters of the
ruins of Jerusalem, and the Romans suffered considerable
losses. Barcochab had chosen the fortified city of Bither

---

* This Messianic idea appears to have originated with the Christian
religion, which, in its earliest stage, was nothing but a Jewish sect;
and there is good reason to believe that neither the thought of a personal Messiah nor of a resurrection was prevalent among the Jews even
in the latter days of the Second Temple. See Jost, Gesch. d. Jud. u. s.
S., pp. 309 and 397.

as his stronghold, which withstood the attack of the enemy for a long time. At last Julius Severus, the ablest general the Romans then had, took command of the army, and the Jews again suffered immense losses. Bither was stormed, Barcochab was killed, and his head carried in triumph to the Roman camp. It was again on the fatal ninth of Ab, says the Talmud, that Bither fell and was razed to the ground.

The Patriarchate. The Mishnah.

After the death of Hadrian, the Jews again breathed the air of freedom, at least of tolerance. The western community was re-established under the "Patriarch," who resided at Tiberias, whence he exercised full authority over his scattered brethren, who sent their annual contributions for the support of his magnificent court; new synagogues were erected, the Sabbath and festivals regularly observed, numerous schools for the study of the law were opened, and rabbinical authority rose to great power. The "Prince of the Captivity" in Babylonia also had his splendid court with numerous attendants, surpassing in splendor even that of his rival in the West. In the latter part of the second century, Rabbi Jehudah, surnamed *Hanassi*, the prince, and *Hakkadosh*, the holy, on account of his great learning and spotless character, occupied the dignified position of "Patriarch," and it was he who compiled the code of traditional laws called Mishnah. This compilation consists of traditionary explanations of the Mosaic law, said to have been given by God to Moses, who taught them verbally to the elders, and these again to the prophets, and so on they were preserved from one generation to another till the time of R. Jehudah who, in order to preserve the traditions from oblivion, thought it necessary to commit them to writing.

This idea that, besides the revealed Law, God had imparted to Moses additional and private instructions concerning the precepts and their proper interpretation, originated, says Dr. Jost (Allg. Gesch. d. Isr. Volkes, Vol. II., 131 and 133), in the time of the Maccabees. And as this period—of R. Jehudah Hakkadosh—is distinguished by the labors of the great Roman lawyers in the formation of a code of jurisprudence for the whole empire, it seems that the Jews desired to follow the example of their masters in providing themselves with a code regulating every act of their religious and civil life. (See Jost as above, and Milman, Vol. III., 157, Lond. Ed., 1859.)

Constantine Adopts Christianity.

For a century or more, the Jews appear to have continued in their peaceful and prosperous state till the time of Constantine the Great. Outside of the Jewish communities, the world at large was then involved in paganism. The Christian religion had made little progress yet during the first three ages of its existence. Jews and Christians often came in furious conflict, and by turns committed horrible ravages upon one another. Still the Jews enjoyed the right of Roman citizenship, and were allowed to observe their religion unmolested. Constantine was the first emperor who embraced Christianity and made it the ruling religion of his empire; and under his rule, and more so by the increased severity of the laws enacted by his son and successor Constantius, the spirit of hostility against the Jews increased, and their condition became gradually worse until the accession of Julian to the throne. This Julian, the fourth emperor after Constantine, in the year 360 renounced Christianity and acknowledged the unity of God. He addressed a letter to the patriarch, calling him "my brother," and assuring him of his earnest intentions to promote the temporal and religious interests of the Jews to the utmost of his power. He even issued an edict for the rebuilding of the Temple on Mount Moriah, and the restoration of the worship of Jehovah to its former splendor. The whole Jewish world was in commotion. Materials and treasures poured in from all quarters to support the holy work. The Christians looked on with amazement and consternation, fearing the total overthrow of their religion, but the early death of Julian, who fell in his expedition against the Persians, reversed matters, and the hopes of the Jews were totally extinguished.

Origin of the Talmud.

Of the occurrences of the fourth and fifth centuries we have but little reliable information; at least no events of great importance, either favorable or contrary, seem to have materially altered the state of Jewish communities; and it appears that, with the exception of occasional outbreaks of animosity between the contending religious parties, the condition of the Jews must have been favorable, as the splendid courts of their spiritual leaders, the wealth of the people, and the flourishing condition of the Mesopotamian schools show the tolerant government of their Persian rulers; but it was during these two centuries especially that rabbinical discussions, which furnished the material for the compilation of the Babylonian Talmud, took place. It should be borne in mind that, as there were two distinct communities under separate heads, so there are two Talmuds, that of Jerusalem, and that of Babylon. The Mishnah, of which we have spoken above, constitutes the text and ground-work of both Talmuds. That of Jerusalem, collected in the third century by R. Johanan, is considered of little importance and is seldom studied or consulted. When, therefore, speaking of the Talmud, it is tacitly understood that the Babylonian is meant. The Talmud, then, consists of very lengthy expositions, discussions, and commentaries on the Mishnah, in which every point is minutely considered and disputed, but not always settled. It is an extensive work of thirty-six books, the result of centuries of labor, and containing, of course, the opinions of men of various talents. Among the Jews it has been always looked upon with great veneration, and very many devoted a lifetime to the study of it, to the exclusion even of the study of the Bible; while the Christians, in the middle ages, looked upon it as "a book very pernicious, abounding with ridiculous fables, insignificant decisions, and manifest contradictions." Not less than ten popes, and some of the kings of France and of Spain, forbade the study of it, or ordered all copies of it they could seize to be committed to the flames.

THE REIGN OF JUSTINIAN. TAKING OF JERUSALEM BY CHOSROES. JEWS CONTROLLING THE SLAVE TRADE.

The most noteworthy events of the sixth century are, the enactments of the oppressive laws of Justinian, and the attacks on Jerusalem by the Persian kings Chosroes I. and II.; also the slave trade carried on by the Jews in the latter half of that century; and it is at this period that the settlements of Jews in different parts of Europe begin to attract our particular notice.

Justinian, having become Roman emperor, commenced a violent persecution of all who differed with him in religious belief. The most noted act of his life was the reformation of the Roman laws, and collecting them in one body called the Justinian Code. Among these laws were some very oppressive to the Jews, and still more to the Samaritans; laws which interfered with their right of property, their liberty, and their religion. Every burden of society was laid upon them, without the return of any reward of interest or dignity. A dispute having arisen among the Jews, whether the Hebrew or Greek language should be used in the synagogue, the affair was brought before the emperor, who decided, to the great vexation of the rabbis, that the Greek might be used; but the study of the Talmud was strictly forbidden. It was also about that time (532) that the computation of the Christian era began; that is, they began to count time from the birth of Christ. While Jerusalem was under the dominion of Justinian, Chosroes I., king of Persia, proposed to conquer the holy city, and the Jews looked with anxious hopes to a relief from their Roman oppressor; but a treaty of peace between the two monarchs being concluded, Jerusalem remained undisturbed. A few years later, Chosroes II. meditated the conquest of Palestine. The Jews, still desirous of a change of government, joined him in great numbers, and those outside of Jerusalem conspired to storm the city on the night of the Christian Easter. The Christians, being informed of the conspiracy, put the city in a state of defense, and threw the most prominent Jews into prison. Those on the outside, seeing the failure of their project, destroyed in the suburbs all the property they could seize; but for every church they set on fire, the enemy inside the city struck off the heads of a hundred Jewish prisoners and cast them over the wall. Twenty churches were destroyed, and two thousand Jews lost their heads. At last the Persian troops arrived, and with them the Jews entered the city to wreak their vengeance on their foes. Every church was demolished; that of the Holy Sepulchre was the chief object of their fury, and the splendid edifice erected by Helena and Constantine did not escape. The Persians, it is said, sold the Christians for slaves, which the Jews bought at high prices, only to slaughter them. Under the mild protection of the Persians, the Jews, though not independent masters of the holy city, remained again in peaceful possession of it for nearly ninety years; then Heraclius sent his troops against Jerusalem to reconquer it, and the Persian king scarcely offering any assistance, Palestine and the Jews passed again under the rule of their former cruel masters, the Romans.

Another notable fact is, that the slave trade in Europe was for more than a century almost entirely in the hands of the Jews, which is owing to the following circumstances. When, about the year 400, the northern barbarians, who were heathen, invaded the southern part of Europe, many wealthy cities and fertile fields were devastated, and their Christian inhabitants slaughtered or sold as slaves. As the Jews were merely sojourners and not attached to the soil, they could easily remove, and suffered little from these invasions. The Israelites, who, notwithstanding their close adherence to their faith, always had a peculiar aptitude and penetrating eye for commerce, took advantage of these revolutions, exchanged with the barbarians the valuable spoils for cheap but more useful articles, and at the same time bought their Christian captives at most trifling prices, which traffic became a source of great wealth to them. Some Christian monarchs and popes looked upon this slave dealing with horror, and issued severe enactments against it; while others, at later times, recognized the right of Jews holding slaves as their property, but ordered that they should be redeemed by Christian individuals or out of the church funds; but as people were not always willing and prepared to obey these mandates at their own expense, and moreover, as these orders were issued in writing, and many officers of the government and even many of the clergy could neither write nor read, these laws produced little effect; and in one of the councils of Toledo a complaint was made that even the clergy sold Christian captives to Jews and heathen.

The Rule of Mohammed. Influence of Islamism upon the Jews.

Hitherto the strife for supremacy in revealed religion had existed only between Jews and Christians; but a new faith, Mohammedanism, was destined to arise, and to surpass, numerically, both its rivals. Mohammed, an Arabian camel driver, born at Mecca towards the end of the sixth century, pretended to be inspired by the angel Gabriel to found a new religion. In the fortieth year of his age he proclaimed his doctrine, which was, "There is but One God, and Mohammed is his prophet." In a few years his followers became very numerous; his religion spread over all Asia, the north of Africa, and Spain, and is now adopted by many millions of people, perhaps more than half of the human race. The Arabs, or Mohammedans, are descendants of Ishmael, the son of Abraham by Hagar. The tenets of their religion are contained in a work called Koran, which, like the word Bible, means book. The successors of Mohammed were called Caliphs, now Sultans, and their religion is also called Islamism. The establishment of the Mohammedan religion caused great changes in the government and religion of the eastern world, and considerably affected the condition of the Jews. The Persian kingdom fell, and their religion, which was the Magian religion, or the worship of fire, was almost extinguished. In the Asiatic provinces, excepting Armenia, Christianity sank to be an inconsiderable and persecuted sect. A magnificent mosque replaced the church on the summit of Moriah, where the Jewish Temple had formerly stood, and Spain came entirely under the dominion of the Mohammedans. To the Jews the change was generally favorable, and especially in Spain, where they entered upon their era of distinction in commerce, in wealth, and in literature. In the peninsula of Arabia, however, uniformity of religion was enforced, and the Jews were still treated with intolerance and cruelty. Later, under the Caliphs, they were generally treated with much consideration, and great honors were conferred upon them. Omar, the second Caliph, intrusted a Jew with the coinage. At a still later period (753) we find Jews intrusted with the office of collecting a heavy fine laid upon the Christians. At the capture of Rhodes, the celebrated fallen Colossus, one of the wonders of the world, was sold to a Jew who, it is said, loaded nine hundred camels with the metal. The rabbinical schools were then in a flourishing condition, and the Prince of the Captivity governed his subjects with undisputed sway.

THE KINGDOM OF KHOZAR.

Historians tell us about a Jewish kingdom under the name of Khozar or Khazar, the most important and accredited points of which are these. It appears that at an early period a tribe of Pagans inhabited the territory along the Caucasus Mountains, between the Caspian and Black Seas, which in course of time became very numerous and formidable. They made rapid progress in commerce and civilization, and from a tribe of nomads they became a settled nation, governed by a king. Their capital, Bilangiar, was situated at the mouth of the Volga, and a line of fortified cities extended from there to the Don. They became so rich and powerful that they were not only respected, but dreaded by the Persians and Greeks. As merchants of all nations were freely admitted, the Khozars became acquainted with the civilized forms and doctrines of religion, and in the year 740, Bulan, their king at that time, after having investigated the merits of the different religions, embraced Judaism, which is said to have happened in this way. He asked the Christians which religion, outside of their own, they thought best, Judaism or Mohammedanism; they answered Judaism, as that was the religion originally revealed by God. Then he asked the Mohammedans which of the two they thought preferable, Judaism or Christianity, and they answered Judaism, which like their own, taught the unity of God. As, therefore, both Christians and Mohammedans agreed in the validity of the Mosaic faith, whilst themselves stood each alone in asserting the superiority of their own creed, the king concluded to adopt Judaism, and make it the dominant religion of his nation, establishing it at the same time as a fundamental law that thereafter no king should be chosen except one confessing the Jewish religion. This kingdom continued to exist for about two centuries and a half, until the year 1000, when the monarchy was subverted, and the country conquered by the Slavi.

Dominion of the Patriarch of the West, and the Prince of the Captivity.

We have spoken before of the two Jewish communities which formed after the destruction of the Second Temple, and which were governed respectively by the Patriach of the West, and the Prince of the Captivity. We will now treat more fully of the office and dominion of these rulers, and the duration of their administration. The exact time when the patriarchate began we cannot say, but it appears to have been some seventy years after the destruction, and that Simon Ben Gamliel was the first who held this dignity. The residence of the Patriarch was Tiberias, in Palestine, and the exercise of his jurisdiction extended chiefly over the religious affairs of his constituents, who were voluntary subjects and tributaries to their sovereign. The Patriarch was acknowledged and supported in his authority by the civil powers of the land, because the whole community tacitly consented to the institution, and though he was not legally empowered to enforce obedience to his decisions by compulsory measures, he had more powerful means at hand, which was that of excommunication—a punishment which all dreaded more than pecuniary fines or bodily chastisement, both of which, however, were also occasionally administered. The Patriarch was supported in his judiciary functions by an Ab-beth-din and a Chacham, as well as by other assessors, thus forming a kind of Sanhedrin, and all minor officials were appointed by him. The annual contributions of the community were such as to enable their spiritual monarch to live in magnificent style, which may have been the cause that some of those rulers looked as much, or even more, to the worldly interests of the position as to the religious welfare of the people. Among those who occupied the patriachal seat, several were ambitious men, who by their severity and overbearance caused strife and disunion in the community, yet there were many of very superior scholarship and excellent character, who had nothing but the real interests of the people at heart. R. Jehuda Hakkadosh, the compiler of the Mishna, is acknowledged as the most illustrious of the whole series of Patriarchs. The institution lasted about three hundred years, and terminated in the year 429. R. Gamliel was the last of the Patriarchs. The position of Resh-Galuta, or Prince of the Captivity, was not unlike the preceding, but differed chiefly in this respect, that the authority of the Resh-Galuta extended over the secular as well as over the religious affairs of the community; in fact, at first his power extended exclusively over secular concerns, while the decisions of all ecclesiastical affairs were rendered at the court of Tiberias. When later,, however, the Babylonian schools produced men equally as well versed in the law as were the Palestinians, the eastern community asserted its entire independence, and still later surpassed its rival in wealth, splendor, and learning, and the Prince of Captivity exercised his royal powers with an authority hardly inferior to that of David or Solomon. The inauguration ceremonies of this dignitary were of truly royal magnificence, and the pomp and grandeur of his court perhaps equally as great as that of his Persian master. Internal dissensions among those in authority prevailed in Babylonia not less than in Palestine; still the eastern schools and colleges increased rapidly and spread all over the country, and general learning grew in proportion; for one of the most remarkable traits in the history of the Jews is the singular devotion they have always shown to mental culture. The most famous colleges were those of Nehardea, Sura, and Pumbedita. Among the many eminent scholars who rose, there is chiefly to be noted Rab Asché, who undertook and accomplished the compilation of the Talmud, which took place about the beginning of the sixth century. In course of time the power of the Romish church increased and the Islam retrograded. The Babylonian schools as well as the Palestinian decreased in number and importance, and the flux of emigration set in towards Africa, to Spain, and other European countries. The office of Resh-Galuta continued in a lingering condition until 1038. The last chief of the Captivity was Hezekiah, who, by order of the Caliph Abdallah Kaim, was seized and ignominiously executed.

THE JEWS IN SPAIN. MOSES IN SACKCLOTH.

We must now turn our attention to the Jews in Europe, beginning with Spain. The settlement of our ancestors in that country is of a very early date, by some believed to have been as early as the time of King Solomon. It is certain, however, that in the early ages of Christianity the Jews in Spain were so numerous and influential that fears of the whole community adopting Judaism were entertained by the Church, and measures were taken by both king and clergy to oppose the influence. As the Jews were always wealthy, their presence excited the envy of their neighbors, while at the same time by their industry they constituted the most important part of the population. The influence of these two qualities—their wealth and their industry—varied and predominated as the sentiments and the circumstances of their Mohammedan or Christian rulers changed. Hence they were often persecuted and exiled in order to rob them of their wealth, and again recalled or readmitted to enrich the country by their industry. This has been the case in most European countries; but the treatment of the Jews under Mohammedan rulers has always been milder than that under their Christian masters, and when in 712 the Arabians (that is the Moors or Saracens) conquered Spain, the Jews hailed with delight the change of government from Christian to Mohammedan, and they are believed to have been instrumental in producing that change. From that time till the end of the tenth century we have but little positive information. But there is no doubt that the Jews shared largely in the splendor and prosperity of the Arabs, and mingled freely with them, and that their common Oriental origin favored the coalition. They soon wrote and spoke in Arabic as well as in Hebrew, and are to this day looked upon by the Christians of Spain and Portugal as their first masters in every department of science. In 980 many Jews came to Spain from Palestine and Mesopotamia, in consequence of the decline of the high-school; and many prominent rabbis opened in Castile and Aragon in Cordova, Granada, Barcelona, and other cities, schools not only of Jewish theology, but also of various sciences. They were treated with great consideration and respect by the Moors on account of their superior learning; and while Christian Europe was enveloped in mental darkness; while Christian barons could not write their names, and Christian priests could scarcely spell out their breviaries; Mohammedan Cordova might be considered the centre of civilization, of arts, and of letters, to which the Jews were the chief contributors. Hebrew poetry began to be more cultivated, and many sublime poems found in our prayer-books, some of which yet bear the stamp of Arabic rhythm, and the Arabic melody of which has even been preserved among the Sephardim, were then composed; and an Arabic translation of the Talmud was made under the direction of R. Moses Ben Hanoch who may be considered as the founder of the great Spanish schools, and of whom the following singular incident is recorded. This R. Moses, together with two other rabbins of great distinction, left Babylonia to settle in Spain, and on their passage were made captives by a Spanish pirate. The wife of R. Moses accompanied him on the voyage, and fearing that she would be ill-treated, looked to her husband for advice. He cited a text in Hebrew, "The Lord said, I will bring back from the depth of the sea," by which he hinted to her that it were better to perish than to yield herself up to the ruffians. Hereupon the high-minded woman plunged into the sea and perished. R. Moses was brought to Cordova as a slave, and was redeemed by the Jews, though his quality and high attainments were not known. One day he entered the synagogue in his coarse dress of sack-cloth, while R. Nathan was presiding and discussing certain points of the law. R. Moses entered into the debate, and showed such profound knowledge that the presiding rabbi and all present were astonished. Hereupon the chief rabbi exclaimed, " I am no more your instructor, this man in sack-cloth is my master, and I am his scholar." Rabbi Moses was then appointed as head of the community by general consent. He was succeeded by his son Enoch, and the latter again by his son Nathan, who was held in such high esteem, and the wealth of the members of his community was so great, that whenever the rabbi went to enjoy a recreation in the beautiful groves and gardens near Cordova, he was followed by great numbers of his scholars and friends, and some 700 chariots followed in the procession.

SPANISH JEWISH SCHOLARS AND STATESMEN.

A full description of the elevated condition of the Jews in Spain and Portugal would fill quite a number of pages, much more than the scope of this work will allow ; we must satisfy ourselves here with a condensed account of it. It is now admitted by all impartial thinkers that the world owes the Jews an immense debt of gratitude, not only for the preservation of the Scriptures, but for their invaluable contributions to the sciences, to philosophy, mathematics, astronomy, and medicine, especially the latter. From the brilliant constellation of literati which adorns our history we can select only a few of the brightest stars, beginning with some eminent theologians and poets. R. Menahem Ben Saruc was a learned Talmudist and author of a Hebrew lexicon, the manuscript of which is preserved in the library of the Vatican. R. Samuel Chophni Hacohen, of Cordova, wrote an exposition on Deuteronomy, still in manuscript. Another R. Samuel, of Barcelona, distinguished himself by the efforts he made to annul the old rabbinical decrees against the study of Greek literature. Another doctor of Barcelona, Judah Ben Levi Barzilai, not long after, wrote a treatise on a subject not well understood in the East, "The Rights of Woman." A very singular coincidence presents itself in a group of five learned men, all of whom bore the name of Isaac: R. I. Ben Geath was the wealthy chief of the congregation at Lucena; R. I. Ben Moses, professor at Denia; R. I. Ben Reuben, of Barcelona; R. I. Ben Baruch, a theologian and mathematician in high esteem for his proficiency in the latter branch at the court of the King of Grenada, and last, the great R. I. Alphasi (*i. e.*, of Fez), distinguished for his elaborate commentary on the Talmud. R. Asher, a German by birth, established himself at Toledo, and, on account of his great learning, was there chosen head of all the schools and synagogues in Spain. The prosperity of the Jews in Castile, and the influence of their nobles reached its greatest height in the fourteenth century. In the counsels and friendship of Alphonso XI., his physicians, Don Samuel Abenhacar, Don Samuel Ben Jaes, and R. Moses Abudiel held a permanent and distinguished place. Spanish historians speak of Don Joseph, called Almoxarife, "the treasurer," who, with Osorio, the Count de Transtamare, long possessed the king's unlimited favor. The marriage settlement of Henry IV., of Castile, with the Princess of Portugal was drawn up by a Jewish ambassador, R. Joseph, the king's physician. In the same century, Abiathar, of Lerida, in Arragon, gained great renown by curing the blindness of King John II. at the age of eighty. This cure is the first instance of the operation for cataract which has been recorded in the history of medical science. The physician ventured to perform the operation upon one eye, and having completely succeeded, felt some hesitation in proceeding; but the resolute and courageous old king compelled him to risk an operation on the other also. In Portugal, the names of Jewish physicians are rarely wanting among the officers of the king's household. The dignity of "Physico-mor," or first physician, was instituted by King John I., of Portugal, in 1385, and bestowed first upon the Jewish physician Micer Moses, together with great privileges for himself and nation. Other Jewish professors of medicine were treated with similar consideration until the reign of King Manuel. When the Jews were banished from Portugal in the year 1497, the new Christians, concealed or baptized Jews, and their descendants continued to distinguish themselves as professors of medicine. For example, Dr. Manuel de Fonseca, and his son, Dr. Lope de Fonseca, whose daughter, Ginebra, was burnt by the Inquisition on a charge of Judaism; Dr. Abraham Zacuto (Zacutus Lusitanus), author of the "History of Celebrated Physicians;" Dr. Immanuel Jacob Rosales, upon whom the Emperor of Germany bestowed the dignity of Count Palatine, and Dr. Roderigo de Castro were equally known by their writings, and celebrated for their enlightened views during the early part of the seventeenth century. Don Samuel Levi was Minister of Finance to King Pedro, successor to Alphonso XI. The ancient Spanish chronicle of that monarch gives an account of the faithful services rendered by this sagacious financier, relating how he enriched the royal treasury by compelling the dishonest tax-gatherers to give in their accounts, and make good their receipts. Pedro, however, was as ungrateful as he was cruel; for his faithful minister, together with other favorites, was condemned to the torture under which he expired in 1360. We rarely find mention made of a Jewish theologian or physician in Spain or Portugal during the middle ages who was not at the same time a poet, astronomer, or mathematician, often all these together. R. Abraham Zacuto was professor of astronomy at the Academy of Salamanca, his native town, till 1492, when, having fled to Portugal, he was favorably received by King Manuel, and raised to a post of honor at his court. He made a perpetual almanac, dedicated to the Bishop of Salamanca, published at Leiria, in Portugal, 1495. He is well-known in rabbinical literature as the author of " Sepher Yochasin " (book of genealogies), a valuable source of reference for the history of the older rabbinical schools of theology. The principal councillors of John II., of Portugal, when undertaking the expeditions that led to the discovery of a new way to India round the Cape of Good Hope, were the two Bishops of Viseu and Ceuta, and three Jewish physicians, José, Roderigo, and Moses. The first idea of the possibility of finding a passage to India was suggested by the observations of two Portuguese Jews, R. Abraham de Beja, and Joseph Zaphatero de Lamego, who had been sent by King John II. to explore Ormuz and the coast of the Red Sea. An investigation as to the best means of encouraging navigation, not along the coast only, but in the open sea, was confided by the government, during the reign of this prince, to the celebrated German, Martin de Behaim, then established in the country, together with the beforementioned Roderigo and José. And let it be borne in mind that we do not depend for our information on these points on the evidence of Jewish writers only, but on the authoritative records of the country as well. From the unanimous testimony of the chronicles of the church, and from authentic Spanish historians, we learn how large a share of influence, wealth, and consideration was at that time possessed by the Jews in Spain. Also in France and elsewhere, Jews frequently distinguished themselves in the medical profession. A Jewish physician was called in to Francis I., and is said to have been the first to recommend the use of ass's milk. Another Jewish physician followed the constable of Bourbon in his exile, and his son was the distinguished chancellor of France, Michel de l'Hôpital, celebrated for his great talent as a legist and statesman. In the eighteenth century, Dr. de Silva, a Portuguese Jew, was highly celebrated in France as a physician, and is one of the very few upon whom Voltaire, the great enemy of Israel, bestowed some words of praise, both in his poetry and his history. We have scarcely spoken of the Spanish Jews as poets. R. Isaac Ben Geath, whom we have already mentioned, was one of the most distinguished poets in Spain. His poetical productions for the penitential holidays are particularly admired. His son, R. Judah, and his grandson, R. Solomon, succeeded him, and both are looked upon as masters of the art by such judges as Alcharisi, and Judah Halevi. R. Bechai Ben Joseph Ben Pekodah also stands high as a poet, and of still brighter fame is R. Moses Aben Ezra, equally celebrated as a Talmudist and professor of Greek philosophy. Although, like his brother poets, he excelled in sacred song, he also tuned his lyre as an inhabitant of the West, and sang at times of love, but more often in praise of the beauties of nature. Alexander von Humbolt, in his "Cosmos," bestows much praise on his sublime description of natural scenery. So, also, Don Santo de Carion, who embraced Christianity, was distinguished as one of the most famous troubadours of the age. Still higher in the scale of poetical genius stands R. Judah Halevi; and the acme, we may say, is reached by the great R. Solomon

Ben Gebirol, who is unanimously allowed to have far excelled all other Jewish poets of the tenth and eleventh centuries. Born in 1031 at Malaga or Saragossa, where he afterwards resided, his life was as short as his talents were brilliant, and his end tragical. His death is said to have been caused by the sanguinary envy of an Arabian rival in song, and the young poet, it is said, was buried by his murderer under a fig-tree, which produced in consequence so great an abundance of fruit of such exquisite flavor as to attract the attention of the caliph, and led to a discovery of the body, and a detection of the crime and its perpetrator. The poetical talents of Gebirol were exercised on many different subjects; hymns, elegies, and confessions of sin, many of which, as well as the compositions of the aforenamed masters, are still retained in the liturgy of the Sephardim. His "Keter Malchut" (Royal Crown) is looked upon as his masterpiece, the sublimity of which, indeed, cannot be too highly estimated, and can be appreciated only by those who have a taste for Hebrew style, though its grandeur appears even in the many foreign tongues into which it has been translated.

ABEN EZRA AND MAIMONIDES.

We have expatiated—perhaps too much, considering the limits we prescribed to our book—on the greatness, the erudition, and the nobility of the Spanish and Portuguese Jews—a subject which we could pursue with an ardor little short of enthusiasm, and for which a sense of national pride in the author may plead an excuse; and yet we cannot take leave of this interesting matter without devoting an additional paragraph to the biography of "the two great lights," Aben Ezra and Maimonides.

Abraham Ben Meir Aben Ezra was born of a noble family at the beginning of the twelfth century at Toledo. He was a man of extensive erudition and wonderful genius, perfectly familiar alike with the Aristotelian philosophy and the closest interwoven textures of rabbinical literature. Taking in consideration the age in which he lived, he was really eminent as a commentator, grammarian, philosopher, physician, astronomer, and poet. In his fiery spirit, in the ardor of his imagination, and in his humorous vein he is unequalled by any of the Jewish literati. His style is pure, expressive, and original; his sentences are elegant, sometimes lively and full of wit, but often so brief as to be obscure. Like many of his co-temporaries, he had a great inclination for travelling. This taste is worthy of remark as presenting a striking contrast to the life led by the monks and the Roman Catholic clergy of that period. This desire of becoming personally acquainted with a world in which they met with so much hostility is especially observable in Aben Ezra. The various places from which he dated his different works show in a literal sense that he was a wanderer on the earth. As a commentator on the Scriptures he is valued without exception by all. His hymn on the Soul is a poetical development of the idea that every night, during sleep, the soul, released from the body, ascends to heaven to give an account of the work done uring the day. His poetical compositions extend also to nuptial hymns, elegies, satires, and even a series of verses on the game of chess. He visited also Palestine, and held converse with the learned men of Tiberias upon the Masoretic text of the Bible. He died on his return from this pilgrimage at the age of seventy-five, much lamented by all who knew him, among whom his friend and admirer Maimonides.

Rabbi Moses Ben Maimon, or with the Greek termination Maimonides, known also among us as Rambam, was born at Cordova in Spain about the year 1130. His father filled the office of judge in his native city, as several of his immediate ancestors had done before him. Maimonides received his early education at Lucena and subsequently pursued his studies at Cordova, where he formed the acquaintance and friendship of the great Arabian philosopher Averroes, which appears to have greatly influenced his mode of thinking. He made uncommon progress, not only in rabbinical literature, but excelled also in mathematics, metaphysics, and the medical science, and added to a knowledge of the Hebrew and Arabic languages that of Chaldee, Turkish, and Greek, and made himself familiar with the writings of Plato, Aristotle, and other famous philosophers. Averroes was, what may be properly called a free-thinker; was persecuted and removed from the chief magistracy of Cordova, and Maimonides, unwilling to betray his friend, submitted to a voluntary exile and fled to Egypt. There for some time he traded in precious stones, but at the same time continued his studies and completed his commentary on the Mishnah in Arabic. His great merit introduced him to the notice and esteem of the Sultan Alphadel Abderrahim who appointed him his physician, which office he continued to occupy under Salaheddin and other Egyptian monarchs till the day of his death. The most extensive work of Maimonides is his " Yad Hachazakah " (the Powerful Hand) which is a complete digest of Jewish law, drawn from the confused compilation of the Talmud. He thus produced a regular code of fixed laws cleared of all the disputations and all extraneous matter with which they are intermixed in the Talmud, thus establishing order out of chaos. The work consists of fourteen books written in pure and elegant Hebrew. The next in importance is his "Moreh Nebuchim" (Guide for the Erring) written in Arabic. This is a critical, philosophical, and theological work, in which the author endeavors to explain many difficult passages of the Bible, and is rendered particularly important by an excellent exposition of the grounds and reasons of the Mosaic laws. Maimonides, like his friend Averroes, was an independent thinker. By looking upon the divine laws in a rational way, and finding a palpable reason for every one of them, he opposed and offended the sentiments of a class of rabbis who believed that we cannot penetrate into the reasons of the laws, and that by endeavoring to do so we detract from their sanctity. The publication of this work, consequently, caused a great commotion in the rabbinical world, and led to fearful results. Some rabbis of France met it with the most violent opposition, and went so far as to burn the books and lay the ban of excommunication on the author; while others as determinately defended Maimonides and his work, and hurled back the anathema. His opponents, still more irritated, ventured on the desperate measure of applying to the Christians for aid, assuring them that certain heretics had come forward among the Jews, who entertained and disseminated dangerous opinions, and expressing an earnest wish that they might be treated as the Christians treated such characters among themselves, by burning both the books and their authors. By these extreme measures the contending parties exposed themselves to great contempt and danger, and the result might have been yet more serious; but the decisive and united action of the Spanish congregation ultimately settled the matter in favor of Maimonides and his writings. The works of this indefatigable author amount to more than thirty in number, and some of them are of great magnitude. His medical profession—as he declared in one of his private letters—occupied nearly all his hours in the day-time; and how he could find leisure to collect and digest materials for the numerous and voluminous works which flowed from his pen is truly astonishing. Our great author died at Cairo, at the age of seventy, and was buried at Tiberias in Palestine, followed by an immense concourse of admirers.

Jews in Arabia, India, and China.

We retrace our steps to an earlier period, to contemplate once more the condition of the Jews in Asia, namely, in Arabia, India, and China. Arabia, in consequence of its close proximity to Palestine, was at an early date (150 B.C.) visited by Jews who sought a refuge there whenever their condition in Judea became threatening or dangerous. They lived with the Arabs on most intimate terms, and in course of time their congregations increased rapidly until they assumed immense proportions. Before the time of Mohammed we find them spoken of in the history of the peninsula as numerous, free, and powerful, constituting a considerable portion of the Arabian population. So close was the intermixture of Jews and Arabs, and so similar their morals and manners, that their rulers, it seems, were chosen indiscriminately from either portion; and the fact is mentioned with certainty that not only Jewish kings were appointed, but that Judaism, that is, in a very limited sense of the word, prevailed. This happy state of mutual toleration continued till 270 (C.E.) when it was disturbed by the Roman Christian emperor Aurelian. Still the Jews maintained their position, at least in some parts of Arabia, for we find that, in the sixth century, Dunaan, the last king of Yemen, was a Jew, and his wars, achievements, and ultimate defeat are described in detail. When Mohammed made his appearance, at first only as a poet and reformer, he found the Arabian Jews in general favorably disposed towards him. Some even joined his ranks, and out of consideration for the Jews of Medina, he even changed some of his precepts; but when he proclaimed himself a prophet, and empowered to annul the Mosaic precepts, the Jews determinately refused all adherence or submission to his teachings, and from that moment they became the special object of his hatred,

We have but little reliable information concerning the Jews in India. What we have been able to glean is, that in the sixth century, in consequence of a persecution raised in Persia, seventy-two families under the leadership of Joseph Rabban (*i. e.*, Joseph our master) sought admittance in India of King Scheram Perimal, and obtained a piece of land near Granganor for the purpose of establishing there an independent principality. Two brazen tablets, to which are attached the names of seven princes as witnesses, contained the privileges granted to the new prince, the first of whom was Joseph. These families henceforth constituted the aristocracy of the community and became very wealthy. Many Indians joined them, and they acquired a great number of slaves, male and female, all of whom were converted to Judaism and who in course of time far outnumbered their masters. The colony increased still more by the addition of new emigrants from various parts of Western Asia, who had heard of the El Dorado of their brethren, especially young men who bought themselves slaves, converted them, and married them, and hence the black Jewish population of India. In language, features, and color these Indian Jews resemble exactly the other inhabitants of the country, yet they have the "Shemah Israel" and some Hebrew prayers; strictly observe the day of Atonement, and various other Jewish institutions. In the latter part of the seventeenth century the Jews of Cochin held some correspondence with the Portuguese congregation at Amsterdam, and information was given of a series of Jewish kings (satraps, we must suppose) who had successively reigned in the country. Another colony of black Jews under the name of "Bene Israel" is found in Bombay, whose ancestors evidently came thither from Persia. A Jewish traveller, J. J. Benjamin, who visited them in 1849–50, gives us information concerning these people much similar to the particulars we just related of the other tribe.

The history of the Jews in China is yet involved in much obscurity. We will give only a few details which are unanimously accepted as true, and some resting on strong probability. It is certain that some of the Mesopotamian Jews in their eastward course settled in Persia, and in consequence of the disturbances in the Mongolian empire wended their way, together with some Christian families, to the far distant regions of China. The first discovery of the existence of Jews in that country was made in 1642 by Jesuit missionaries who met with Jews at Pekin, Nanking, and Kai-fung-foo. The whole population of the Chinese Jews sprang from seven tribes, or families, whose unpronounceable names seem to be derived from those of the different emperors under whom, at successive periods, these families established themselves in China. The Jews there are distinguished by a Chinese name which signifies, "the people that cut out the sinew." They have at Kai-fung-foo a fine Synagogue, a Sepher, and several, but not all of our books of the Scriptures; and the initiation into the Abrahamic covenant, as also the Sabbath and festivals, are observed by them. The religion and history of Christ is entirely unknown among them, but some have been found great admirers of Confucius. Some inscriptions testify that several Jews had been highly honored with the imperial favor and had attained the rank of Mandarin; and we read especially of one named Chao, or Chong, who was much praised for having rebuilt at his own expense a synagogue destroyed by fire. We will only add that the source of all these Asiatic Jews must be traced back to Babylonian origin, and they are not to be considered as parts of the Lost Ten Tribes.

JEWS IN AFRICA.

Africa—the cradle of Israel's nationality, the birthplace of their great legislator, the place where they dwelt for centuries, and from the small number of seventy men rose to more than half a million, is interesting in point of history, not only for the events related in the Bible, but also for the condition of the Jews there in the middle and the latter ages. Long before the dissolution of the Jewish state, a large colony had settled down in Egypt and established a rival temple there as we have seen.. Two distinguishing characteristics of the Jewish people have always been—their love of learning, and their ambition for commerce; and as Alexandria offered particular advantages for the exercise of both, it became a resort for them both in times of peace and of war. We have no room to consider the condition of our people in Africa through the different stages of our history, suffice it to say that, with the spread of the Mohammedan religion over Africa, many Jews accompanied the Arabian hordes into their new settlements, where they were often subjected to much ill-treatment, while at other times their usefulness was recognized and important positions intrusted to them. At a later period their numbers were considerably increased by an influx of emigrants from Spain, who joined their brethren at Tripoli, Tunis, Algiers, Fez, and all over the empire of Morocco, where they found numerous synagogues and seminaries noted for their men of learning. Their intelligence and industry secured to them the first position in society as merchants, as statesmen, and as men of letters, and yet were they subjected to severe and oppressive laws. The most important branches of industry were in their hands. They were occupied chiefly in vine-culture and fisheries, in weaving, especially gold and silver-cloth, and in the manufacture of gold and silver articles, of which they had a monopoly, and the coinage was, and is even now, entirely intrusted to them. In literature they distinguished themselves, not only as theologians, but as linguists, mathematicians, and astronomers, particularly in the schools of Fez and Morocco. We may mention the able Isaac Ben Schescheth from Saragossa, who in 1391 was appointed by the king as chief of the community at Algiers. Cotemporary with him was Simon Ben Semach Duran, a highly cultivated and liberal-minded scholar, and adherent of Maimonides, who administered to his congregation for fifty-three years. He labored indefatigably for the improvement of the elementary and higher branches of instruction, and opposed the mystic speculation of the Cabalah, the interpretations of dreams, and all superstitious practices to which the Jews of Barbary even now attach much importance. During the administration of that worthy leader, the number of emigrants from Spain was so great that the use of Arabic was partly supplanted by the Spanish tongue, and to the present day we hear the Jews of northern Africa express themselves either in bad Arabic, in corrupt Spanish, or indifferent Hebrew. Among the labors of this spiritual chief was his endeavor to establish union among the various congregations; for it is to be noted as a peculiarity of the Jews in those states, that the different communities keep themselves quite distinct from each other; occupy different parts of the city, each having their own rabbi, who is not only their leader in religion and representative by the government, but at the same time their superior judge in all civil matters, and from whose decision very seldom an appeal is made. Thus the later emigrants from the peninsula keep aloof from the earlier settlers—that is, their respective descendants do—and both are distinguished from the European Jews whom they call Franks. The ancient congregations enjoy the privilege of a smaller capitation tax than what is laid upon the others. In the second half of the seventeenth century the Jews were subjected to persecution and driven from the country by Muley Archey, who succeeded in dethroning his brother Ismael. The Jews of Morocco and Tetuan suffered most, their synagogues were destroyed and themselves obliged to flee to Fez. And yet a few years later, Joseph Ben Hamoshet was appointed as Sheik by the same prince. When Ismael regained his throne, Don Jos.

Toledano of Mequinez, with whom Ismael had found a refuge, was elevated to the position of minister of state, and sent to conclude a treaty of alliance between Morocco and Holland. The affairs of finance and the negotiations with European powers were almost entirely intrusted to the Jews, who were often used as the instruments of the emperors or sultans, and seldom allowed to die a natural death. They attained distinction and wealth and were then frequently betrayed into some political snare, accused of misdemeanor, and ordered to be executed. At Oran, which was conquered by the Spaniards under Cardinal Ximenes in 1507, the Jews from Spain were permitted to reside upon sufferance. They were exemplary in their fidelity to the Spanish government, and gained its esteem by their personal services. The valiant families of Casino and Saporta, originally from Arragon, served the King of Spain against his Moorish enemies in Africa; so that when in 1669 the Spanish governor forbade the Jews to remain any longer in Oran, he granted letters patent to the Saportas, making honorable mention of the services that family had rendered, ending with the remarkable declaration, that they were banished for no other reason than "because it was absolutely impossible for his Catholic majesty to allow a Jew to remain within his dominions."

In 1775, a Jewish nobleman of Morocco, named Masahod de la Mar, was sent as ambassador to the court of England, and there treated with distinction and honor on account of his talents as a diplomat and his courteous demeanor. Being once out on a hunting tour with George III., the ambassador saved his majesty from some impending danger and was rewarded with the uncommon privilege of driving about the town with six-in-hand. He was sent in a similar mission to Holland, and subsequently established himself with his family at Amsterdam, where he resided the remainder of his life. In 1817, Masado Ben Leaho was minister of foreign affairs in Moran; Meir Ben Manin of Fez obtained in 1823 the general consulship of all foreign courts; and yet are those who do not attain to any such distinction obliged to appear in different dress, are not allowed to ride on horses or mules, not to use umbrellas or parasols, which are privileges reserved for certain dignitaries. Algiers has often been the scene of horrible persecution and suffering for the Jews, of which the following instance may serve as a sample. The Dey—governor of the province—had issued an order requiring all Mussulmans to carry a lighted lamp when out at night. Jews, however, were to carry a light, like all others, but were not allowed to use a lantern. On a stormy night, therefore, the poor Jews were exposed not only to the danger of burning their hands badly, but also to the ridicule and amusement of police agents, who delighted in inflicting a bastinado or a fine on the offender whose light was extinguished. Since 1830, however, when Algiers came into the power of the French, the Jews enjoy full liberty and equality of rights. We find in the Barbary states and in the Ottoman empire generally a curious admixture of intolerance towards the Jews with an appreciation of their talents and business capacities which render them indispensable. Thus they were rigorously compelled to wear the black turban, and a different kind of shoes, so as to be distinguished from the Mohammedans; they were exposed to immense taxations, and to the uncivil treatment of the populace; and yet many were employed by the sovereigns of the respective states in important missions and intrusted with the management of state affairs. Towards the end of the sixteenth century, Don Samuel Palache was sent by the emperor of Morocco as his agent to the Hague, where he died in 1616 and was followed to the grave by the Prince Maurice, the States-General, and the councillors of the United Provinces.

Jews in Italy.

As we have previously spoken of the dwelling of Jews in Rome, it is evident that the date of their settlement in Italy is very ancient. Pompey, as we have said, having invaded Jerusalem, brought Aristobulus and his family to Rome as prisoners, and doubtless many more were made captives and sold as slaves. They were, however, soon emancipated, we know not by what means, and that they soon became numerous and wealthy is likewise evident, for we find that Cicero, a cotemporary of Pompey, in one of his orations before the senate, recommends the measure of forbidding the Jews to send their annual contributions to Jerusalem, as the exportation of so much treasure was detrimental to the welfare of Italy. After the dispersion, when the Jews were literally scattered to almost every habitable part of the globe, emigrants from Palestine joined their brethren in Italy as well as in other countries, though we have no certain information of their establishment at that time in any other provinces of the Roman empire. From that period down to the sixth or seventh century, we almost lose sight of the Jews in Italy, though there is reason to believe that during this interval they were never very flourishing nor did they suffer much from the animosity of their neighbors. The Popes generally, with some exceptions, appeared kindly disposed toward them, and more than once stood forth as their protectors when menaced and ill-treated by the populace and the clergy. Gregory I., in the seventh century, proved himself the friend of Israel both in his writings and decrees. By this time the Jews had spread over many of the Papal States, and their position varied; but in commerce as well as in literature they improved rapidly, and in the twelfth century we find them not only possessed of great riches, but also engaged in the production of many literary works. Their prosperity was owing mainly to their commercial enterprise, but also to banking speculations, and to the money-lending business which subjected them to the hatred of the population; yet in this branch of industry they were far surpassed, in Italy at least, by the Lombard bankers, so that complaints were often made that where the Jews did not manage the financial affairs, usury was carried on to a more hateful excess by nominal Christians. Persecutions took place from time to time in the kingdom of Naples, where they settled about the year 1200. The Portuguese Jewish historian Samuel Usgul speaks of one in particular, about the middle of the eighteenth century, the result of which was the compulsory baptism of many Jews, and the conversion of their synagogue into a church.

Jewish literature prospered more in Italy than in other parts of Europe during the middle ages—Spain always excepted. Eleazar Ben Jacob Kalir, a native of Cagliari in Sardinia, was distinguished as a poet, and many interesting pieces of his composition have been preserved in the Jewish liturgies of Rome and other communities. R. Nathan Ben Jechiel presided over the Hebrew academy at Rome, and undertook a work which attained much celebrity in the literary world, namely his Lexicon of the Talmud, entitled "Aruch," which evidently forms the ground-work of Buxtorf's celebrated Chaldee, Talmudic, and Rabbinical Lexicon. Elias Levita, of German birth, philosopher and professor of Grammar at Padua for thirteen years, stands pre-eminent as a scholar among his cotemporaries, and his works are to this day much appreciated. Many more names of celebrated Italian scholars of the middle and latter ages might be added here, but space does not permit. At the end of the fifteenth and beginning of the sixteenth century, a new element as it were, streamed from Spain and Portugal into the Jewish population of Italy which seemed to infuse fresh life and vigor into the community, transplanting there the love of science and literature which they had inherited from their fathers, and one striking consequence of this emigration seems to have been the establishment and multiplication of printing presses in more than one Italian city. No sooner had the blessing of this invention dawned upon mankind, than the Jews availed themselves of it for the purpose of diffusing that universal knowledge of which they had been the champions, and in our libraries may be found many beautiful specimens of printing executed within the first half-century after the invention. When in 1471 the Jews in Italy began to set up Hebrew presses, their example was soon followed at Lisbon. The first Hebrew book printed in the peninsula is dated, Lisbon 1485. It is the "Sepher Orach Chaim" (Path of Life) by R. Jacob Ben Asher. In 1489 a Hebrew Pentateuch was printed at Lisbon; and in 1494 a second press was set up at Leira, which produced the Greater Prophets in the original. Three years after this, the edict of banishment was promulgated in Portugal as it had been in Spain, and this abolished forever the printing of Hebrew in the Spanish peninsula. Alas! the Inquisition had been founded—to rob and to torture were the chief aims of this priestly institution. In the place of schools and colleges were found palaces of human woe, where fierce Dominicans lived in boundless luxury, and where the wisest and purest of their species often suffered torture and death at the hands of the most infamous and the most degraded. Knowledge and virtue perished at their approach, and Spain sank into an almost irrevocable decay.

JEWS IN FRANCE.

In none of the European countries has the condition of the Jews been more variable than in France. The first notice found in history of their presence in that country is under the reign of Childebert I. (540), who ordered that in Paris no Jews should be seen in the street during the whole of Passion week. Chilperic (562), one of the most wicked and most foolish monarchs of his time, ill-treated his jeweler Priscus and threw him into prison because he refused to adopt Christianity. The council at Paris, under Clothair (615), declared all Jews unfit to hold any government office; while in Rheims the slave-trade was forbidden them; and among the many inconveniences they were put to, not the least was that they were required to listen to the Bishop's wretched sermons. King Dagobert (628) issued an edict that the Jews should receive baptism or be banished from the country; but this order soon lost its effect. This king had nevertheless Jewish tax-gatherers. Under Clovis II. we find mention made of the Jews with the following circumstances. · A capitation or poll-tax having been imposed on all citizens, some of the poorer families sold their children to satisfy this demand, but the queen forbade the Jews to make any such purchases. In the eighth century, however, under the reigns of Pepin and of Charlemagne, the Jews rose to great opulence and power. Their commerce became more and more extensive; the port of Marseilles and of Narbonne were crowded with their vessels which kept up a constant communication with the East. Their warehouses and their Christian slaves were numerous, and the trade was almost entirely in their hands, so that by their influence certain markets or fairs which were kept on the Sabbath, were changed to other days. In Narbonne one of the two prefects or mayors of the city was by prescriptive right a Jew; and the best and finest part of the city of Lyons was the Jewish quarter. "In that Christian city," says Professor Milman, "the church seemed to veil its head before the synagogue." The Jews were restricted only to the observance of certain state-laws regarding intermarriage and the treatment of their slaves, but their general prosperity was such as to rouse the jealousy of their Christian neighbors, and especially the clergy. Agobard, bishop of Lyons, indignant at seeing the great advancement of the Jews, used

all his influence to oppose them. He accused them of
cursing the Christians in their synagogue, of selling unwholesome meat and spoiled wine to the Christians; and
ordered his people to have as little intercourse as possible
with the Jews; not to sell them any slaves, not to eat or
drink with them, nor to buy their meat or wine. The Jews,
feeling offended at this, complained to the king, and the
bishop was comanded to withdraw his orders. He then
offered a petition to the king, and tried by every possible
argument to persuade him to withdraw his favors from the
Jews, but it was all in vain. He then went to Paris and
asked an audience with the king. He was ordered to wait
in an ante-room while his appeal was laid before his
majesty, and then received permission to retire. Charlemagne, whose wise and benevolent rule and whose greatness
of mind is universally admired, was very favorably disposed
towards his Jewish subjects. His father had already
granted them many privileges, as the right of holding
landed property, and under his own reign their prosperity
considerably increased. Wishing to send a communication
of a strictly private nature to the Caliph Haroun-al-Ra-
schid, he made choice of a Jew named Isaac, who, accompanied by two Christian counts, Sigismund and Lanfred,
was sent to convey the imperial message from Aix-la-
Chapelle to Bagdad. Isaac spent four years in the fulfilment of his mission, returned with very rich presents for
his master, and acquitted himself of his duties with such
ability that he was afterwards sent on a similar commission
to the court of Persia. While we ascribe such fair treatment
generally to the good sense and the justice of their rulers,
the chief cause of it is to be found in the superior intelligence and education of the Jews in a period when nobles
and kings, officers, and even the clergy could not always
write their own names. It is because the Jews, from the
earliest period of their history, always fostered knowledge

and learning, that they were selected for offices of trust and responsiblity which others were unable to fill ; they were chosen as the physicians, the ministers of finance, to nobles and monarchs because of their superior ability. During the reign of Louis I., the son and successor of Charlemagne, the Jews were so powerful that their influence was courted by the presents of nobles and princes. The king's physician, named Zedekiah, and the chief of the Jewish community enjoyed the privilege of residing within the precints of the court. During the reign of Charles the Bald the Jews still maintained their power and influence; but when, about the latter part of the ninth century, the weak-minded Louis II. ascended the throne, and the feudal system became more firmly established; when the country was virtually ruled by barons, counts, and dukes, who paid no allegiance to their king, the Jews were no longer under the protection of a powerful sovereign, the clergy began more and more to assert its authority, and the Jews gradually lost the advantages they had so long enjoyed. When Philip Augustus ascended the throne (1197), he passed a decree by which all debts due to the Jews were cancelled, and the pledges ordered to be surrendered; and shortly afterwards an edict followed which confiscated all landed property of the Jews, and commanded them instantly to depart from the kingdom. They were then re-admitted upon certain conditions, one of which was the obligation to wear a little wheel upon their dress as an ignominious distinction. These unjust and barbarous decrees were repeated by his successors, Louis VIII. and Louis IX., and by others who alternately readmitted them when in need of funds and drove them out again after they had plundered them.

The literary attainments of the Jews in France were never equal to those of the Spanish, yet the French Jewish schools produced some very eminent men, and literature was more cultivated in the southern provinces than elsewhere. Paris,

Montpellier, Marseilles, Narbonne, and Lunel were prominent seats of learning. Among the most distinguished theological doctors which these seminaries produced we may name R. Gershon, a thorough Talmudist, who distinguished himself particularly by his instrumentality in having a synodal act passed concerning the Levirate law,* by which it was decided that the marriage or dismissal of a brother's widow be not optional with the levir, but that in such cases the ceremony of Chalitsah always take place. R. Solomon Ben Isaac, better known by the initials of his name, Raschi, was born at Troyes and is famous, not so much for deep research or independence of thought, as for his assiduous labors in writing commentaries on all the books of the Bible and on all of the Talmud. Like many of the great Rabbis of the middle ages, he was a great traveller, visited Germany, Italy, Greece, Russia, Tartary, Persia, and Palestine; and is held in high esteem as the "chief of commentators." He died in the latter part of the twelfth century, and was buried in Prague, Bohemia. R. Solomon of Montpellier is distinguished as having been the leader among those Rabbis who so strenuously exerted themselves to oppose the works of Maimonides, especially his Moreh Nebuchim. The French seminaries took the part of the traditional school, against the majority of those in Spain and in Provence. Another French rabbi of no ordinary celebrity was David Ben Joseph Kimchi, descended from a Spanish family which had produced many learned men, who gained great reputation as linguists and grammarians. This R. David Kimchi undertook and succeeded in the laudable task of reconciling the contending parties in the case of Maimonides and his works; and lastly, we name the excellent poet Judah Alcharisi, whose work exhibits such warmth of expression, lively imagination, and such versatility of style and taste.

---

* See our explanation of that law *postea*.

Jews in Germany.

When the Roman empire spread its power over nearly all the nations of Europe, many Jews who were Roman citizens, together with Christians, settled in different parts of the vast realm, and of course also in Germany. An edict of the Emperor Constantine shows that in the year 321 they were already established at Cologne, where they soon became numerous and prosperous in commerce, while they continued to enjoy many important privileges. In the course of succeeding centuries, from the fourth to the tenth, their condition varied according as their rulers were kindly or unfavorably disposed towards them, but no occurrences of great importance seem to have affected their position. But when in the tenth century Germany became an independent state, the position of the Jews assumed a different aspect. At the establishment of the German empire it was laid down as a fixed rule that the Jews and all they possessed were to be considered as property of the State, and as such they and their goods could be sold, pledged, or otherwise disposed of, as the interest of the state required; and this power was vested in the emperor as liege-lord of the realm, wherefore the Jews were designated by the name of "special servants of the imperial chamber." This was by no means intended to imply anything like a state of slavery; on the contrary, it denoted an exemption from any other authority except the imperial power, and that at the same time their rights and privileges were secured, so that no prince or other power could encroach thereon without the emperor's express permission.

On the accession of a new emperor to the throne, the Jews were required to show their obeisance in welcoming the new monarch, and likewise in Italy, whenever a new pope was inaugurated. This latter ceremony was performed by a deputation of the Jewish community offering the pontiff a scroll of the law (Sepher) with an address in Hebrew, to which the pope, returning the scroll, answered in Latin. Neither one understood the other, but such was the custom.

The internal or religious affairs of the Jews were not interfered with as long as they came not in contact with the rules of government. This, after all, was not so bad in *theory*. But it must be remembered that this new situation assigned to the Jews was but part of the feudal system just then introduced into Europe by the German and Gothic tribes; an institution by which a country was parceled out to numerous barons, dukes, or other noblemen who held their respective portions as a loan from the king or emperor to whom they were responsible, and for which privilege they were to yield a certain annual tribute. With these titles granted by the sovereign to his vassals the right of holding Jews with it was sometimes granted, and sometimes not. Now although the Jews in Germany seldom had to complain of oppression proceeding directly from the emperor, they were subject to the caprices and often to the extortions and cruel treatment of the nobles under whose immediate control they were, without having an opportunity of laying their complaints before his majesty. In this manner were the Jews in Germany, and likewise in other European countries, from the eleventh till the sixteenth century, though nominally under royal protection, subject to the most cruel oppression; existing only for the benefit of their masters, for the payment of taxes and fines and all sorts of extortions. Justly has this period of our history been termed "the iron age of Judaism." The records of these inhuman barbarities, unheard-of cruelties and outrageous crimes, committed, too, under the name of religion, and of which every honest Christian now feels ashamed, constitute the blackest pages in the history of mankind, and baffle all description. Before attempting to give any instances of these atrocities practised on the Jews, not only in Germany, but generally, we will state the causes that led to them, which were chiefly two : Hatred on account of difference in religion, and jealousy of the riches which the Jews always knew how to accumulate. As true religion and rational religion is a blessing to man, so when carried to the excess of fanaticism it becomes a curse ; and this is always the case when religion is not supported by enlightened education. In those dark ages, when the very ministers and teachers of religion were ignorant of almost everything except the dogmas of their faith, their limited understanding could not grasp the grand idea that the essence of religion is the aspiration after the perfect and sublime, and its end the happiness of man ; they believed that God could be served only in that particular way they were taught, and that all who held different views were God's enemies, and to destroy them was the most meritorious act they could perform. Under these erroneous impressions, ignorant preachers harangued their still more ignorant audiences, teaching them that it was their duty to clear the community of all unbelievers, and often inciting them to deeds of violence. The populace is easily put in commotion when their political or religious prejudices are stirred up, and the flame is always fed by the prospect of plunder. In ordinary cases, however, the mob is opposed by the better classes and nobility, but when the latter find it to their interest to encourage rather than allay the sedition, the tumult will run its full course until passion have exhausted itself. As the Jews were excluded from all honorable pursuits, nothing was left them but the sordid business of money-lending at the highest possible rate of interest they could obtain (50 or 60 per cent per annum was no unusual figure). The nobles who thought all business and trade, and every profession except the military, below their dignity, who lived—

as *nobles* always live—on the toil and products of others, and often wanted large sums of money to keep up their idle and luxurious mode of living; who especially wasted immense sums to carry on the wicked crusades, of which we shall speak further on, these nobles were indebted to the Jews to a very great extent, had pledged to them the greatest part of their property which they were unable to redeem, and were ignoble enough to wish to have their debts cancelled by any means. Thus hatred and prejudice, jealousy and avarice combined to arouse and maintain the bitter feeling against the Jews. To form a better idea of the position of the Jews in Germany, we begin by stating that as a rule they were excluded from holding any civil office, and altogether from military service; were not allowed to hold landed property, nor to practise as physicians or apothecaries, and as they were not allowed to hold slaves, they could neither engage in agriculture. In short, almost every honorable and legitimate occupation was forbidden them. To these rules exceptions were often made, for which the Jews sometimes paid heavily. Some emperors, more indulgent than others, did not always enforce the law, and often intrusted them with responsible positions; but under these restraints only were they suffered to live, and in most cases were obliged to occupy a separate quarter of the city. It will be easily understood now that, under such circumstances, it needed but little to bring the populace in open assault against the oppressed Jews, and in the absence of any real offences that could be laid to their charge, to bring forward some imaginary ones. And what is quite remarkable here is the absurdity, the folly which was joined to the wickedness of the accusations. It is too well known that the Jews religiously abstain from the use of "all blood" which is most strictly and repeatedly forbidden in the Mosaic laws. Yet a hundred times were they accused of killing children in order to use their blood in Passover-cakes, which it was alleged Jews required for that purpose. When a city or territory was visited by a pestilence, from which the Jews suffered alike with their fellows, they were accused of having poisoned the wells, though they themselves drew water from the same sources; and incredible, preposterous as it may sound, they were once, in real earnest, accused of having poisoned the Rhine and the Danube. So was every public calamity or visitation attributed to the direct doings of the Jews or to their magical spells. Another absurd and oft-repeated accusation was, the Jews had stolen the Host, and pierced it so as to draw blood from it. The misery, the woe, the sufferings brought on the Jews by these monstrous charges cannot be fully described. Only a few data. In 1283, the Jews of Maintz were charged with the murder of a child for the purpose mentioned, whereupon they were assaulted, plundered, and ten innocents killed. Two years later a similar charge was made in Munich, with more pernicious result. All efforts of the police to quell the sedition being ineffectual, the Jews were advised to take refuge in their synagogue. The mob set the building on fire and 180 persons perished. A like accusation made in Paris in 1238, and disseminated in various towns, cost 2500 Jews their lives. In Ratisbon, Bavaria, where the Jews had lived for more than a thousand years, accumulated wealth, and improved the city with fine dwellings, and where their number almost equalled the Christian population, the jealousy of the impoverished populace and their thirst for the Jews' gold prompted them to accuse the latter of having killed seven children in order to use their blood for Passover. The Jews' houses were searched and blood stains pointed out; their owners were put to the torture, and a general massacre and pillaging ensued, in which all, the higher and lower classes, participated. Not only their houses, schools, and synagogues were destroyed, even the hallowed repository of the dead was not too sacred for the villains' hands.

No Jew was allowed to remain in the city, and a little chapel was erected on the ruins of the principal synagogue. Similar scenes occured in various other cities and towns, too many and too horrible to relate. In 1348, a pestilence broke out and spread over nearly all Europe. The Jews, perhaps in consequence of their dietary, had cleanly habits, suffered less. They were suspected as being the cause of the evil and were persecuted. In Basle a number of them were placed in a large hogshead, closed up, then set on fire, and the vessel sent to float on the river. In other parts of Switzerland all the Jews were guillotined or otherwise massacred. From Switzerland the mania spread to Alsace, and the magistrates of Strasburg refusing to yield to the demand of the ruffians, were compelled to resign, and the new mayor gratified his constituents by having 2000 Jews burnt alive in the market place, and dividing their property among the poor citizens. Thousands and thousands were thus launched into eternity, and neither the monarchs, the magistrates, nor even the clergy were able to stay the mad fury. Also the accusation of stealing and abusing the Host often spread desolation and death in the Jewish circles. In the cities of Würzburg, Nuremberg, and other towns of Bavaria and Austria, the sacrifice was not less than 100,000 souls. We will give only one particular case to conclude this dark chapter. About the end of the 14th century, it is related, a Jew named Jonathan, living at Enghien, France, bribed a poor Christian to steal the Host for him. When the Jew got possession of it, he assembled his friends to ridicule and insult the sacred article, but they did not then injure it. Later, Jonathan moved to Brussels, and on Good Friday the Host was brought to the synagogue and there treated with the grossest indignity, and—so runs the story— when they pierced it with their knives, the blood flowed from it in profusion. Having satisfied their vengeance, the holy thing was intrusted to a woman to take it to Cologne, but this woman, having been secretly converted to Christianity, betrayed the trust and informed the clergy of the whole affair. Thereupon the Jews were arrested, put to the torture, condemned to have their flesh torn from them by red-hot pincers, and then be burned alive. This story is even yet circulated and swallowed whole by true Catholics, and in the city of Brussels, as late as 1820, it has been commemorated with great satisfaction as a triumph of the Catholic religion.

In 1613, in Frankfort, three hot-headed vagabonds, Fettmilch, Gerngross, and Schopt, after having caused considerable disturbance in the community by inciting the people to demand certain changes in the municipal government, proceeded to demand also a public reading of the statute concerning the Jews, wherein it was laid down among other restrictions that, during the time of the annual fair, the Jews were obliged to wear a certain mark on their dress, not to appear in public on the Christian holidays, nor to be seen at public places of amusement; not to keep Christian servants ; to make sworn statements of their personal property and business transaction; and many similar oppressive regulations. On the 9th of January, some desperadoes entered the Jewish quarter with threats of violence, but they were yet kept in awe by the authorities. The rioters, however, gained in numbers and strength. Repeated menaces were held out also against the city-council, and on the 6th of May, on the occasion of an election of a new mayor, the mob surrounded the city-hall and demanded the keys of the treasury which were given up to them. Even the imperial troops could scarcely overawe the multitude. Several mandates for the arrest and punishment of the offenders were proclaimed, but hardly heeded. On the 22d of August, the robbers again entered the Jewish quarter, committed fearful depredations, destroying the best property and stealing all they could carry away. This general pillaging went on for some time, until at last new troops arrived to enforce order. On February 28th, 1616, Fettmilch and his consorts were arrested and executed; having first two fingers cut off, were then beheaded and quartered; the parts of the body exposed on the four principal streets; and the head stuck on a pole; and on the place of execution a column was placed with an inscription as a warning for offenders in future. Some 1400 Jews who had been driven from the city were, by imperial order, brought back in procession, with banners and music and under military escort; and their losses, estimated at 175,919 florins, refunded by the city, and the day (20th Adar) henceforth celebrated as a second Purim. A similar attack was made at this same period (April, 1615) on the Jews of Worms. Several corporations joined in a petition to the magistrate that the Jews might be altogether expelled. Not finding these wishes gratified, they assembled on Good Friday and announced to the Jews, whose community numbered 14,000, that they were to leave the city immediately, if they would escape pillage and murder; allowing them, however, to carry away their property. No sooner had the Jews left their quarters, when the populace entered and began their work of destruction by tearing down a synagogue which had stood 767 years, desecrated the burying ground, and committed further depredations. Directly after Easter, the imperial troops came forward, headed by one of the princes of the royal house, who punished the ring-leaders, and notwithstanding all opposition on the part of the municipality, reinstated the Jews, who on the 9th of January took possession again of their remaining property.

THE CRUSADES.

The crushing effect of the institution of the Crusades upon the Jews in Europe was overwhelming indeed. It was the beginning of a long continuance of oppression, murders, and tortures which lasted for two centuries. About the end of the eleventh century, some Christians were inflamed with the idea of gaining possession of Palestine, because it was the place where Christ was born and buried; they proposed to dispossess the infidels, as they called the Mohammedans, of that sacred spot, and to exterminate all enemies of Christianity. Great results are generally brought about by small beginnings. A fanatical monk of Amiens, Peter the Hermit, having made a pilgrimage to Jerusalem, on which occasion he met with difficulties and with insult, returned emboldened with the thought of snatching the tomb of the crucified Nazarene from the hands of its illegitimate possessors, and making Christianity the ruling faith, the only religion of the world. He was encouraged in his project by the pope, promulgated his views among the multitude, and the success of his enthusiastic harangues was proportionate to the boldness of his scheme and the ignorance of his auditors. The mania spread over all Europe; more than six millions of people, says a contemporary authority, professed themselves the soldiers of the cross. In 1096, the first expedition was set on foot and headed by count Godfrey of Bouillon. Nothing was too dear, nothing too sacred to be applied to this grand purpose; the highest and the lowest alike exhausted their means in contributing to the support of the Crusades; and many a thousand the Jews must have made in supplying the adventurers with funds and with the necessary articles; but little did they think of the dark cloud that hung over them. While these good Christians were busy preparing themselves for the holy war, it occurred to them that, before going to Palestine, they ought to get rid of the unbelievers who were near, and among them the Jews, the murderers of the Lord. Accordingly the above-named Peter, Walter the Penniless, and one named Gottschalk, at the head of a horde of fanatics, opened the campaign with a massacre of the Jews. They marched on Trier (Trèves) and began a merciless slaughter of all Jews they could find. Driven to desperation, men slew their children and themselves rather than give themselves up into the hands of their murderers; women tied large stones to their necks and threw themselves into the river. A few sought refuge in the castle of Bishop Egelbert, where the prelate took occasion of reproaching them with their unbelief, and promised them protection on condition of baptism, to which in their agony they assented. The same bloody scenes were repeated in almost all cities on the Rhine, in Metz, Cologne, Maintz, Worms, and Spire. In Cologne two hundred were dragged from the river and cut in pieces. In Worms they took refuge in the bishop's palace, but it was besieged, and to escape worse horrors, they slew each other. In Spire they defended themselves valiantly, and then succeeded in buying the protection of the bishop for a large sum. A repetition of the tragedy was performed in the cities on the Maine and the Danube by a troop under Count Emice. The emperor Henry IV. was one of the very few who showed some humanity for the unfortunate; in an edict issued from Ratisbon he permitted those that had been involuntarily baptized to return to their religion, and restored to them some of their property. About this time many Jews fled to Silesia, Moravia, and Poland, where their numbers increased with incredible rapidity. The Jews had half a century of respite. In 1146 began the second crusade, to which the Western Emperor Conrad III., and Louis VII., king of France, lent their royal support. An unworthy monk, Rudolph, stirred up the populace of Cologne, Strasburg, and other towns of Germany to renew the horrible atrocities against the "remnant of Israel," and the scenes of murder and robbery under the cloak of religion were repeated. On this occasion, however, Conrad III., though in favor of the expedition to Palestine, showed mercy to the Jews and endeavored to protect them; so did Frederick II.; Pope Eugene III. espoused the same humane part; and indeed more than once the voice of humanity issued from Rome by the mouth of her popes, such as Gregory IX., in 1240, and Innocent IV., in 1250, who are specially noticed in pleading the cause of the Jews with nations and kings. But the most sincere and the most eloquent advocate who pleaded the cause of the oppressed Jews before the beginning of the second crusade was the celebrated Bernard, Abbot of Clairvaux, a man eminent for the spirituality of his writings, as well as for the sanctity of his life. His great merits, which had secured him almost universal respect, enabled him to exercise considerable influence both in the Church and over the crowned heads of Europe. We regret not having room to reproduce his excellent exhortation to the clergy which is well worth perusing. These Crusades were repeated from time to time; the sixth and last was in 1248 under St. Louis, king of France, and the horrors they brought upon the Jews are incalculable; yet, notwithstanding the ill consequences it bore to our nation and to the whole world, the question whether the Crusades exercised a baneful or a beneficial influence on the state of society has engaged the attention of some eminent scholars, some of whom maintain that they have been favorable to the intellectual, commercial, and political interests of the world, by establishing a general intercourse between nations, and by breaking up the feudal system which, it is alleged, laid the foundation of the civil liberty now enjoyed by all European communities; while others hold that the evil results of the Crusades far overbalanced the good that followed from it; considering the great waste of life and labor without an adequate return; the affliction and privation caused to almost every family in Europe during two centuries; and withdrawing the attention of the inhabitants from all legitimate pursuit of industry. There are many other points of consideration brought forward by the contending parties, for which we have no room. Suffice it to say that the French Institute, in 1806, proposed the question as a subject of general competition to the learned of all countries, and the prize was awarded jointly to the essays of Heeren and Choiseul d'Aillecourt, who think that the Crusades, in spite of their evil consequences, have materially contributed to the advancement of learning and civilization in Europe. (But Palestine is after all in the hands of Mohammedans.) When those holy wars had terminated, another species of religious insanity sprang into existence which failed not to have its baleful result upon the Jewish population, and which is especially worth mentioning on account of its eccentricity. In the middle of the 14th century, a set of mad enthusiasts was formed at Cremona in Italy, and in a few years the contagion spread throughout Europe. The name of the sect was Flagellants, from *flagellum*, a whip. Believing that they could make their peace with God only by severe penance, they went about the streets in procession, naked from the loins upward, with high pointed hats partly drawn over the face and on which a red cross was painted; switches in hand, with which they scourged themselves till the blood flowed freely. Had their religious ceremonies been confined to these self-inflictions, we might look upon them with mere ridicule, but they thought their services incomplete without an intermixture of massacre and plunder among the Jews. Accordingly they entered the streets of Frankfort and other cities, and made a furious assault upon the enemies of Christ, who, however, seized their weapons in self-defense, and a terrible slaughter ensued. The citizens interfered, and the Flagellants were driven back; still the Jews refused to lay down their weapons, fearing, presumably, that the mob would take advantage of the occasion to commit further depredations. Then a skirmish between them and the citizens followed, the alarm was sounded, the city-hall set on fire, and many Jews lost their lives. In the mean time many of the rich had escaped with all the valuables they could carry. The emperor appropriated the remainder of their goods to the use of the city, with the privilege, however, to the fugitives to receive them back if they chose to return, and moreover a remission of their taxes for two years, which proves the justness of the Jewish cause.

JEWS IN ENGLAND. JEWISH WEALTH AND USURY.

The Jews are known to have lived in England already in the beginning of the eighth century, and their condition in that country was very similar to that in France and Germany, with this difference, that the kings of the latter two countries frequently opposed the cruelties practised on the Jews by the churchmen and the populace, while the kings of England were themselves foremost in tormenting their oppressed subjects and draining from them their ill-gotten gain. Edward the Confessor declared the Jews, by their own request probably, to be the property of the king, the same as in France. Many of them seem to have come over to England from Normandy with William the Conqueror, who introduced the feudal system, but issued no special laws concerning the Jews. We find especial mention of them made in the time of William Rufus, the second king of the Norman line. This king, himself the enemy of the clergy and very indifferent towards the Church, permitted the Jews to defend their religion in public as much as they pleased. What, however, he liked best in them was their wealth, which, for his own sake no less than theirs, he gave them every opportunity to amass, especially from the clergy. At that time the Jews possessed in London and elsewhere considerable mansions, resembling the castles of the nobility. The greatest part of Oxford belonged to them, and streets were named after them.

Now, before continuing the thread of our history let us stop awhile to consider how it was possible that the Jews, amidst their deep degradation, cruel oppression, and almost entire exclusion, should still have been able to gather up such immense wealth, not only in England, but everywhere, which must appear incredible unless we take a view of the general state of things in those ages. In the history of France, several instances are recorded of enormous special taxes having been laid on the Jews to replenish the exhausted exchequer. At one time, the most valuable estates of Paris and of the whole of France were mortgaged to the Jews. Paris of the middle ages was almost a Jewish city; the dawn of its magnificence was due to Jewish capitalists. Their wealth adorned its narrow streets with fine mansions, and cultivated its environs into groves and gardens. Louis X., after his father's death, being much pressed for money, re-admitted the Jews into his realm on the payment of a considerable price. King John and king Charles V. drew large sums of money from them, either by taxation or in loans. The most sacred objects of the church, golden relics and crucifixes with precious stones, were pledged to the Jews, and the Christians could not redeem them. In England, also, the most unreasonable and exorbitant exactions were made of them, and when in 1188 a parliament held at Northampton fixed upon a tax to defray the expenses of a Crusade, the whole Christian population was assessed at £70,000, and the Jews alone at £60,000. Now whence did all this wealth come, and why did the Jews hoard up that which they were allowed so little to enjoy? They were not originally a commercial nation, but shepherds and husbandmen; during their long sojourn in Palestine their condition was nearly the same; their change of occupation, when they became men of commerce, must be viewed in connection with their position as wanderers over the earth. When they entered upon their new career, trade or traffic was far from being what it is now. The Romans had early looked upon commerce as unbecoming the dignity of a warlike and conquering nation; the northern tribes, who in their migrations during the fifth and succeeding centuries had taken the place of the Romans, manifested still greater contempt for all matters of finance and traffic. The free men possessed the land, the rest of the population were either peasants, serfs, or artisans. Thus all trading, banking, and financial operations fell naturally into the hands of the Jews, who, considering themselves as strangers, and looked upon as enemies by the Christians, were more and more excluded from the possession of land, and the pursuit of agriculture. In the situation in which the Jews were then placed, commerce itself soon took a more ignoble aspect, and sank into petty traffic, while their financial speculations not infrequently degenerated into usury. Thus persecution drove them to the meanness of becoming usurers, and, in turn, their undignified occupation increased the hatred of their oppressors, who looked upon them, not only as a degraded race, but as their extorting creditors.* Crushed and confined by the Christian nation within the very narrowest circle in which existence could be endured, the Jew was forced to confine his inventive genius to financial speculations only. We must not, however, imagine that everything to which the name of usury was given in the middle ages, when the science of finance was unknown, really deserves that name. To understand this accusation of usury, and to pass sentence upon it with fairness, we

---

* " To justify the Jews from the accusation of having established an almost universal system of usury, I need not repeat—for it is a truth no longer contested—that they gave in to this vice only in those countries where the ill-treatment of Christians compelled them to resort to such expedients."—Beignot, Les Juifs d'Occident. The Jews of Spain and Portugal, during the centuries of their sojourn there, were never charged with being usurers.

must further take into consideration that the prejudices of the time did not allow men to consider that property in money, as well as in land or any other possession, ought to bring in some return to its owner. The Jews, it is true, contributed largely to establish this misunderstanding, by changing a fair interest into a detestable system of usury; but Christians, on the other hand, were no less to blame; and the impartial judge, when considering the financial operations of the Jews, and fairly analyzing the charges against them, will at any rate acknowledge the science and talents, as well as the cupidity and avarice, which they displayed. While admitting the infamous abuse of interest which the Jews practised, we must at the same time recognize the services rendered by them both to the theory and practice of finance. While the enormous rate of interest exacted—the scriptural *Neshech*, the biting, corroding interest—cannot be justified, even towards a stranger; and while there is no doubt that the Jews were often guilty of the basest fraud, and scrupled not to employ any means whatsoever in order to amass riches, these offences may be nevertheless easily accounted for as unavoidable evils. Excluded by the feudal system from every honorable and legitimate career, his life continually threatened, his property and means of subsistence defenceless against injustice, is it to be wondered that the Jew employed without scruple the only weapons which were left him? He encountered violence and force with artifice and finesse; he opposed the law of the stronger with calculations and deep-laid schemes; he brought to bear the power of gold against that of iron. By their superiority in financial affairs the Jews excited popular fury to the very utmost. Doubly detested as the murderers of Christ and the vampires of Christian wealth, they were a special object of severity to the laws, both ecclesiastical and civil, of hatred to the nobles, and of violence to the populace. The sovereigns who gave them protection usually made use of them as of a sponge, which they allowed to fill with the money of their subjects, and then squeeze its contents into the royal treasury. Sometimes, however, their protection availed nothing, and they were obliged to leave them to the fury of their enemies, when a single sermon from a fanatic or malevolent monk, or an absurd report of a murder committed on a Christian child to celebrate their passover with his blood, or even a mere outbreak of blind fanaticism among the populace, was sufficient to bring death and desolation upon the whole Jewish quarter. What indeed did this nominal thing of royal protection amount to, when they were debarred by law from holding landed property, from exercising any civil or military office, or even from the right of citizenship, while the most humiliating restrictions were imposed upon them? They were shut up within the narrow bounds of a peculiar quarter, often locked up at night like cattle in a yard. Conspicuous marks of degradation were imposed upon them, such as yellow patches on their clothes, peaked hats, and the like. In Bohemia there was an edict issued prescribing a peculiar manner of hanging Jews, that a distinction might be made between their body and that of a Christian criminal who might share the same fate.

Was it possible that such a classification and such treatment should fail to produce an effect upon the moral character of the Jews, and tend to enervate and harden the subject of such cruel oppression? Can we be surprised that he whose toleration in society depended only on the amount of money he possessed, should cling to that possession with the greatest tenacity, and, next to his religion, centre all his activity, all his delight, in the hoarding of gold? Can we be surprised that his outward appearance should have suffered, as well as his inward character; that is, his countenance should come to wear the expression of that timidity, and trembling of heart, which belongs to the man of distrust, who feels no security for his property, his life, or for those that are to him dearer than life? To retain their equanimity, their integrity, and an evenness of character under such circumstances would have been superhuman indeed.

Having thus endeavored to show in its proper light the position of the Jews in those ages, we resume the thread of events as they occurred in England. The rather favorable condition in which they appear in the beginning of this article was interrupted by fearful outrages after the reign of Henry II. When the coronation of Richard I. was to take place, the whole population prepared to join in the festivity; but the Jews, being suspected of sorcery, were strictly forbidden to make their appearance in public. A few strangers, however, ventured to enter the church to witness the grand ceremony. They were detected, and dragged out of the church almost dead. This roused the people to a tumult, and a general plunder of the Jews' houses ensued. The example of London was followed in several other towns, where the Jews were robbed and murdered. At York many of the unfortunate took refuge in the castle, where the governor admitted them, but when the latter was absent, the Jews, suspecting that they were betrayed, closed the gates against him, and boldy manned the citadel. The indignant governor gathered an armed force and gave the signal for attack. The populace, urged on by the clergy, shouted: "Destroy the enemies of Christ! destroy the enemies of Christ!" The besieged resisted manfully during several days, but finding their fate unavoidable, their minister addressed them thus: "Men of Israel! the God of our fathers calls upon us to die for our law. Death is inevitable, my advice is that we voluntarily render up our souls to our Creator, and fall by our own hands." The greater part of them consented, burned or buried their most valuable effects, set fire to the castle in many places, cut the throats of their wives and children, and then their own. The minister and his friend Joachim alone were left. The latter fell by the hand of the rabbi, who then stabbed himself to the heart. The next morning, when the enemy approached for a new assault, they found the castle in flames, while the few wretches who remained were running to and fro, crying for mercy, and offering to submit to baptism. The terms were accepted; but when the gates were opened, the multitude poured in and put every living being to the sword. No less than 500 families perished.

John of England, known for his cruelty, rapacity, and cowardice, being again and again in want of money, threw all prominent Jews into prison, and subjected them to most cruel torments, in order to make them pay. A Jew of Bristol, being suspected of having some hidden treasures, was required to pay ten thousand marks.* He pretended to have no money, and the king ordered that he should have one of his teeth drawn every day until he should tell where his money was. He resisted for seven days and lost seven of his teeth, then saved the rest by paying the sum demanded. Henry III., in the beginning of his reign, treated the Jews with much consideration, but the people, and especially the clergy, remained their inveterate enemies. The wearing of two strips of white cloth, as a mark of ignoble distinction, was again enforced. A crime was now laid to their charge—much more probable than the tales of their crucifying children—their tampering with and clipping the coin of the realm. In 1230, one-third of all their movable property was demanded and taken from them. A few years later, several heavy taxes were again laid upon them, and so inexhaustible seemed their resources, that it was commonly believed the Jews obtained their wealth by magical or supernatural means. The king, being ever in want of money,

---

* A mark equal to 13*s*. 4*d*.

sold the Jews to his brother, Richard of Cornwall, for 5,000 marks, giving him full power over their property and persons. When Richard was elected king of the Romans, Henry again sold them to Prince Edward, who re-sold them to the merchants of Dauphiny. But Henry, devoid of even common honesty, broke his bargain and took the Jews again under his own power, to satisfy his insatiable thirst for money, and subject them once more to his barbarous extortions. After the death of Henry III., they were treated with equal injustice by Edward I. He issued an edict, however, which had a tendency to wean the Jews from their usurious practices All usury was forbidden, but the Jews were allowed to transact all other kinds of business, and to cultivate farms, and were therein promised the royal protection. This, however, did not suit the taste or convenience of the Jews. Many were now found guilty of having clipped the coin, and in London alone two hundred and eighty of them were executed in one year for this offence. At last an edict was issued (1290) for the total expulsion of the Jews from the realm. All their property was seized for the benefit of the king, and about 16,000 of them were mercilessly driven from their homes and their country, to which they were never allowed to return, nor their descendants, until three centuries afterwards.

THE INQUISITION.

It is with reluctance that we begin the story of the Inquisition. In casting a cursory glance over the whole of this horrible chapter; the injustice, the inhumanity, the systematic infliction of so much unmerited suffering, the agony of so many inoffensive creatures roasting and writhing over the flames of the auto-da-fè, or dragging out their existence in loathsome dungeons; all rise before the imagination, and the mind is shocked to think that so much depravity can dwell in the human heart. We have in the preceding paragraphs described much cruelty and suffering; but in those cases the perpetrators were mostly the uncultivated, unprincipled populace, hungry wolves ready to seize their prey wherever it could be found; while the sufferers were comparative strangers to their foes, looked upon as intruding on the rights of old inhabitants; sometimes wanderers driven from place to place, who did not feel themselves at home and knew that they were living on the sufferance of their fellow-men.

Aware also of the mutual antipathy that ever existed between them and their neighors, they expected no kindness at their hands, and when the blow came, they were more or less prepared for it. But how widely different from this was the condition of the Jews in Spain when the thunderbolt of the expulsion came upon them. The Jews in Spain had been settled there for many centuries; they constituted part of the aristocracy of the land: they were the nobles, the statesmen, the councillors of kings, the companions of princes, the pre-eminent scholars; they had been the great benefactors of the country, had elevated it by their talents, and enriched it by their industry; while their enemies were not of the vulgar multitude, but the highest dignitaries of the church, they whose avowed profession it was to enlighten the people; to teach benevolence, charity, forgiveness, and so many virtues which the Church vainly claims as her own, and their wickedness was performed under the cloak of that very religion they pretended to teach. Now, before entering upon the facts of the inquisition, that is, of the Spanish Inquisition, let us look for a moment into the causes of it. Inquisition, as the word inplies, is the title of a court established to inquire into offences against the established religion. The idea originated with the tyrannical pope Innocent III., who in the twelfth century commissioned St. Dominic to persecute the Albigenses, a sect in the south of France, who entertained views different from the Roman church. After these people had been entirely conquered, a regular and permanent inquisitorial tribunal was established in France in the thirteenth century; it was subsequently introduced into Italy, Germany, and various other parts of Europe, though not without meeting with strong opposition even on the part of the bishops and clergy. It must be borne in mind that the Inquisition, when first established and while it remained under the immediate control of the popes, had none of those horrible features, did not aim at those unheard-of barbarities which it assumed afterwards. The first instructions were simply to labor for the conversion of heretics; to acquire information of their numbers and their rank; to examine and report whether priests and magistrates were zealous in the performance of their duties: but when the power of execution was delivered into the hands of the detestable orders of Dominicans and Franciscans, the ambitions and the barbarity of these monsters knew no bounds, and the Inquisition became a cause of terror even to the papacy which authorized and upheld it. In Spain it was not introduced until the latter part of the fifteenth century; and then the Cortez, the nobility, the great cardinal de Mendoza, and various eminent dignitaries were opposed to it; but the Dominicans, at whose head was Thomas de Torquemada, the first inquisitor general, were determined to have it, and they were supported by the lowest orders of the populace. You will remember that Spain was then divided into different monarchies. Isabella, daughter of John III., inherited the throne of Castile, and espoused her cousin Ferdinand, king of Arragon, and by this union was founded the united kingdom of Spain, though the consorts reigned independently of each other. Isabella was the stronger-minded of the two. Ferdinand was subtle and perfidious in his dealings, insidious in his policy, crafty in his schemes; while the queen was amiable and frank, her temper was firm, her intentions upright. Neither of them, especially not Isabella, entertained any hatred for the Jewish race; she befriended them and felt attached to them. She herself had Jewish blood in her veins, by her descent in the female line from John I. of Portugal, whose mother had been a Jewess. Her court, as well as that of the kings who had preceded herself and consort, had always been surrounded by Jews, in the capacity of physicians, treasurers, councillors, and ministers of state; individuals of that nation had many times proved their fidelity to Queen Isabella and her husband. Don Abraham Senior, in a moment when their succession seemed doubtful, had exerted himself on their behalf with so much energy that, when a great diminution of favors and pensions was decreed, he was among the few to whom a continuation of his pension was considered due; and Don Isaac Abarbanel long enjoyed the confidence of the "Catholic sovereigns," as they were pre-eminently called. But Queen Isabella was also a sincere devotee, and this was her weakest side. To vanquish her strongest resolutions, to persuade her to the adoption of any measure whatever, it sufficed to alarm her about her salvation. Cardinal Ximenes, at the same time prime minister, was the queen's confessor, and no doubt used his influence to poison her mind. Torquemada had filled that office to the infanta when she was quite young, and on the occasion of her receiving the sacrament for the first time, a moment when the mind and soul of the young candidate is entirely given to God and to religion, the crafty monk exacted from her the promise that, if ever she should come to the throne, she would maintain the Catholic faith with all her power, and extirpate heresy to the very root; and it is no wonder that, under these circumstances, and under the power of these two influential men, even the strong-minded Queen Isabella was made to yield. Consequently, when in 1478

Pope Sixtus IV. issued a bull for the establishment of the Inquisition in Castile, the institution was accepted by the king and queen. The powers granted to this new inquisition were far more extensive than any of which similar tribunals in other countries were possessed, and the institution was such as to strike terror into the hearts of the whole population, from the lowest to the highest, the king himself not being exempt from its prowling searches. The fury of the inquisition was directed at first against heretics and infidels among its own ranks, and its suspicions rested especially upon those Jews who from time to time had been converted, and upon the descendants of converts whose number was quite extensive. The proceedings of this tribunal were the most arbitrary, surpassing all bounds of justice and equity. It had a number of spies spread over all cities, towns, and villages in search of victims. No one connected with the institution was amenable to the civil law for any of his acts. Any one suspected or reported could be seized without any warning, without being informed who accused him, without being told of what he was thought guilty. Apprehended in the midst of his family, his friends, and domestics, nobody dared to move in his defense. The moment he passed the threshold of the Inquisition, he was dead to the world; terror chained the tongue even of his nearest relations. A man was obliged to inform against his father, his brother, his wife, his children, if a suspicious word or phrase should escape their mouth, under pain of excommunication, and of being treated as an abettor of heretics. The property of an accused person was immediately seized, and if found guilty it was confiscated. Penitent offenders were subjected to imprisonment, scourging, confiscation, and infamy; those who were condemned were burned at the auto-da-fè. Few escaped the voracity of the blood-hounds of the "Holy Office;" even the bodies of those who died under sentence of condemnation were, hyena-like, taken from their graves, insulted, and burned; and if perchance some escaped their clutches, they were burnt in effigy. In one year two hundred and eighty were burnt in Seville alone, seventy-nine were condemned to perpetual imprisonment, 17,000 suffered lighter punishment.

Thus this horrible scourge of the nation went on from year to year, multiplying its victims, and increasing its terrors, and yet twelve years intervened between the introduction of the Inquisition against concealed Jews and the edict of banishment for those who were so openly. During the interval, the latter continued on good terms with the government, and were still admitted to high offices at court, and too confident perhaps of their high-standing, acted incautiously and gave cause for complaint and even for alarm in the ranks of their enemies. For example, in the year 1480, when the Cardinal de Mendoza had published a catechism for the use of baptized Jews, there appeared from the pen of a Jewish author a virulent attack upon the Roman Catholic religion, as well as upon the Catholic sovereigns. The Jews were also accused of endeavoring to make proselytes, not only among the new Christians, but among the old, whose descent could be traced to Jewish parents, and in some cases they seem to have succeeded. So formidable were they by their number, their riches, their influence, and their relationship with the *conversos* in all parts of the country, and the unanimous testimony of both Jewish and Christian writers establishes the fact, that there is scarcely a family of note in Spain or Portugal which is not descended, either in the male or female line, from Jews who had embraced Christianity. At last the fatal edict, which had long been threatened, was proclaimed on the 31st of March, 1492, commanding all unbaptized Jews to vacate the Spanish dominions within four months. The effect of this cruel mandate upon the Jewish communities baffles description. They made a strenuous effort to avert the blow. Don Isaac Abarbanel, a man of great learning and unblemished reputation, and highly respected at court, threw himself at the feet of the king and queen, begging them to revoke the fearful edict. He knew that Ferdinand was ambitious, and that the royal treasury was nearly exhausted by the late wars against the Moors. In the name of his people he offered the king an immense sum if he would withdraw the decree; he counted also upon the tender-heartedness of the queen, and might have gained his point, but the monster Torquemada placed himself before their majesties, crucifix in hand, exclaiming: "Behold him whom Judas Iscariot sold for thirty pieces of silver, sell ye him now for a higher price and render an account of your bargain before God." The sovereigns trembled before the unrelenting demon, and the Jews had no alternative but baptism or exile. They were allowed to dispose of their property, but not to carry away gold, silver, or jewels beyond a certain amount; for their sales they were to accept bills of exchange. In the great need of the moment, and the short time allowed them, their enemies naturally took every advantage of the situation. "A house was sold for an ass, and a vineyard for a piece of linen." It is estimated that not less than 300,000 Jews were thus most cruelly driven from their own native country. They left the homes of their youth, the scenes of their early ancestors, the more recent tombs of their own friends and relatives. They left the synagogues in which they had so long worshipped their God; the schools where those wise men had taught who had thrown a lustre which shone, even through the darkness of the age, upon the Hebrew name.

NEW SETTLEMENTS OF THE SPANISH EXILES.

Let us follow the exiled Jews in their wanderings over the different parts of the world where they were now obliged to seek a refuge. Portugal had no inquisition yet, and being the nearest by, many Jews directed their steps to that country. They were admitted by Joam II. on the payment of eight golden crowns per head, but were to remain only eight months. After that time those who were possessed of means went towards Africa, but the poor, or those who were afraid to travel further on, were made slaves, and children under fourteen years of age were torn from their parents' arms and forcibly baptized. A number of these were sent to colonize the island of St. Thomas. Don Emanuel, who succeeded John II., was at first very lenient towards the Jews, and made the slaves free; but when he sought in marriage the infanta Isabella, daughter of the catholic sovereign of Spain, one of the conditions of the alliance was that he should banish the Jews from his country, to which Manuel agreed. Thus, against the advice of the king's councillors, the choice was offered to the whole body of Jews in Portugal, either to receive baptism or leave the country forever. This decree, you will observe, had reference, not only to emigrants from Spain, but to the whole community which had been established there for centuries. The consequences were the same as in Spain—a general exodus. The Jews were divided in opinion as to what course to take; some abandoned forever the soil of Portugal, others, not fewer in number, embraced or feigned to embrace the Roman Catholic faith. Thus Spain and Portugal had been cleared of all Jews avowing their religion, but there was a multitude of concealed Jews who bore the name of New Christians, Conversos, or Marranos. Being outwardly attached to a religion which they detested in their hearts, because they had learned how bitter and cruel is that love and charity which that religion teaches, the nominal Christians embraced every opportunity secretly to observe the ceremonies of their own faith, and inculcated its principles in the minds of their children with the more vigor. Some ten years after the expulsion, a number of them were detected celebrating the Passover, which aroused the popular fury against them. That same year there had been great drought and scarcity in the land, and as a means of consolation a deceiving monk exhibited to the superstitious populace a crucifix on which a hidden light had been made to reflect which the impostor declared as a manifestation of the Deity. One of the New Christians in the audience observed incautiously that "if God would manifest himself by water instead of fire it would be more acceptable." The multitude rushed upon him and murdered him right out, and his brother, who stood by lamenting his death, instantly shared his fate. The houses of the converts were assailed and ransacked, and a general massacre ensued.

It did not fare better with the fugitives who escaped to Morocco. They were not even permitted to enter the town, for fear that they might bring famine and pestilence to the citizens. They were left on the sea-shore without food or drink, and obliged to live on a few roots or a little grass they could find there. And so firm were they in their religious principles that on the Sabbath they would not even pluck the grass, but they laid on their knees to eat it off like cattle. Some sold their children for bread, others killed them with their own hands rather than see them pine away. Some were landed by a barbarous captain, and left naked and desolate on the African shore, where the wild beasts came to devour them, and they could save themselves only by plunging into the sea where they remained till the animals retired. For five days they were left in this condition, until the captain of another vessel sent his boat to their relief.*

Hardly were those who went to Italy more fortunate. When they reached the coast of Genoa they were perishing with hunger. The clergy came to them with the crucifix in one hand, and provisions in the other. The unfortunates had to choose between baptism or starvation; they yielded to the cravings of nature and were baptized. In Rome they were received unfriendly even by their own brethren, who were afraid that the increase of their number would bring evil on the community. Even the wicked monster, Pope Alexander, was moved with indignation, and to relieve himself of the sight of so much distress, ordered all Jews to leave the country; and they were allowed to stay only on the payment of a large sum of money.

The Turkish empire, particularly its European dominions, was the great final retreat of those who fled from Spain and Portugal. As the Mohammedans have always been more friendly to the Jews, generally treated them with consideration, often with distinction, so they were in these hours of tribulation well received by their half-brothers. They settled down in Constantinople, Salonica, and other commercial towns of the Levant, where they breathed again the air of freedom; re-established their rabbinical schools; and soon availed themselves of the new invention of printing for the publication of the Hebrew Scriptures and the literary works of their ancestors. There also they established extensive connections with their brethren in Italy and in other parts of the world.

---

*An author of our days cleverly observes the striking fact, that, "ere a century had passed, the flower of the youthful nobility of Portugal, with king Sebastian at their head, were slain or made prisoners on the same coast of Africa to which the Jewish exiles had been so barbarously driven, and happy, by comparison, was the lot of those Christian captives who fell into the hands of African Israelites, from whom alone they received any compassion and assistance in their misfortunes."

THIRD PERIOD.

FROM THE TIME OF THE SPANISH INQUISITION TO THE PRESENT DAY.

The Reformation.

With the dawning of the Reformation (1520) began a new era which brought about great changes in the political and ecclesiastical history of the world, and at the same time affected the condition of the Jews very materially. Though not immediately connected with our history, it will be necessary to give a concise account of that important turning-point, its causes, and the circumstances which attended it, that our young readers may be able the better to understand the results thereby produced, and how they were produced.

From several of the foregoing articles it appears how strong a hold the Catholic religion—till now the almost exclusive religion of Christians—had on the public mind. The pope, as head of the church, claimed—and still claims—to be the representative of God upon earth, and the claim was tamely submitted to. The pontiff exercised absolute authority, not only in religious matters, but in secular affairs as well. Kings and emperors were made and unmade by him, and if any ruler dared to oppose his authority, the pope had only to tell the people that they owed no allegiance to their king, who then and thereby lost all control over his subjects. The pope was supposed to hold the keys of heaven, and to have the power of granting pardon to sinners who paid for the immunity, and even to grant the privilege of committing a sin or a series of sins if paid for in advance. In this way an immense business was carried on, and vast amounts flowed into the treasury of the church. As the pope could not attend to all this traffic himself, numerous delegates were authorized by his holiness to sell indulgences, as it is called. It can be well imagined that these salesmen were not always strictly honest and pious men. Many indeed there were of such dissolute morals, so profligate and corrupt, as to bring disgrace on the profession. This practice had existed for ages, still no one dared to oppose the holy See. In the beginning of the sixteenth century, Pope Leo X., being in want of more money, put up for sale a number of indulgences which were disposed of in so shameful a manner as to attract particular attention and indignation. It was then that Martin Luther, formerly an Augustinian monk, now professor of divinity at Wittenberg, boldly and publicly began to expose the corruptions and abuses of the church. He, of course, met with strong opposition, was summoned, threatened, excommunicated; but he soon gained adherents, whose number grew stronger from day to day; the Catholic church was shaken to its very foundation, and the Protestant religion had taken root. About the same time, though quite independent of Luther's labors, an attack on the Roman church was made in Switzerland, and occasioned likewise by an excess of this unwarrantable religious traffic. Shortly afterwards, John Calvin, another eminent reformer from popery, began to teach different doctrine in France, and while the Christians were thus quarrelling among themselves, the Jews were allowed a little repose. Not that the changes which were going on had an immediate effect on their condition, only the spirit of the age began to incline a little towards toleration; something of that deep darkness and blind fanaticism of which the Roman church was possessed began to be removed. Luther, though not free from the common prejudice against the Jews, often spoke kindly of them, was opposed to violence against them, and reprobated all means of converting them except those of gentleness. In short, the whole procedure gave a different turn to a great portion of the public mind, which was beneficial to the Jews. Another circumstance which contributed to a better recognition of the Jews, their religion, and their literature was, that mighty instrument of civilization—the printing press, had begun to do its work, and the Jews had not been slow to avail themselves of its advantages. The Scriptures, which hitherto could be read only with such commentaries and constructions as popery chose to put on them, appeared in a new light. The unintelligible Talmud, which was believed to be full of blasphemies against Christ, and to contain mysterious and dangerous secrets applied by the Jews to illegitimate purposes, and to the injury of Christians, was found to contain much wisdom and much folly, but nothing hurtful; the immense literary labors of the Jewish doctors of the middle ages were given to the world, and made it evident that these people were not all money-lenders and small dealers. Christian scholars began to seek a knowledge of Hebrew at the hands of Jewish masters; eminent men, such as the Buxtorfs, applied themselves to the study of rabbinical literature and recognized the services these writings had rendered and might still render to science, as well as to the proper interpretation of Scripture. The celebrated prince John Pico de Mirandola, towards the close of the fifteenth century, was so deeply devoted to, and so much prepossessed in favor of these works, that he looked upon them as the source of all wisdom, and labored to prove by their means the truths of the Gospel.

Already a few years previous to the reformation, the merits and demerits of rabbinical writings had been the cause of very serious debates among Christian theologians. John Pfefferkorn, an apostate Jew of Cologne, had obtained from the emperor Maximilian a decree authorizing the destruction of all Hebrew books except the Bible. An edict to that effect was issued in 1510, but through the intervention of Professor Reuchlin, the execution of it was suspended until the opinion of the Archbishop of Spire should be obtained. In the mean time, Reuchlin employed his pen in defense of Jewish literature, making a distinction between those of general utility and those that might be injurious to Christianity. Eminent scholars of different parts of the world took part in the dispute, and the contest became very animated, lasting not less than ten years. Reuchlin, not in the least daunted by the strong opposition he met with, brought the matter before the judgment seat of Pope Leo, and now his adversaries thought themselves sure of victory. But the pontiff was a friend and protector of science and literature, and appointed a committee of investigation. The emperor Maximilian, having come to a better conviction of the truth, threw the weight of his influence in favor of Reuchlin, and a decision for the preservation of the Hebrew books was soon rendered.

We must further bear in mind that the discovery of the New World, at this same period, opened for the dispersed of Israel a new sphere of which they failed not to avail themselves very shortly after the discovery, and that within the same century Holland renounced its subjection to the Spanish government, and opened its doors for the reception of the Jewish refugees, all of which contributed to the amelioration of their general condition. Yet it must be also remembered that these various causes worked but slowly and gradually, that the fury of persecution which peculiarly characterized the middle ages had only slackened; that the Jews were no longer massacred, tortured, pillaged, or arbitrarily expelled as in the time of the crusades; at least such events were now of rare occurrence; but the anathema of public contempt, humiliation, and exclusion from every public or private connection still lay heavily upon them, until the commencement of the revolutionary period in 1789, when a brighter horizon rose to view, as much for the whole civilized world as for the scattered remnant of Israel.

JEWS IN THE SCLAVONIAN COUNTRIES.

The history of the Jews in the Sclavonian countries, Russia, Poland, Bohemia, and the Austro-Hungarian monarchy, acquires an especial interest only in the centuries succeeding the middle-ages, though they lived very early and in great numbers in Poland, and were numerous in Prague before the end of the tenth century, where Boleslaus II. granted them permission to build a synagogue in recompense for their services in his wars against the Pagan tribes, and to Boleslaus V., duke of Poland (1264) the Jews were indebted for peculiar privileges. His great-grandson King Cassimir showed them still greater favor, out of love, it is said, for a beautiful Jewess named Esther. An authority before us courteously says, "The beauty of the Polish Jews, both men and women, is remarkable, partly as the characteristic feature of their nation, and partly as an endowment which they share in common with the population of that interesting country," and further compliments them on their extraordinary sagacity, which, we presume, will not be disputed. The condition of the Jews in those countries was not unfavorable, at least tolerable. They enjoyed the protection of their kings, and, with exception of the usual restraints, were under the general law. Banishments and persecution rarely occurred, except by an invasion of Tartars and Moscovites.

They were allowed to have their synagogues and talmudical schools, and even the civil and criminal judicature over their own people was left in the hands of their rabbinical leaders. The royal protection was here also more of a reality and more effectual than in the German states. Any infraction of their rights was duly punished, and at the call of "Help!" during the night, the neighbors were required by law to give their assistance or be accountable for the results of their neglect. Though excluded from many profitable pursuits on account of not being admitted to the guilds or corporations together with the Christians, they could peacefully follow the trades of baker, butcher, brewer, tailor, shoemaker, and the like. The government found these regulations to its interest, since the Jews were more profitable to the community as merchants than as mechanics. It was considered a peculiar privilege to the Jews in Poland that any of their nation who embraced Christianity and distinguished himself in the army became by right a noble; and to this day many of the Polish nobility acknowledge their descent from Jewish families. Privileges, elsewhere conferred upon the nobility alone, were in this country granted even to unbaptized Jews. In the Sclavonic countries the Jews continued for centuries to form an essential element of society by means of their extraordinary activity. They formed the middle class between the nobility and the rest of the inhabitants who were no better than serfs, and commerce and retail trade were entirely in their hands. But they were not always exempt from false accusations and consequent persecution. Thus in 1541 they were accused of having been the cause of a series of incendiary fires which at that time desolated Bohemia, and they had already received orders from the emperor to leave the country, when fortunately the real culprits were discovered and the Jews cleared from guilt. Soon after a new persecution was raised with threats of expulsion; while an inquiry was set on foot whether the Jewish prayer-book contained curses against the Christians. They gained but little in being absolved from this new accusation, for a decree of banishment was on the point of being hurled against the whole community, when one of them, Mordecai Temak, obtained the intervention of Pope Pius IV., and by this means averted the execution of the decree. Another disaster was, about the same time, added to their misfortunes by a fire which at Prague consumed the whole Jewish quarter, and when in 1648 the inhabitants of Prague had to defend their city against the Swedes, the Jews suffered much from the bombardment of the city by the enemy; their quarter having been most exposed to the attack, but when the war was over, the emperor bestowed much praise upon the Jews for their efficient services in the erection of fortifications and batteries, and their general zeal and activity in the defence of the city, and presented them on the occasion with a clock to adorn their synagogue. When peace was established, the Jews gained permission to take part in the public festivities, and join the procession with two banners which had on a former occasion been presented to them by the emperor of Germany. The same year, however, brought great calamity on all the inhabitants of Poland in consequence of an insurrection of the Cossacks, caused by some oppressive measures adopted by Vladislaus. The Jews seemed to be the especial object of their fury, and suffered fearfully. Scarcely a town in Poland which did not share in the disaster, and great numbers of Jews were driven from their homes to seek a refuge among strangers; many of them could not find a resting-place until they reached Holland or England. The year 1744 seemed likely to bring upon the two hundred thousand Jews of Bohemia a catastrophe more terrible than any they had experienced for the space of two centuries—a banishment in perpetuity from that country. The States-General of the Netherlands, at the request of the synagogue of Amsterdam, took a lively interest in their case, and, supported by the English government, succeeded in making manifest the innocence of the Jews, and persuading the emperor to reverse this terrible decree—not, however, before thousands of Jews had left the country.

The Jewish population of the countries now under discussion was made up of emigrants from different lands. The Hungarian Jews came mostly from Italy, the Polish from Germany, while the Bohemian and Moravian communities consisted of Jews from France and Italy; but we find no accounts of very early Jewish settlements in Russia or in the Muscovite territory. Peter the Great admitted them in his domain, but in the reign of Elizabeth (1745) their residence in Russia was again forbidden on account of a correspondence which had been discovered with the exiles of Siberia. The large portion of the Jewish population of Poland which is under the sceptre of Russia has been often tyrannized over, but never driven out by the government.

We hear also of another part of Russia in which a body of Jews have not only existed, but attained destinction in a peculiar manner. In the Ukraine they have devoted themselves to agriculture and the study of natural history, and are said to have attained a high degree of civilization. Also in the Crimea there have long been whole villages of Jews distinguished by their prosperity and mental culture. One peculiar feature in the history of Jewish population of Poland is, that some of them belong to the sect of Karaites. It appears that still greater favor was shown them than to the rabbinical Jews because of their aversion of the Talmud. The Karaites seem to have come into Poland from Tartary; and King Stephen in the year 1578 issued an edict in their favor. Before the beginning of the seventeenth century, Prague was the principal seat of rabbinical learning. It was there that the celebrated R. Jacob Falk taught, and gained renown by introducing a new method of debating and sifting, requiring the scholars to dispute, if necessary, with the master every minor point of the subject under discussion, in order thereby to sharpen their wit and allow full scope to their mental powers. The peculiar way of intonation or chanting in the study of the Talmud is also ascribed to this master. In Prague also flourished R. David Ganz, author of a well-known work, "Zemach David," on Jewish history and chronology; R. Judah Bezalel, R. Mordecai Jaffé, and many others. Also Bohemia had its distinguished academies during the same period; but at the commencement of the seventeenth century, the seminaries of Poland rivalled and subsequently surpassed their sister-colleges, and from that time forward supplied the German congregations with teachers and Rabbis. We must not omit to observe here that the studies pursued in colleges, and more especially the Polish, were confined almost exclusively to the Talmud; besides the great waste of time given to the study of Cabbalah, and even worse than waste, for this study laid a strong foundation in the student's mind for the reception of superstitious ideas: for the belief in the supernatural, power of talismans, amulets, and the like. And herein we notice the striking difference between the Spanish and Portuguese schools and those of Poland and Germany. While the latter occupied themselves with the hairsplittings of the most trifling phrases of the Talmud, the best result of which was that it sharpened the senses, the former combined with a study of the Talmud that of Jewish theology, a searching into the spirit of the Jewish religion, the writing and the study of commentaries on the Scriptures, poetry, and, what is by no means the least, an earnest and steady application to the sciences. That these were thus better fitted for a social intercourse with their Christian fellow-men, and gained a better reputation as accomplished scholars, while the others by their superstitious practices often exposed themselves to accusations of using magical spells drawn from the Talmud to the injury of Christians, need hardly be said.

Shabbetai Zebi and Joseph Frank.

The following account will serve as an illustration of the pernicious results proceeding from a partiality for the Cabbalah, though the hero of our story issued not from Poland or Germany, but from Turkey. In 1625, Shabbetai Zebi was born at Smyrna. In childhood already he gained the admiration of his circle on account of extraordinary intelligence and cleverness; at fifteen he was considered a perfect Talmudist; and at eighteen commenced his career as a teacher of the Cabbalah to which he drew large audiences of disciples. He made himself conspicuous by frequent fasting and bathing, often at the mysterious hour of midnight, in which ablutions his disciples joined; gradually he assumed the character of a saint or a prophet. The story runs that he was endowed with extraordinary personal beauty which, in spite of his severe penitential practices, increased from day to day, and that his presence imparted a delightful perfume which was owing, he said, to his having been anointed by the Patriarchs. At the age of twenty-four he declared himself the Messiah who would soon deliver Israel from the oppression of Christians and Mussulmans, and in token of his authority he ventured to pronounce the name Jehovah, which was then considered one of the boldest crimes a Jew could perpetrate. His fame began to spread far and wide, but the saying that "nobody can be a prophet in his own place" held good in this case also, for the rabbinical authority of Smyrna declared him an impostor and an outlaw, authorizing any one who dared to take his life, and declaring themselves prepared to pay the fine which the government would impose for such an act. Hereupon the man fled to Salonica, where he was honored by the populace, but likewise denounced by the rabbis. Again he was obliged to flee from place to place until he reached Jerusalem, where he contrived to remain for a number of years promulgating his cabbalistic ideas. After living for fourteen years in comparative obscurity, he reappeared in his native city, where he was now received with great enthusiasm. People came from all points to do homage to the Messiah. The fanaticism rose so high in the community that young men and women felt elated beyond themselves, joining in song and dance to the honor of the great prophet. Even his opponents had changed sides to a considerable extent. At last the report of his doings and his pretentions reached the sultan, who ordered his arrest. When the royal messenger appeared before Shabbetai to seize him, he himself was so over-awed that he dared not lay hands on him and returned trembling to his master. A second officer was sent, but with the same result. Shabbetai then had the good sense to surrender himself; he was admitted to the presence of the monarch, and the man before whom so many had trembled, stood himself dumbfounded in the presence of the grand seignior. Being ignorant of the Turkish language, a Jewish apostate was appointed as interpreter. The sultan asked of Shabbetai if he was the Messiah; he stood in trembling silence. The sultan then proposed a practical test of his messianic qualities; he said he would shoot three poisoned arrows at the Messiah, and if these would leave him unhurt he would acknowledge his title and join in his ranks. The cowardly Messiah, seeing the sultan in earnest and fearing for his life, snatched a turban from one of the pages and put it on his head, exclaiming, "I am a Mussulman," stating at the same time that he had only waited for so favorable an opportunity to publicly embrace Islamism. The sultan was not only satisfied with this declaration, but ordered him to be treated with distinction and conferred a title of honor on him. Having escaped this danger, he was yet emboldened in his imposture and stated to his followers that by the will of God he had thus changed, and cited Scripture and Talmud in support of his act. For some time he sustained his double character with great success ; many Jews followed his example and adopted Mohammedanism; the rabbis became alarmed at the result, and succeeded in laying before the sultan the confusion and damage caused to their communities by the strife and conversions which took place in their midst. The Messiah was then seized and confined in a castle where he died of a colic in the year 1676. It might be supposed that the influence of Shabbetai ceased with his death. This is far from being the case. His teachings became more firmly rooted in the minds of his followers, and Shabbetaism forms to this day a sect whose faith and practice rest on the " bruised reeds " of the Zohar and the Cabbalah.

The career of another adventurer furnishes us an additional and rather stronger proof of the danger and perplexity in which a departure from the plain rational principles of religion, and a speculation of things beyond the reach of our understanding will necessarily involve those who engage in it. Scarcely a century after the disappearance of Shabbetai Zebi, Joseph Frank, a native of Poland, and distiller of brandy by trade, organized a new sect under the name of the Zoharites. He publicly renounced the Talmud, rejected and burned it, and in the mystical teachings of the Zohar he discovered the doctrines of the *trinity*, of *original sin*, and the *appearance of God on earth in the person of Christ ;* it is uncertain whether he meant Jesus Christ or Shabbetai Christ. He readily consented to be baptized, and had an immense number of followers, who did so likewise, chiefly in Poland, his principal field of activity. The bishop of Camentz gave his support to the matter, and the new departure gained general favor. The bishop soon after died and the church of Rome, stirred up by the rabbis, began to look upon this sect as dangerous, and it was persecuted on account of its Jewish cabbalistic proclivities, as it had been by the synagogue for its Christian dogmas.

The government interfered; condemned some to hard labor, and others to have one side of the beard shaved to expose these half-and-halves to ridicule; while Frank was imprisoned in a fortress, from which he was delivered by the Russians who took the citadel in 1777. Frank now travelled through Poland, Bohemia, and Moravia with a large retinue and great pomp, and established himself in Vienna, where immense quantities of treasure flowed constantly into his coffers, enabling him to maintain a truly royal magnificence. He died of apoplexy in 1791, having attained the age of 78. With his death the influx of wealth ceased; and his sect sank into insignificance, though remnants of it are still existing in Poland, Moldavia, and Turkey. Quite a number of persons might be named who from time to time presented themselves under the claim of being the deliverers of Israel or regenerators of the world at large, and who in the end proved to be either wilful deceivers or deluded zealots, and not one of these pretenders ever fulfilled the mission they proposed to accomplish; on the contrary, they brought about nothing but disturbance, bloodshed, and utter disappointment.

Jews in the Netherlands.

One of the places of refuge where the Jewish exiles from Spain found a safe asylum, and where they attained to great opulence and distinction, is Holland. As we have not hitherto spoken of their dwelling in that country, it will be necessary to begin with a short account of their residence there prior to the fifteenth century.

The history of the Jews in the Netherlands during the middle ages is, on a smaller scale, much like that of Germany and the north of France. They were early settled in the provinces of Belgium and the northern part of the Netherlands. The records of history bear witness that, after the invasion of the Normans, the commerce in those provinces was all carried on by Jews, and that the entire failure of trade in Liege must be attributed to their banishment from that city. Jews were living in Flanders already at the time of the crusades. Later some fugitives from France and England established themselves there. They were driven out in the twelfth century, but by the fourteenth had already settled there again in great numbers. In Guelderland the Jews were numerous and enjoyed the protection of its counts, especially at Zutphen, Doesburg, and Arnheim; still, a noble lady of Guelderland was burnt at Cologne for having married a Jew, which was considered a crime equivalent to adultery. In Utrecht the Jews resided till 1444, at which time they were completely driven out of the town; and till the revolution of 1795 in Holland, a residence in that city was still forbidden, though they were numerous and wealthy in surrounding towns and villages. But the history of the settlement of the Jews in Holland becomes most important and interesting at the beginning of the sixteenth century. Several families of the new Christians emigrated from time to time into Holland whenever a favorable opportunity offered, without however, removing the mask of Christianity.

The first indication of their settlement in the southern part of the United Provinces after the expulsion is found to have been in 1516. At that time some refugees from Spain petitioned Charles V., the grandson and successor of Ferdinand and Isabella, for permission to reside and exercise their religion in his dominions. Their appeal was unheeded, for several edicts entirely excluded even new Christians from Holland, as well as from Spain. And yet many Jews were to be found in these provinces holding the same position as those who remained in the peninsula. Their religion was not tolerated; but by practising it with the greatest secrecy they lived and prospered under Spanish names. Both at the court of Madrid and in the government of the Spanish Netherlands at Brussels, descendants of Israel were to be found, who, afterwards, renounced Catholicism to make an open confession of their true faith at Amsterdam. Also, during the reign of Philip II., the Dutch were strictly forbidden to give an asylum to the Jews; but when, in 1579, the Netherlands threw off the Spanish yoke and gained their independence, which result was greatly promoted by the immense riches the Jews had brought into the country, they were not only allowed more freedom, but rose to high estimation. Their talents and their noble descent were recognized; their number gradually increased, and their refined manners procured them an introduction in the best society, so that they subsequently became the associates of the princes and nobles of the land.

Among the many families who eagerly looked for opportunities to escape the tyrannical despotism to which they were subjected, was the family Rodriguez Lopez, of Portugal. Lady Rodriguez sent her son Manuel, and her daughter Maria, who was exceedingly beautiful, in company with a few others, to find a safe home in Holland. The ship which conveyed them was taken by an English man-of-war under command of a duke, who became enamored of Maria, and offered her his hand, which, however, she refused, saying she preferred to live like a Jewess. The whole party were put in prison on their arrival in London. The beauty of the imprisoned Jewess, and the circumstances under which she arrived, became the general subject of conversation in the town, and the eccentric maiden queen Elizabeth, the promoter of Protestantism in England, desiring to see the young lady who was bold enough to refuse a duke's hand on the ground of religious principles, sent for her, and drove with her in an open carriage about the town. Shortly afterwards the party were allowed to proceed to Holland, and landed at Emden. From there ten individuals came to Amsterdam in the year 1594; resumed their original Jewish names, as well as the open profession of their religion. They were accompanied by a German rabbi óf Emden, who aided and instructed them, and in gratitude for his services the synagogue granted him and his posterity many privileges, and a perpetual right of membership.

Henry II. in 1550 encouraged many Conversos, not only to settle in France, but allowed them to throw off the disguise of Christianity and establish congregations of their own; but as Holland offered better inducements for the extension of their commerce, a goodly number of Jews came to Amsterdam, Rotterdam, Antwerp, and other maritime towns, and were later joined by Conversos who had been driven from the peninsula by Philip III. At Antwerp, the concealed Jews were quite numerous, and the ancestors of many families who later settled at Amsterdam and The Hague had long resided there. Among them was Don Manuel Alvarez de Pinto y Ribera, gentleman of the household to the king of Spain and knight of the order of St. James, from whom descended the family of de Pinto, well known in the Dutch synagogue; Don Francisco de Silva y Solis, afterwards marquis of Montfort, who at the head of his company, when serving under the emperor Leopold I., contributed greatly to the defeat of the French marshal de Créqui, in the campaign of 1673; Don Antonio Lopes Suasso, agent of the king of Spain, and invested by that prince with the barony of Avernas le Gras, in Brabant. It was this baron Suasso, who, when afterwards established at The Hague, offered to William III., in 1628, a million of florins for his expedition to England, to be repaid only in case of success. From various records of the Portuguese congregation at Amsterdam, it appears that in 1596, for the first time, the Day of Atonement was celebrated by a small number of men. The mayor of the city having surprised the assembly, took it at first for a meeting of Roman Catholics, which was at that time forbidden, but, being better informed, left them unmolested. In 1598, the first synagogue was erected; and R. Joseph Pardo, of Salonica, engaged as their chief rabbi; ten years later, another synagogue, was built, and in 1618, a third. In 1639, the three which had hitherto been under separate administration were united to form henceforward a single community of Spanish and Portuguese Jews, under the name of Bet Jahacob. In 1675, they erected the splendid large structure which now is one of the finest buildings in the city, much admired by the inhabitants and by visitors from abroad. It is the largest synagogue in Europe, having a capacity to accommodate about 5,000 worshippers. The Portuguese congregation of Amsterdam has been always distinguished for the vast capital it had at command, and even now we think it no exaggeration to say that its treasure amounts to millions. The number of scrolls of the law, the solid silver and golden ornaments for the same, the heavy chased and very antique lavers, some of which could not be bought for 100,000 florins, the splendidly embroidered coverings and other temple-furniture, form the finest collection of the kind to be found in any Jewish congregation. The ancient burying-ground of the congregation is still at Ouderkerk, a village about five miles from town. The first man interred there was Manuel Pimentel, the playmate and confidant of Henry IV., and two years later the body of Elias Rodrigo Montalto, physician to queen Mary of Medicis, was by order of that lady embalmed and sent to Amsterdam for interment. A Hebrew printing press was soon established, and some of the finest specimens of Hebrew printing yet extant were issued there. After Amsterdam, the prosperity and esteem gained by the Jews in Holland has been highest at The Hague, and one of the first Israelites to whom letters of naturalization were granted, in 1672, was of Polish origin; his descendants, the Polak Daniels, are still living and highly respected in that city. The Spanish and Portuguese community of the Netherlands have been noted for the extensive commercial relations in which its members were engaged with Spain, Portugal, Italy, the Levant, Brazil, etc.; by an unblemished reputation for probity and honor, ever accompanying their immense riches, and by the loyal services they rendered in more than one critical situation to the country, and to the House of Orange. It is not, therefore, to be wondered that the Dutch government appeared at all times the protector of the rights of its Jewish subjects among foreign powers; and to the present day there is hardly any of the princes of the house of Orange and Nassau who failed to pay at least one visit of ceremony to the great synagogue at Amsterdam.

Among the archives of that congregation there are several records showing that a correspondence was held, in the year 1622, between Christian IV., of Denmark, and the Parnassim (directors) of the Portuguese community, for the purpose of inviting some of its member to establish themselves in his dominions, with a promise of entire liberty of conscience, freedom of commerce, and special privileges. Similar invitations were received from the duke of Savoy, and from the duke of Modena. It is a fact that, early in the seventeenth century, families and synagogues of Portuguese Jews were settled and flourishing in the Danish states, chiefly at Holstein. At Copenhagen also they had a community, but their settlements at Gluckstadt and Altona have long been their chief establishments in that part of the world.

At Hamburg their well-being has been even more remarkable, and the protection granted to Jewish refugees by the king of Denmark seems to have been one of its principal causes. From the history of commerce, we know the spirit of rivalry which has ever existed between this free imperial city and the commercial towns of Holstein. Altona in particular was feared as a rival by the magistrates of Hamburg, when they beheld her enriched by the establishment of a Jewish population, with its wealth and important mercantile connections. Notwithstanding the opposition of some of the citizens and the Protestant clergy, and in spite of the complaints of the emperor—that a city which had expelled Roman Catholics should admit Jews—the magistrates of Hamburg considered themselves compelled, by their commercial position with respect to Altona, not only to admit, but to confer many privileges upon the Portuguese Jews. This social prosperity was much advanced by the high honor awarded to some distinguished families, who were employed as agents or residents, by different foreign powers. The kings of Denmark, the kings of Portugal, and queen Christina, of Sweden, employed notable members of the synagogue as their representatives in Hamburg.

The success of the Portuguese Jews in Amsterdam drew a great many emigrants also from Germany and Poland, and the accession was so considerable that in a short time the latter far outnumbered the former. The Jews of Poland and Lithuania had endured great cruelties from the Cossacks and from popular disturbances, and no less than three thousand of them embarked at one time for Holland, and received hospitality at Amsterdam. This increase, however, was far from pleasing to the Portuguese Jews. They looked upon the new-comers as intruders, and would not allow their claims to equality and fraternity. We must bear in mind that the Sephardim came with great wealth, with titles of nobility, with refinement and general scholarship, and with no small share of that haughtiness so peculiar to the Spanish, which spirit they especially imbibed in their intercourse with the aristocracy at home. The new emigrants, on the other hand, were not provided with that universal passport "money;" from generation to generation they had been compelled to live in exclusion; were oppressed, degraded, crushed; and as circumstances form man's character, theirs had become debased in their own estimation; they had lost their self-respect. Precluded from all honorable pursuits, they had been obliged to resort to the meanest occupations in order to support themselves. Their naturally bright intellect had been kept under the bushel of cruel oppression; and their unqualified prejudice to all that was not strictly Jewish debarred even the few gleams that might have entered to enliven their spirits. Hence the Portuguese Jews could not recognize in them their brethren of the house of Israel. They spoke a different language; neither understood the other; and even the common password, "Shemang Israel," as the Germans pronounced it, sounded like spurious in the ears of the Portuguese. No wonder, therefore, that they not only declined all association with them, but considered their presence as injurious to their own interest and reputation. For a long time the German Jews in Holland had to contend with many difficulties, and did not obtain equality of rights with their more fortunate brethren; still they were protected, and enjoyed full liberty of conscience. But they were persevering and industrious. In 1636, permission was at last granted them to appropriate to themselves a piece of ground for a burial-place, and in 1656, they were allowed to erect a house of prayer. Thus the Jewish population of Holland was divided, and to the present day consists of two distinct and separate bodies.

It might be supposed that the exiles from the peninsula, now transplanted on the free soil of the Netherlands, would have gained new energy in the pursuit of literature and the sciences; that they would have exerted themselves for the benefit of their less favored brethren; but this was not so. The zeal and activity which they had formerly evinced in various departments was superseded in many by the indolence which accompanies an excess of luxury, the result of their great prosperity and complete security. Their manners changed and became more corrupt; and the glory of their former greatness degenerated into an object of vanity and party spirit, in which the origin of these distinctions was forgotten, while the aristocracy of money exercised the greatest influence. In the mean time, the German Jews had learned better to appreciate the blessing of liberty, and took advantage of the privileges they enjoyed. They felt that they had a great object to accomplish; they advanced, while the Portuguese retrograded; and to-day many of their members fill some of the highest and most responsible offices in the kingdom, while their proud brethren have little more left than the boast of their past ancestral glory.

Eminent Scholars of Holland.

The degeneracy of the Portuguese Jews in Holland, spoken of above, must, of course, not be supposed to have begun at once with their settlement in their new home; it was a thing of slow progress, and the seventeenth and eighteenth centuries produced some eminent men, without a notice of whom our history would be quite incomplete.

Among the great men brought up in the synagogue of

Holland, no one has been more generally known by his learning, his literary productions, and his public acts than Menasseh Ben Israel. Born at Lisbon in 1604, he came to Amsterdam when yet a child, with his father Joseph Ben Israel, who had greatly suffered from the Inquisition, and escaped with great difficulty and the loss of his whole fortune. Young Menasseh was brought up in strict Judaism, and received a liberal education. Gifted with an enlarged and penetrating mind, he early became familiar with the elements of Jewish theology and acquired also a knowledge of the Castilian, Portuguese, Greek, Latin, and Arabic languages. At the age of fifteen he was already listened to with interest as a public speaker, and several prominent Christian scholars, as well as Jewish, were admirers of his talents. At eighteen he was appointed chief rabbi of one of the three synagogues at Amsterdam, in which office he continued until he was chosen as delegate of the whole community to represent the same before the protector Cromwell, with a view of gaining a readmission of the Jews into Great Britain, the particulars and success of which undertaking we will speak of further on. His son Samuel accompanied him on his voyage to England, and was honored by receiving the degree of Doctor of Philosophy and of Medicine from the University of Oxford. R. Menasseh returned in 1658, and settled in Middleburgh, where the tomb of the son, who died before his father, is still to be seen. Among the numerous works written by the father, some in Spanish, Portuguese, Latin, or English, we notice his "Treatise on the Frailty of Human Nature," and "Man's Inclination to Sin," in which he combats the doctrine of Pelagius, a monk of the fourth century, who denies original sin, and asserts man's perfect freedom to choose the good or evil; "Three books on the Resurrection of the Dead;" and "The Conciliator," in which he endeavors to reconcile the apparent contradictions of the Bible. This last work gained him much reputation among Christians also, and the year after its publication, a Latin translation of it by Dionysius Vossius, appeared in print. He died at Amsterdam in 1659

Uriel da Costa (in Portugal called Gabriel da Costa, also A Costa) was a contemporary of the above subject. Born at Oporto about 1590 of noble and wealthy parents of the class of New Christians, he was brought up in the Catholic faith, and at the age of twenty-four held the position of canon and treasurer of a collegiate church in his native city. As his conscience could find no rest in the profession of the Catholic religion, he determined to yield his rank, his wealth, and his country in order to adopt in Holland the Mosaic religion, and thus find rest for his troubled soul. His mother and younger brothers, led by his influence, accompanied him on his journey to join the synagogue at Amsterdam, where the family has ever since been established. Da Costa, however, did not find in Holland what he eagerly looked for, namely, the Mosaic religion in its purity. He had left the church which he thought too much burdened with Roman traditions and inconsistencies, and found instead a Mosaic religion overloaded with rabbinical traditions and superstitious practices. Being excommunicated for his too liberal views, he learned to his sorrow that free thought and the expression of it was as dangerous here as it was in Spain. He wrote a book under the title of "Examination of Pharisaical Tradition," in which he expressed his views on the Books of Moses as being divine, but denying the resurrection of the dead, and the life to come, and all rabbinical tradition. While the book was circulating in manuscript among friends, Dr. Samuel da Silva took up the pen and wrote a "Treatise on the Mortality of the Soul" in order to expose Da Costa's errors and bring him to a better conviction. The latter, however, wandered still further on the path of error, and became a complete deist. Tired of a contest in which all were against him, and forsaken even by his nearest relations, he resolved on a reconciliation with the synagogue, at least outwardly, but the contest was soon rekindled, and with more fierceness than ever. Seven years the philosopher remained in seclusion. A second reconciliation followed, which was effected, however, on the condition only that the unbeliever should submit to the public chastisement of receiving the "forty stripes save one." The penalty was inflicted, but the mind of Da Costa could not bear up under such a degradation, and a few days after this exposure he put an end to his life with a pistol, leaving behind him his own biography in excellent Latin, in which he protests with the greatest vehemence against the proceedings of the synagogue.

Baruch (Benedict) d'Espinosa, more generally known as Spinoza, was born at Amsterdam in 1632, of parents belonging to the Portuguese congregation. He early engaged in the study of theology and philosophy, and was led to doubt the principles and the authority of the religion to which by birth and education he belonged. He questioned the public teachers, and disputed with them on points of religion, and finding no satisfaction in the answers he received, he candidly expressed to them his skeptical views, though he did not altogether desert the synagogue and its ceremonies. Every effort to induce him to give up his opinions having proved unsuccessful, he was publicly censured and excommunicated by the ecclesiastical authorities. Being now looked upon as an outcast, a fanatic was soon found who thought it would be a meritorious act to rid the community of so dangerous a person as Spinoza, even at the risk of transgressing the sixth commandment; and one evening, coming from a public meeting, the assassin met him, dagger in hand, which he endeavored to plunge into the philosopher's breast; but Spinoza happily perceived the foul attempt and escaped unhurt. Seeing the danger of his position, he determined to leave his native city and went to live at Rynburg, and finally settled at The Hague. He voluntarily gave up his claim to any share of the family property, and earned a scanty livelihood by grinding glasses for microscopes and telescopes, employing every leisure hour to the study of philosophy and the sciences. As his talents and erudition became known, he received an invitation from the elector palatine to occupy a professor's chair in the university of Heidelberg, but Spinoza, whose only wish was literary retirement, declined the offer. Baruch d'Espinosa stands foremost in the rank of modern philosophers, and may be considered, if not the founder, at least the reviver in a new form of the natural theology called Pantheism. We cannot now dwell at length upon Spinoza's system, but will give the essence of it, as it appears from his various writings. By strictly mathematical reasoning, based on a few axioms, he deduces the principles that "there can be no substance but God; whatever is, is in God, and nothing can be conceived without God." In other words, taking the ground that God is everywhere, in everything, and pervades every particle of everything, he concludes that God is everything, and ergo everything is God. There is, therefore, but one substance with its modifications and ramifications, having within itself the necessary causes of the changes through which it passes; and this universal substance Spinoza calls God. Spinoza left several works in manuscript as well as in print, the most celebrated of which is his "Tractatus Theologico-Politicus." Though living in complete retirement, he maintained an extensive acquaintance and correspondence with friends and literary men, both in his own country and elsewhere.

All that is known of the private and domestic character of this extraordinary man bears the same impress of calmness, moderation, and dignity; and even his enemies admitted the greatness of his mind and the excellence of his character. Spinoza died at the early age of forty-five, in full persuasion of the truth of his system; and lest reports might be circulated that he had recanted some of his opinions, he charged his hostess not to allow any clergyman to approach his death-bed. A monument in memory of the great philosopher has been lately erected in the city where he labored and died.

Isaac (formerly Balthasar) Orobio de Castro was the son of Jewish parents who lived as new Christians at Braganza, and afterwards at Malaga, where Isaac was born in 1616. Having studied the scholastic philosophy, he was appointed professor of mathematics in the university of Salamanca; and later taught medicine and metaphysics at Seville; but had the misfortune to be accused before the inquisition of infidelity and Judaism. Through the tale-bearing of a Moorish slave, who reported that a distinction of meats and other tokens of Judaism were to be met in the house, Orobio fell into the hands of that fearful tribunal. After he had endured three years of imprisonment and the infliction of the usual tortures, the Inquisition, not being able to produce a confession, nor finding any direct evidence against him, declared him only suspected but not convicted of Judaism, and he was at length discharged; and as may be supposed, seized the first opportunity for quitting the Spanish territories. He first settled at Toulouse, where he was appointed professor of medicine and councillor to Louis XIV. and there he conformed to the religion of the country; but wishing to enjoy the free exercise of his religion, he left France, and at the age of forty removed to Amsterdam, relinquished his Christian name Balthasar, and submitting to the distinguishing rites of Judaism, took that of Isaac. He continued to practice as a physician in that city till the year of his death, 1686, and his descendants are to this day in the capital of Holland. Among his numerous polemical works in defence of the Jewish religion, his controversy with Philip of Limborch was published by that learned remonstrant under title of " Friendly Discussion with a learned Jew on the truth of Christianity." Other writings of Orobio against Christianity remained to our day in manuscript, and have circulated so among the Portuguese Jews.

The Jews of the peninsula continued to set a high value upon the poetry of their ancestors, and many more names might be given of persons who distinguished themselves by their poetical and other literary productions. Even the synagogue witnessed within its walls the representation of certain pieces of poetry, much in the same fashion as the ancient mystery-plays of Spain in the middle ages. Such a piece of poetry, composed by Rehuel Jesurun (formerly Paulo de Pina) was recited in the synagogue Bet Yahacob, by several of its most learned and distinguished members. In this poetical dialogue the seven mountains, Sinai, Zion, Hor, Nebo, Gerizim, Carmel, and Senir (Sirion), mutually dispute the right of pre-eminence, which is decided at last by king Jehoshaphat. Such entertainments, however, though not considered actually unlawful, were soon thought inconsistent with the sacrednes of a house of prayer. Among the poetical geniuses at Amsterdam we find also the names of two distinguished women, Isabella Henriquez, and Donna Isabella Correa; the latter wife to the lieutenant-colonel Don Nicholas de Oliver y Fullana, then in the Spanish service, and much esteemed as a cosmographer. The interest for literary attainments, however, gradually decreased, and the eighteenth century witnessed an almost entire extinction of poetical génius among the Spanish and Portuguese Jews of Holland, nor could they in other branches of science and lettters ever vie with their ancestors. Perhaps the intermingling of prosperity and oppression; perhaps also the climate had exercised a happier influence than the repose which they afterwards enjoyed without interruption.

Re-establishment of Jews in England.

In the preceding article on the Jews in England, we stated that they were banished from that country by an edict of Edward I. at the end of the thirteenth century; and we know also that toward the middle of the seventeenth, the Spanish Jews were firmly and extensively established in Holland, where they had formed commercial relation with different countries. They had long since looked for an opportunity of extending their traffic to England, but as long as the parliamentary act of their banishment was in force, this seemed impossible. When Oliver Cromwell came to hold the reins of government of Great Britain, the time seemed to have arrived for the country to reopen its ports to a people that had already been favorably received on the continent, both by Roman Catholic and Protestant powers. For this purpose the Jews of Amsterdam delegated one of their ablest members, the celebrated Menasseh Ben Israel, of whose character and talents we have already spoken. He presented a petition to the Lord Protector, in which he complimented him and the nation on their humanity and enlightenment, and requested permission for his people to reside and enjoy the free exercise of their religion in England; and at the same time issued a pamphlet to circulate among the public, in which he stated the grounds upon which he based his request, and the financial advantages which would accrue to the nation by a consent to his proposition. Hereupon

Cromwell called together an assembly of lawyers, clergymen, and other citizens to consider the matter, but on account of the hesitation and the prolonged debates of the clergymen it was left undecided; yet from time to time some Jews entered quietly into the country without meeting with opposition or molestation, until the reign of Charles II., 1666, when they were lawfully readmitted to dwell in England. It is quite probable that this permission was effected by the circumstance that the negotiations for the king's marriage to the infanta Catharine of Portugal had been carried on by General Monk, through the intervention of a Portuguese Jew. It is an ascertained fact that the infanta was accompanied to England by two Portuguese brothers, one of whom, Dr. Antonio Mendez, had been professor of medicine at Coimbra, and at the request of the infanta established himself in London, where, from that time, both brothers openly professed the Jewish religion. They obtained a piece of ground for burial, built a synagogue, and were joined by several distinguished families from Spain and Portugal, but especially from Holland. Their number was soon increased by other Jews from Germany and more yet from Poland, who, together, formed a new congregation. The presence of the Jews in England was frequently discussed in public, and though no parliamentary act for their legal readmission was issued, still no measures were taken by the government to hinder them. They were allowed to remain as strangers, and were obliged to pay a capitation-tax. Under James II., they obtained relief from this charge, but it was again imposed under William III. Hitherto Jews could not be admitted to citizenship, because they could not in truth take the oath required on such occasion, which prescribed the candidate to swear " upon the true faith of a Christian." This difficulty was removed in 1723 by an act of parliament, which allowed the Jews to omit the objectionable clause, and to be allowed henceforth to hold landed property. In the American colonies, the Jews had long since been admitted on a footing of equality with the English inhabitants, and in 1739, George II. declared all those who had been established there for seven years as entitled to English citizenship on taking the required oath with the omission as granted. Thus the Jews steadily gained ground in England; still they were far yet from enjoying equal rights with their Christian neighbors. In 1753 a bill was brought into Parliament "granting to all Jews who had resided in Great Britain or Ireland for the space of three years the right of English citizenship, with the exception of patronage and admission to parliament." Notwithstanding a violent opposition both within and without the House, the bill passed by a considerable majority; but before it was yet confirmed by the royal sanction, public feeling against the measure was so loudly expressed that Parliament, in its next session, found it necessary, for the preservation of peace and order, to repeal the act; and, what is remarkable, the Jews themselves, at that time about 12,000 in number, were not anxious for the success of the measure, and were rather opposed to it, for fear that such an equality might be injurious to their religion; which fear was perhaps supported by the circumstance of a prominent Jew, Simpson Gideon, adopting the Christian faith, and being subsequently chosen a member of Parliament. Still the Jews persevered and became eminent in every commercial enterprise. They aided once more in building up the financial supremacy of the country, and slowly won their way to a respect that was at length awarded them. Strong was the opposition on the part of the churchmen and Tories, but stronger still, because supported by justice, was the brilliant defense made in their behalf (1830) by Macaulay and the united force of the whole Liberal Party. The friends of freedom and humanity everywhere assumed the defence of the Jews; the conservative faction in church and state was everywhere their bitterest foe. Ten times the Liberal party in the British House of Commons, by great majorities, carried a bill for their enfranchisement, and ten times it was thrown out in the House of Lords. Long was the struggle, but glorious was the victory. In 1835, one of the leading members of the synagogue, Mr. David Salomons, was elected sheriff of London, being the first Jew that ever held this high office, and an act was passed by Parliament enabling him to serve. Moses Montefiore, Esq., was elected sheriff of London in 1837, and on the 9th of November of that year was knighted by the queen, being the first English Jew on whom this honor was ever conferred. In 1849, Baron Lionel de Rothschild was elected to Parliament for the city of London, and in 1857, alderman Salomons was returned for Greenwich. Rothschild was again returned for the capital in 1852, and at the two general elections in 1857; but neither of these gentlemen was able to take his seat on account of the form of the oath which was still objectionable to them. In July, 1858, Parliament passed an act, which received the royal assent, and which by a kind of compromise enabled Jews to sit in that legislative body; and on the 26th of that month Baron Lionel de Rothschild took his seat as the representative of the city of London. In 1855, Alderman Salomons was elected Lord Mayor of London, the first Jew ever chosen to that office, and in 1865 Alderman Benjamin Samuel Phillips became the second Jewish Lord Mayor. At last, in 1860, Parliament adopted an act permitting Jewish members to omit the words "on the faith of a Christian" from the usual oath, and now the election of Jews to almost the highest offices of the state is, so to say, of daily occurrence. The Master of the Rolls in England is an officer of the court of chancery, second only to the Lord Chancellor; is appointed by the crown, and holds his office for life, with an annual salary of £7,000, and has the power of hearing and determining cases the same as the Lord Chancellor. Sir George Jessel was appointed to that office in 1873, and, as if England were anxious to make amends to the Jews for past injuries, Lord Beaconsfield, born a Jew, though in his infancy given to the Church, now virtually rules the country as the head of that conservative party which was the last to persecute his race.

THE JEWS IN FRANCE AND ITALY AFTER THE MIDDLE AGES.

Shortly after the expulsion from the Spanish peninsula, many Jewish emigrants sought a refuge on the northern side of the Pyrenees; and we never find that their tranquillity was in any way disturbed by the French kings. Half a century later, these emigrants obtained from King Henry II. letters patent securing to them, under the denomination of *Portuguese*, their entire liberty and many desirable rights and privileges. These letters were registered by Parliament, in the year 1550. Subsequent kings confirmed these rights, and at all times protected their Jewish subjects from any violence on account of their religion. When the edict of Nantes was revoked by Louis XIV. (1685), this legal toleration seemed for a moment in danger, but no evil consequences ensued. An effort made in the reign of Louis XV., to cut short their privileges, likewise fell to the ground. In consequence of the annexation of Alsace to France towards the close of the seventeenth century, that kingdom contained three or four different classes of Jews within its territory: those who belonged originally to France, those of Alsace, who were German, the Italian Jews of Avignon, and the Spanish and Portuguese Jews who were settled chiefly at Bayonne and Bordeaux. The

Spanish exiles who established themselves in France were, generally speaking, more distinguished for probity and by their great wealth than, as elsewhere, for their learned men and literary productions; yet some names of note have already been given, and to these we may add that of Jacob Rodriguez Pereira, a native of Spanish Estremadura, to whom belongs the honor of having anticipated the celebrated Abbé de l'Espée in his plans for instructing and communicating with the deaf and dumb. As a recompense, Louis XV. bestowed on him a pension of 500 francs in 1751, and appointed him his librarian, and later he was rewarded by a patent for the office of royal interpreter. We may also mention (though not by way of eminence), the famous banker, Samuel Bernard, the Rothschild of his time, who joined the Catholic Church. French memoirs of his time speak of the great financial services he rendered to Louis XV., and how the haughty and aged monarch might be seen condescending to conduct the Jewish banker over his palace, and showing him the curiosities of the royal mansion, at Marly. On the annexation of Alsace, Louis XIV. extended the privileges of free commerce, that had been granted to the Jews in the southern provinces, also to those of Metz, for which they paid a tax of forty francs annually for each family, afterwards compounded for by a payment of 2,000 francs per annum. Under Louis XVI. (1784), this tax was abolished, and in 1788, a commission was appointed, with the wise and good Malesherbes at its head, to devise means for remodelling, on principles of justice, all laws relating to the Jews. But the revolution burst upon France before the measures could be drafted, and the tribunals of the republic were more rapid in their movements than the slow justice of the sovereign. In 1790, the Jews, who had watched their opportunity, sent in petitions from various quarters, claiming equal rights as citizens. The measure was not passed without considerable discussion, but Mirabeau and Rabaut St. Etienne ably pleaded their cause, and, as if by magical influence, eighty thousand inhabitants of France, hitherto dependent on the will and the whims of their rulers, were recognized as free citizens of the great republic. It is indeed to the French revolution, more than to any other cause, that the European Jews owe their final and entire emancipation.

When Napoleon ascended the throne, he not only confirmed the position of the Jews as being on an equality with their fellow-citizens, but desired that the Jewish people should speak for themselves, and declare authentically, upon the authority of their own law, in what relation they stood to their fellow-men of another creed; what were their obligations towards non-Israelites; and whether the laws of their religion required from them any duties contrary to the laws of the land they inhabited. For this purpose an edict was issued (30th May, 1806), for the convocation of deputies from all parts of the country, to assemble at Paris and debate and decide upon certain questions that should be put to them. One hundred and twelve delegates met as directed, on the 26th of July following, and twelve questions were propounded to them: 1st, Whether, according to Jewish law, polygamy was allowed? 2d, Could divorces be established, independent of the state laws? 3d, Can Jews intermarry with Christians? 4th, 5th, and 6th, Regarding the relations of Jews to other citizens and to their country. 7th, 8th, and 9th, Concerning the appointment and jurisdiction of the rabbis. 10th, Are there any professions which the Jews are not allowed to follow? 11th and 12th, Concerning the laws on usury between Jews among themselves, and between them and others. The assembly of deputies, presided over by M.

Abraham Furtado, entered upon the debates and sent in their answers, which were entirely approved of by the emperor; and in order to give full authenticity to the decisions rendered, the emperor ordered that a committee of 71 members, of whom 46 were clergymen and 25 laymen, should be appointed, and to which committee the appellation of *Great Sanhedrin* was given, that they might ratify, in conformity with ancient Jewish usages, that which had been decided by the general assembly. The Sanhedrin, of course, met and ratified; and the decisions were received with joy and acclamation; but in honest truth it must be confessed that this Sanhedrin had no authority as of old to legislate for the whole nation, since it represented only a small portion of the Jewish body; and further, that the answers given were not without some ambiguity, not without some evasion; and it is evident that both the general assembly and the so-called Sanhedrin, in framing their decisions, kept steadily in view the great and good purpose of firmly establishing the emancipation of their people, even at the sacrifice of a little honesty. The excellent result, however, which followed these proceedings can hardly be over-estimated, as not only they placed the independence of the French Jews on a firm basis, but also served as an example and an impetus to others. It aroused the people to a higher sense of self-esteem, it gradually cured them from that detestable practice of usury, they applied themselves more and more to labor, to agriculture, to the arts and sciences; though a special edict against usury, for those of the Rhine provinces, was still deemed necessary (17th March, 1808). Statistical returns of the same year showed that of 80,000 Jews under French dominion there were 1,232 landed proprietors, not including the owners of houses, 797 military, among whom some officers, 2,360 artisans, and 280 manufacturers.

The extension of the French dominions, and the annexation of tributary kingdoms were highly beneficial to the Jews. In Italy, in Holland, in the kingdom of Westphalia, the old barbarous restrictions fell away, and the Jew became a citizen, with all the rights and duties of the order.

The laws of France relating to the Jews have remained unaltered, with the exception of this improvement, that the law of the restoration (7th Aug., 1830), which enacted that ministers of the Gospel alone should be salaried by the state, was modified at the accession of Louis Philippe, so that Jewish ministers should thenceforth also receive a stipend from the state. Minister Merilhou, in proposing the amendment, said, "The Jews have, for the last quarter of a century, in all public positions filled by them, whether under our glorious banners or in the arts and sciences, or in the ordinary walks of life, most nobly refuted the calumnies which their oppressors had raised against them." Though the political aspects of France have changed since that time, yet neither under the empire of Napoleon III. nor under the present republic has the relation of the Jews towards their country suffered any change, while their internal condition has continued to improve with the general progress of the age.

Not so favorable an account can be given of Italy during the first three centuries after the reformation. It is true that, in the Papal States, the persecutions of the Jews were never carried to such excesses as they were in other parts of Europe, and that some of the popes granted them protection and certain privileges, but not till within the last few years can it be said that the Jews were placed on an equality with their fellow-men of the other creed. As late as 1823, the ordinance was renewed that the Jews must live apart in a ghetto, and every Sabbath three hundred of them were required to attend a conversion sermon preached for them. Leo XII., in 1827, was very severe towards his Jewish subjects, and in 1829, there were brooding murmurs of an expulsion from the ecclesiastical states; which, however, was not effected. The French revolution of 1792 brought some relief also to the Jews of Italy, but after the restoration they again lost ground, and as formerly, so again, four elders of the synagogue were obliged every year humbly to supplicate the pope for permission to reside in Rome. Pius IX. abolished this custom, and further showed some liberality to the Jews by allowing them the free use of the city; and on the evening of the 17th of April, 1849, the ghetto was solemnly opened, as if to proclaim that henceforth the wall of separation between the Jewish quarter and the rest of the city was thrown down. Still, notwithstanding these indulgences, the hand of the church lay heavily upon the Jews. Though the inquisition had been abolished in Italy by a decree of Napoleon in 1808, the spirit of it was by no means crushed even so late as 1858, when the papal church was permitted to exercise its last act of bigotry and cruel oppression towards a certain family under its tyrannical authority. Mr. Mortara, an humble but respectable manufacturer of Bologna, Italy, was the happy father of eight children. One evening, his house was visited by several emissaries of the archbishop who claimed and forcibly carried away one of the children, named Edgar, a boy about seven years old, on the plea that it belonged to the church, and could therefore not be allowed to remain under the guardianship of its Jewish parents. It appeared that a servant of the family had made a confession that, some time ago, she had baptized the child when it was ill of a dangerous disease. When the mother saw her dear boy torn from her arms, she fell fainting upon the floor, the father remonstrated, supplicated, the neighborhood was alarmed by the cries of the children, but the heartless officials were unrelenting: the child was placed in a carriage and hurried off to Rome. The affected parents followed him, but were not even allowed to see their child again. The archbishop and Cardinal Antonelli, the pope himself were appealed to; the most tender pleadings of humanity, of outraged parental feelings were employed, but they found no entrance in the cold hearts of these ecclesiastics. The story of the abduction of Edgar Mortara spread all over the world and created quite a furore; indignation meetings were held, and the liberal press of France, England, Germany, and America, even calm and enlightened Catholics denounced the act; but the pope refused to give up the child, even at the solicitations of foreign courts and powerful diplomatic influence. Edgar Mortara was brought up in a convent, forgot his parents, and, it is said, has become a priest. With the fall of the papal throne (1870), God be thanked, and the liberation of Italy under Victor Emanuel, the Jewish inhabitants also began to share the blessings of liberty. Quite a number of them now sit in Parliament, some occupy professors' chairs at the principal universities, and many bear titles of nobility; while the number of those who are prominent at the bar, in the pulpit, as journalists, and in the learned professions generally, as well as those who cultivate the liberal arts, is quite considerable. As a counterpoise to the affecting Mortara story we have just related, we take the following from the "Archives Israelites," 15th of September, 1871. On the 14th of June, a noisy crowd assembled in that quarter of the city of Rome called Moriti, in front of a convent appropriated as a refuge for neophytes. The entrance was guarded by a number of soldiers and policemen, and the doors having been forced open by order of the city authorities, three nuns came forth who entered a close carriage, and drove away under a strong escort of police. The fact was this. A Jewish girl, daughter of Samuel Ascarelli, of Nettuno, had been enamored of a young Christian, and in order to remove every obstacle to her marriage on the part of her father, resolved to become Catholic, and was aided by the clergy to go to Rome and reach the convent above named. It was not until after several weeks and by dint of diligent searching that the father discovered the whereabouts of his daughter; but his request to see and communicate with her was positively refused, and he was told that he could not possibly see her until after she should have received baptism. It proved, however, that some months ago the girl had already been baptized by Vice-cardinal Patrizi at St. John de Latran, since which time she had been kept at the convent. According to the opinion of the sisters, marriage was out of the question, and Enrichetta Ascarelli would have been made to take the veil, were it not, fortunately, that the Italian laws of 20th of September opposed such transactions. The father now applied to the government, requesting that his daughter be restored to him, which request was immediately granted. Still the clerical authorities refused to recognize the decision of the court, and it was found necessary to resort to forcible means. Not less than seven doors had to be broken before the young lady was found. She was then conducted to the mayor's office, where her father awaited her, and her opinion on the matter was asked. Filial affection was stronger than the pious exhortations of the nuns, and Enrichetta laid off her monastic habit and returned home with her father.

So strong has become the spirit of toleration, of freedom of conscience, and of universal emancipation in the present century, that even Spain and Portugal had to yield to its influence; and though the number of Jews now inhabiting these countries is exceedingly limited, the laws regulating their condition and the general sentiment towards them have materially changed. A royal decree of 13th November, 1831, granted permission to English Protestants to inter their dead in a ground set apart for the purpose; and the 29th of August, 1855, a law was established in Spain by which permission was granted to all non-Catholics to have their own cemeteries. In 1865, some French Jews residing in Spain thought it necessary to apply to the minister of the interior for a similar permission, and were informed there was no obstacle to their laying out a special burying ground, provided that there should be no chapel on it or connected with it, nor any public or private religious services held on the occasion. In 1869, the provisional government under General Prim virtually abrogated the decree of banishment of 1492, and a petition of one hundred and forty Jews of Amsterdam, of Spanish and Portuguese descent, asking that this decree might be entirely repealed and the abolition of it made public, was followed by an eloquent address by one of the deputies, E. Castelar (12th April, 1869), which had the desired effect. In the same year, perfect freedom of religious exercises throughout the dominions of Spain was proclaimed, but our people have thus far scarcely availed themselves of this right. We learn, however, that in Lisbon, a Jewish community of about fifty or sixty families, some three hundred or four hundred souls, hold divine service in a house rented for the purpose. The grand cross of the order of Isabella the Catholic was, in 1872, presented to Mr. D. Weisweiler, a Jewish banker connected with the house of Rothschild; and in Portugal an English Jewish baronet possesses a noble estate, and bears the title attached to it. It would seem, indeed, that the Spanish of the present century feel ashamed of the barbarity of their ancestors, and are anxious that it be effaced from man's memory; for in the same periodical from which we have just quoted we find the following anecdote. A French lawyer, M. Jules Lan, writes that, being on a visit in Madrid, he was informed that the building formerly occupied as the Holy Office of the inquisition had been turned into a hotel, and its dungeons into wine-cellars. M. Lan had the curiosity to visit the place, and inquiring of the proprietor as to the truth of the fact, was answered that this was merely a trick which his French competitors played on him, to injure the reputation of his house; that there never had been any inquisition in Spain; that this was but one of those fanciful tales invented to frighten children.

JEWS IN THE EAST. THE DAMASCUS BLOOD-ACCUSATION.

It is an admitted fact that the progress of civilization has been ever tending westward, consequently the eastern countries, generally, are to this day much enveloped in darkness, and our brethren in that part of the world, as everywhere else, sharing the influence of the country they inhabit, have made but little advance. The Jews of Palestine, notwithstanding the strong effort made in their behalf by their brethren in the west, are almost in the same condition as they were a thousand years ago. The very venerable and celebrated philanthropist Sir Moses Montefiore, as president of the Board of Deputies of British Jews, and from the particular interest he takes in the fate of the Jews of Palestine, has sacrificed a great deal of time, personal efforts, and large sums of money for their benefit; the Board of Delegates of American Israelites (established 1859) has ever shown its readiness to promote the well-being of the wretched Jews of the Holy Land; the "Alliance Israelite Universelle" (established in Paris in 1860) has taken a deep interest in the affairs of the Palestinians, and established schools, agricultural societies, and other useful institutions among them; but the results produced have been by no means adequate to the vast amount of labor, talent, and treasure employed. These people have yet to learn the lessons of independence, civilization, and the dignity of manhood.

There is so much sameness in the general condition of our brethren in Asia and Africa that it is hardly necessary to enter into details as to their circumstances in any particular country. Ignorance and superstition prevail to a great extent, and the Jews are often suffering from the prejudices entertained against their race. Within the last few years even (in 1872) we have had in Smyrna a repetition of the absurd rumor that Jews need human blood for their Passover cakes, and a Catholic journal of Tunis industriously circulated and confirmed the falsehood. A similar accusation made in the capital of Syria in the year 1840 caused such a universal sensation, and drew forth the eloquence and activity of so many prominent men, non-Israelites as well as Jews, that we deem it necessary to reproduce the particulars of the case. A certain monk, named Father Thomas, who practised medicine at Damascus, had suddenly disappeared. On the 5th of February his body was found, and it was soon suspected that the Jews had murdered him. A Jewish barber was imprisoned, closely questioned, and put to the torture. At last they drew from him a confession that some of his people had tempted him by the offer of a sum of money to assassinate Father Thomas. This statement, extorted from a man on the rack and supported by no evidence whatever, was considered enough to warrant the arrest of the most prominent Jews of the community. Many of them, foremost the rabbis, were put to the torture, the aged and weak sank under the horrible torments inflicted on them; while others allowed a false confession to be drawn from them; and some in despair embraced Islamism, though most of them persisted with constancy in declaring their innocence. The furious populace, taking advantage of the occasion, pillaged the synagogues, robbed the people in their houses, and were not hindered but abetted by the police. The French consul, Count Menton, who conducted the search of the case, was cruel enough to imprison even the school-children and put them in chains. The rumors of the accusation spread to Rhodes and to other places, and were made the pretexts for persecution even there. The afflicted Jews communicated with their brethren in Europe to enlist their sympathy, and immediately found a response, not only in every Jewish heart, but the European powers interested themselves in their behalf. England distinguished itself for its zeal in demanding an impartial examination of facts to show the innocence of the ill-treated Jews. The emperor of Russia and the government of the United States acted in concert with Great Britain, with the object that henceforth such abuses and such horrors should not be repeated. The interest and co-operation of all religious and political parties in England was general, and on the 15th of June a large meeting was held in the synagogue to devise means for the relief of the oppressed. This meeting had decisive results. Sir Moses Montefiore, accompanied by several learned men, and furnished by his government with the necessary credentials, set out on his mission to Syria, and passing through France, was joined by the celebrated advocate, now senator, Adolph Crémieux. Wherever they came the benevolent missionaries were received with enthusiasm, and all over the world public prayers were offered for their success. On the 4th of August, they landed at Alexandria and soon obtained an audience. Supported by the representatives of all the European powers—excepting France, whose government preferred upholding the inexcusable conduct of its consul—they obtained a firman from the pasha ordering the release of nine persons who were yet in prison at Damascus. M. S. Munk, the interpreter of the company, having observed that the word "pardon" had been used in the deed, and fearing that, if allowed to pass, the question of their guilt might be considered as undecided, persevered in his efforts until he had it altered. On the 16th of September, 1840, the liberated Jews were conducted in procession to the synagogue, where they wished to render thanks to God before returning home. Sir Moses and Senator Crémieux took advantage of the occasion to establish schools at Alexandria and Cairo, to provide for a Jewish hospital, and to procure many privileges for their oppressed brethren. Our noble heroes, Sir Moses, now in his ninety-seventh year, and M. Crémieux, in his eighty-fourth year, are still the ornaments of their respective communities and the pride of the Jewish people. An account of their incessant labors for the benefit of the Jews in the East would fill a volume. God bless them!

The condition of the Jews in Persia has been hitherto very deplorable, and perhaps the worst feature of the case is with them, as with the Eastern Jews generally, that, in consequence of their prejudices and want of enlightenment, they often refuse to accept such assistance as the European associations think most beneficial and most suitable to them; they deem acceptable scarcely anything but gifts of charity for immediate relief. They frequently suffer, like the rest of the population, from famine, sometimes from earthquakes, and, in addition to this, from the crushing oppression of their petty rulers. On the late occasion of the Shah's visit to Europe (1875), various petitions were offered to his majesty requesting him to ameliorate the condition of his Jewish subjects; the French and English Jewish delegations were graciously received by the emperor, and the promise obtained that measures would be employed for improving the condition of the Persian Jews.

Similar favors were sought, and similar promises obtained from the Sultan, in 1840, by Sir Moses Montefiore and by M. Albert Cohn from the same monarch after the Crimean war. But the greatest victory these indefatigable gentlemen and the associations they represent have lately achieved is, the resolutions passed by the Berlin congress (1878) in which body it was unanimously decided that perfect liberty of religion, and entire equality of all persons before the law, should be established in the Danubian Principalities; and the venerable octagenarian Crémieux, in addressing the last meeting of the "Alliance," in deep emotion and unspeakable joy, announced as the result of so many years' labor that "now, all over the East, liberty of religion for the Jews, civil and political equality for the Jews, is established; the Jews of the Orient are now citizens in the respective countries of their birth."

JEWS IN GERMANY, AUSTRIA, AND THE SCLAVONIAN COUNTRIES IN THE LATTER AGES.

The emancipation of the Jews in Germany has been very slow and tardy. What was established in France, as it were in a moment, was not accomplished in Germany except in a long series of years and through many hard struggles. The example set by Napoleon in granting the full right of citizenship to all Jews under his dominion was not without effect upon the German states, but the Jewish inhabitants of Germany, in consequence of the deep degradation to which they had been so long subjected, were not quite prepared for, nor willing to accept an entire emancipation. The emperor Joseph II. was the first who evinced much enlightened liberality in reducing the power of the Church, in granting full toleration to the Protestants, and extending the privileges of his Jewish subjects. In 1782, he issued an edict which abolished all the old obnoxious regulations.

The Jews were allowed to fix their residence in any town they pleased; no more distinctive marks on the dress; no exclusion from festivals and public walks; no confinement to any particular part of the town; the military profession as well as those of the law and medicine thrown open to them; the right of wearing a sword, and bearing titles of nobility was granted, though without the power of holding landed property; all trades were permitted, though without admission to the guilds; and protection to their children against the proselytism of the Roman Catholics. On their side the Jews were required to adopt surnames, or family names; to acquire a knowledge of and make use of the German language instead of the so-called *Jüdisch Deutsch*; and to send their children to the public institutions for instruction, whether Christian or Jewish. This edict, which was received with great applause by the Jews of Germany and Austria, formed quite a turning-point in their history; still they, for whose benefit the edict was intended, in consequence of their long habituated degradation, were not yet ripe fully to enjoy these improvements. What the emperor Joseph II. undertook in his Austrian dominions, was carried out with far more beneficial results in Prussia by king Frederic William II., in 1787. Under the reign of his predecessor, Frederic the Great, some very curious and absurd enactments regarding the Jews were in vogue. As for instance, when the king in hunting had taken more wild boars than could be consumed in his own household, the Jews were obliged to purchase the superabundance of the royal venison at fixed prices; and as they could not use this forbidden meat, they gave it to be consumed at the hospitals. The law allowed only a limited number of Jews in the kingdom and these were under the king's protection, as it was called. This protection descended to one son; for the second an additional tax was demanded. This tax consisted in the obligation of the father to purchase at one of the royal porcelain factories 300 thalers' worth of porcelain, and that for foreign exportation. Frederic William abolished these and similar arbitrary institutions, and by an edict of March 11th, 1812, granted to the Jews the right of Prussian citizens, though not without some conditions and restrictions. The French revolution, and the influence of the French imperial government, considerably aided the cause of the Jews throughout a great part of Germany. Those inhabiting the cities on the western side of the Rhine had now been fully emancipated; the example reflected on the other side of the river, and the spirit of it penetrated into the interior and to the opposite boundary of Germany. Especially in Westphalia, in its capital Frankfort-on-the-Maine, were the improvements noticeable. It was there that the worthy philanthropist Israel Jacobson, formerly chamberlain to the duke of Brunswick, distinguished himself by his unceasing efforts and very large pecuniary contributions for the elevation of his co-religionists. The abolition of a personal toll imposed on the Jews the same as on cattle; the prohibition of a drama in which the Jews were loaded with insult and ridicule, and the endowment of free schools, were some of the fruits of his benevolent activity. By a decree of 27th January, 1808, Jerome Napoleon declared the Jews of Westphalia to be free citizens. Besides many of the smaller states, the grand-duke of Baden in 1809, the duke of Mecklenburgh-Schwerin in 1812, the king of Bavaria in 1813, issued ordinances admitting the Jews to civil rights. The act for the federative constitution of Germany, passed at the congress of Vienna in 1815, pledges the diet to turn its attention to the amelioration of the civil state of the Jews throughout the empire.

That the newly acquired rights of the Jews met with strong opposition on the part of a certain portion of the population may be well imagined. Some of the ablest writers employed their pens for the purpose of counteracting the emancipation acts. Professor Ruhs openly declared his opinion that the admission of the Jews to civil rights would be pernicious, in consideration of their existence as a nation; of the inherent and deeply rooted vices of their character; and of the very nature of their religion. With the exception of any attacks on the life and persons of the Jews, he advocated the reproduction of those enactments of the middle ages which tended to purge Christendom of its Jewish population. In the absence of such measures he foretold that in less than forty years all Christians would be in a state of dependence on the Jews. In a like spirit, and if possible more violent, one Frederick of Frankfort published his opinion in an anonymous pamphlet. Many voices then arose in defense of the Jews; among themselves, Zimmern, of Heidelberg, and Herz, of Frankfort; and among the Christians Johann Ludwig Ewald of Carlsruhe and August Krämer of Ratisbon. While even some members of the Catholic priesthood stood up in defense of the Jews, Professor Paulus of Heidelberg distinguished himself as the bitterest opponent of the Jews and declared his opinion in favor of their entire exclusion. It was thus that during the period of reaction from 1815 to 1830, the question of emancipating the Jews considerably retrograded. Not only in the monarchial states of Germany, also in the free towns of Frankfort, Lubeck, and Bremen measures were taken to restrict and revoke the rights of their Jewish inhabitants. At Lubeck, as early as 1815, they had already concocted the design to drive the Jews from the country and as far as the precincts of the city were concerned, the plan was carried into effect in 1819. In other places the excesses of the middle ages seemed likely to be revived; in some towns the old death-cry of "Hep, Hep" arose; the houses were pillaged and demolished, as in Hamburg, where a similar outrage was repeated as late as the year 1835.

But in the year 1830, fresh revolutionary movements arose in France, which spread afterwards over Europe, and influenced Germany more especially. The old tendency to a union of the German States under an Imperial Government again revived. At this time, a second and even a third generation of the liberal Jews had arisen. They were no longer the same men who in the beginning of the nineteenth century had felt themselves encumbered by their recently acquired rights, and who had been prevented to take their position in society by the various prejudices of Jews and Christians. Now, on the contrary, united with "Young Germany" in a system of radical liberty, the new generation of Jews enforced its claims to a complete emancipation on the ground of its forming an integral part of the nation. They maintained that, if hitherto all efforts to organize for the Jews a limited and conditional equality had failed, it was precisely on account of this limitation that it had fallen to the ground. Then only can the Jewish population fulfil its duty to Germany, and Germany be what it should be to its Jewish and Christian inhabitants, when, without any reserve or restriction whatever, liberty and equality shall be insured alike to all. The question was frequently discussed by the press, in the cabinets of kings, and in the different assemblies in the states of Germany, but not until the revolutionary changes of France and Germany in 1848 was the emancipation of the Jews effected to its full extent. Since then the relation of the German Jews to their government has not suffered any material change, but their internal condition has been steadily improving; and if the enfranchisement of the Jews has been of a slower pace in Germany than in some other countries, they surely have not been tardy in taking advantage of every step they gained. The rapid progress made by them in the paths of science and literature has no parallel. In medicine, astronomy, and mathematics, they not only equal, but, in consequence of the progress of science during so many centuries, surpass the great models of their nation in Spain in the middle-ages. Rabbinical theology, by reason of the multiplied studies and rigid examinations exacted by the government, has assumed a truly scientific character. Germany now forms the great centre of Jewish learning; it is to her schools and seminaries that the Jewish world partly owes its emancipation, or rather its fitness for emancipation, and that we Americans are specially indebted for the excellent preachers which fill our pulpits, the rich literature which she has given us, and the many accomplished teachers who labor in our religious schools.

The Jews under the dominion of the emperor of Russia have hitherto not been so fortunate as to attain to the full enjoyment of their rights as citizens. Alexander, in 1805, and again in 1809, granted them some privileges in pursuing different branches of business and in agriculture, but in that vast empire, where the subjects are at so great a distance from the monarch and left to the control of subordinates, and where the prejudice of the people against the Jews is very strong, these imperial decrees effected little or no good. The enterprise of a certain philanthropist, Nathan Funkelstein, in 1818, to establish Jewish settlements met with considerable success, and found favor with the emperor, who granted the new settlers an immunity of taxes for twenty years. Several thousands of Jews availed themselves of the opportunity, and seven villages, to which Hebrew names were given, became the happy homes of these people who devoted themselves to agriculture and the raising of cattle. They were farmers in summer and talmudical students in winter. In the districts of the Caucasian mountains similar settlements were formed which became so flourishing that several thousands of Russians embraced Judaism in order to join them. The emperor Nicholas, not so favorable to his Jewish subjects, recalled into force some of the old regulations which determined the residence of the Jews; drove them from the capital and many other cities; and otherwise restricted their movements and occupations. The old blood-accusations, which were renewed about this time, were, however, discredited and disdained by him, and the instigators punished. Under the reign of the present emperor, the condition of the Jews has somewhat improved, owing to the general progress of the times, and more through the intervention of Sir M. Montefiore and other benevolent friends of humanity who interested themselves in their behalf, but it is far yet from what it ought to be. The great misfortune is that a very large portion of the Russian population are yet in a state of semi-barbarism. General education and the enlightenment of the present age have scarcely penetrated these. In some parts of the country no school can be found within a hundred miles or more, and wherever there is ignorance, there is prejudice, there is intolerance; and considering that nearly half of the Jewish population of the world, nor far from three millions, are under Russian dominion, we may conclude that there is a great deal to be accomplished yet, by those noble individuals and by the various Jewish societies in Western Europe, whose aim it is to ameliorate the condition of their brethren.

Moses Mendelssohn and his Cotemporaries.
Modern Jewish Reform.

The life and labors of Moses Mendelssohn have been of such great influence on modern Judaism and on Jewish emancipation that we deem it necessary to devote a separate article to the same. The various causes which brought about the successive changes in the condition of the Jews in Germany and other parts of Europe, as the Reformation, the revolutions and changes of government between 1789 and 1848, the accession of Napoleon and of Joseph II., all these acted, as it were, from without, leaving the internal state of the Jewish communities unchanged; but the life of Mendelssohn and his co-laborers mark a very decisive period in the history of our nation, inasmuch as the labors of these great men produced such an internal change in the condition of their brethren as to make them fit recipients of the emancipation that was in store for them. Let us trace the life of this wonderful man through its different stages of boyhood, adolescence, and manhood, like the life of a tender but precious plant, whose growth we watch with solicitude.

Moses Mendelssohn was born at Dessau, September 6th, 1729. His father was in very humble circumstances and earned a scanty living by teaching Hebrew and transcribing the Pentateuch on parchment. Young Moses, who was of a delicate constitution and somewhat deformed, received his early instruction at home, but at the age of ten he had already acquired such a familiarity with the Hebrew language and literature that his father found it necessary to place him under the instruction of an abler teacher than himself. Not without emotion do we read in the history of his life how, in the cold winter mornings before daybreak, with scarcely clothes enough to keep him warm, the father carried the tender child to the school of R. David Frankel, where Moses received his first talmudical lessons. At that time he began to entertain a partiality for the writings of Maimonides and especially his Moreh Nebuchim; and it was the study of these works which caused the development of his philosophical genius. So intense was his application to study that it prostrated him on the bed of sickness, from which he was scarcely expected to rise. His teacher Dr. Frankel being called to Berlin, the boy Mendelssohn determined to follow him, and provided with but a few small pieces of coin, without recommendation, without friends, and with a natural timidity and averseness to ask favors, he entered the metropolis of learning in search of more knowledge. But there also poverty stared him in the face, and though but fourteen years old, he was obliged to relinquish his studies and work for a living which he but scantily gained as a copyist and corrector of the press. But no difficulties whatsoever could repress in Moses the indomitable desire for learning. In his leisure hours, and often after midnight, he pursued his studies, if it happened that he was fortunate enough to have a lamp or candle by which to read. Ever occupied with the Talmud and other Hebrew works, he now began to feel the necessity of a *correct* knowledge of the German which at that time was possessed by only very few of his co-religionists; and so well did he master that language that his contributions to German literature stand to this day as proud monuments of his genius. He next thirsted for a knowledge of mathematics; but how to obtain the books, and where to find a teacher? Just then he made the acquaintance of Israel Samos, a Polish Jew who had been persecuted and driven from his home because he had expressed too liberal opinions, and depreciated the Talmud and some rabbinical institutions. This man came to Mendelssohn one day and said, "My friend, I am without money, but here I have six volumes of Euclid I wish to dispose of, buy them of me." Mendelssohn eagerly grasped the treasure, turned over leaf after leaf in deep and sad silence, while the impatient visitor resumed, "I haven't had a mouthful for twenty-four hours, and wish to buy a meal with the proceeds of these books." "My good friend," said Moses, "I am as poor as you are, gladly would I take the books at any price, but I have no means to buy them, but here is some bread and fruit which I set apart for my supper; take it, I shall have a good meal to-morrow." "I accept it; hunger knows no shame," said the other. "Now, young man," continued he, after having somewhat satisfied his craving appetite, "you have given me all you had, let me do as much for you; I not only give you the books, but I shall assist you in studying them, for I have acquired some proficiency in mathematics." The study of the classical languages and authors was his next step, then of the modern languages, and thus our young philosopher mounted step by step the ladder of science with astounding rapidity. His bright intellect and the progress he had made on the path of learning could not fail now to attract the attention of other scholars, and he soon gained the acquaintance and friendship of Lessing, Nicolai, Abbt, and other distinguished German literati. His Phædon, on the Immortality of the Soul, by which he acquired the surname of "The Jewish Socrates;" his work "On the Sensation of the Beautiful," and a volume of "Philosophical Dialogues" were particularly admired, and gained for him greater fame among Christians than among his own people; indeed, some of his works rather gave offence to the rabbis who saw in these writings a deviation from orthodox Judaism. But his subsequent publication of a commentary on parts of the Scriptures, and other Hebrew works, and more especially his strict adherence through life to all the observances of rabbinical Judaism, allayed the uneasiness of his pious friends about his suspected tendency to free thought. Some zealous Christians, in order to claim him as one of their own, have ascribed to him strong proclivities for the Christian faith, and some have been bold enough to say that he embraced Christianity, but these imputations are entirely without foundation. Among others Lavater, the celebrated physiognomist, urged him to join the Church, in reply to which he published "A letter," remarkable for its calm, dispassionate reasoning, and a firm vindication of his adherence to his paternal religion. Mendelssohn distinguished himself by his mild, amiable disposition, and his readiness to serve his friends, and by an extreme aversion to animated controversy. In 1771, he was chosen a member of the royal academy; but the king disapproved the choice, on hearing which, Mendelssohn mildly said, "Better the academy think me worthy of membership and not the king, than if the case were reversed." The scriptural passage, "The man Moses was very meek," may be very properly applied to him. Mendelssohn died January 4th, 1786, deeply lamented by the literary world and a host of admiring friends.

The fruitful results of this great man's labors upon Jewish society can hardly he overestimated, and to appreciate them we must consider that the Jews of that period—especially in Germany—lived, as we before observed, in a state of exclusion. Hated and repulsed by their neighbors, and withdrawing themselves from the world around, they lived in the midst of society as a separate body, enjoying the satisfaction that, under the rule of Providence, they were not excluded as unworthy, but kept apart as a sacred people. Hence all intercourse with strangers, except as their pecuniary interests for self-preservation required it; all familiarity with what was not strictly Jewish, they thought an infraction on their religion; in short, all that was not Jewish was anti-Jewish to them. It was the task of Mendelssohn to remove this deeply rooted impression; to show the people that there were things worth knowing besides the Pentateuch and the Talmud. This he did, not so much by preaching or teaching, as by his own example; by diving into the depths of philosophy and metaphysics, and attracting to himself the master spirits of the age, and yet remaining in practice an orthodox Jew. We look upon Mendelssohn as the first mover of modern Jewish reform, yet he did not propose to introduce anything like reform such as we have it now. Had he made the attempt, he would have accomplished nothing, just as many well-meaning men frustrate their own plan by attempting to do too much. Mendelssohn did for his people just as much as was necessary and suitable for the time : he removed the first barriers that separated them from their fellow-men; he bridged the chasm that lay between them by making them acquainted with their native language in its purity through the very channels of the Holy Scriptures, of which he furnished an elegant and correct German version. Even that brought down upon him the censure and anathema of some benighted, over-pious rabbis, who burnt some of his Bibles in the courtyard of the synagogue at Prague. But his works spread, nevertheless, and were received with favor, not only in Germany, but in Holland, France, England, and Italy likewise. Thus Mendelssohn awakened in his people a desire for knowledge, a taste for branches of learning hitherto unknown to them; he opened for them the road to mental improvement, to refinement, to civilization. And when the question is asked, " What good has reform done to Judaism?" it may with justice and propriety be answered that it has rendered the Jews fit to receive the blessings of entire and universal emancipation, which otherwise would have been—as indeed in the beginning it was to them—an embarrassment, a burden, rather than a blessing.

The good work which Mendelssohn had begun was taken up also by several of his cotemporaries, among whom we notice especially the following : Hartwig Wessely (born in Hamburg, 1725, and died 1805) distinguished himself by his zeal to promote reform among his co-religionists. Being engaged in a business-house at Amsterdam, he employed his leisure hours in study, and acquired several modern languages, but excelled in the knowledge of Hebrew. He wrote several useful books, among which his "Hebrew Synonyms" is well known and appreciated. Not being successful in business, he consoled himself by following the path of literature ; went to Berlin, and formed an intimate acquaintance with Mendelssohn, and, like the latter, adhered closely to the synagogue. He interested himself particularly for education, and, in consequence of the edict of toleration by Joseph II., being asked to furnish a plan for regulating the new schools to be established, he gave it as his opinion that the study of the Scriptures should be made primary, and the Talmud secondary; and that a secular education should be joined to the religious. This called forth a severe condemnation from the pens of the Polish rabbis, but Wessely's plan was adopted. His fame as a Hebrew poet stands high, and his epistolary publication in favor of the training and instruction of youth are considered valuable contributions to the cause of Jewish reform.

Isaac Euchel, born at Konigsberg in 1756, was an excellent scholar of the same period, and in the knowledge of Oriental literature excelled even Mendelssohn. He was the first who undertook a German translation of the Jewish liturgy, urging the necessity of people understanding their prayers. He wrote a translation and commentary on the Proverbs of Solomon, and a biography of his friend Mendelssohn. This clever and talented author also was obliged to support himself by trade till the time of his death which happened in 1804.

David Friedlander, born at Konigsberg in 1749, was another of those friends of Mendelssohn who, by their indefatigable activity and valuable works, acquired a name among their brethren in Germany. He settled in Berlin in 1780, and lived in society with the most distinguished persons of his age, both Christians and Jews, without ever losing sight of the main object he had in view, viz., to seek the improvement of his nation by every means in his power. With this view he translated several German classical works into Hebrew, and several portions of the Bible into German. He also made an improved translation of the prayers, and by the establishment of schools for the poor he conferred a benefit which long survived him. Always active, sometimes too precipitate in his zeal for a true and thorough reform of Judaism, some of his writings, in which he vigorously opposed existing prejudices and abuses, elicited severe criticism. When Frederic William II. issued orders for the amelioration of the Jews in his kingdom, and desired a statement of the opinion of the Jews themselves on the subject, Friedlander, who presided over a committee appointed for the purpose, drew up a document in which he displayed unusual vigor and ability. He candidly stated the faults and deficiencies which still prevailed among his people; the connection of these with the imperfect state of freedom the Jews hitherto enjoyed; and the disadvantage to the state of having in its midst a class of people who cannot enjoy an equality of rights with their fellow-citizens. Even to the advanced age of seventy-five, Friedlander ceased not to labor in the cause of his people in the different relations in which he was placed or to which he was called. His long career of activity and usefulness closed in the year 1834.

The seeds sown by Mendelssohn in the field which his friends and followers continued to cultivate now began to produce fair and abundant fruits. The spirit of learning and investigation which he had awakened began to spread widely among the new generations; many applied themselves to the study of polite literature, and the production of many a profound scholar who became the pride of his nation was the result of the initiative steps taken by our great reformer who has been justly styled "The third Moses." We have already made mention of the enlightened and wealthy gentleman, Israel Jacobson, who at his own expense established a seminary in Cassel. He it was also who first introduced reform into our synagogue-service. He erected an elegant temple, and inaugurated it with pompous ceremonies on the 17th of July, 1810, and it was there that after eighteen centuries the sound of instrumental music and a well regulated choir was again heard to accompany the prayers of a Jewish congregation who were delighted and edified by what we may call an indispensable concomitant of divine worship. In the absence of a regular minister, Mr. Jacobson often ascended the rostrum to address his friends, and thus set an example to others who not unfrequently entertained the audience with eloquent discourses. Urged by political circumstances, Mr. Jacobson moved to Berlin and there established a synagogue on a small scale and on the same principles as that in Cassel; where some changes were introduced, and some German prayers substituted for the Hebrew. In 1819, a reform temple was established at Hamburg, where Dr. Kley, and afterwards Dr. Salomon, both profound scholars and eloquent preachers, enlightened their audiences with stirring and impressive discourses. The liberal movement spread further and further, and with the immigration of Germans into America was introduced into this country, where daily it gains strength and stability. Outside of these countries there exists very little reform yet in Jewish congregations. In London, in the year 1840, a number of Jews, at the head of whom stood Sir Isaac L. Goldsmith and other prominent gentlemen, organized a reform congregation, and called it "The Congregation of British Jews." The Rev. D. W. Marks was elected and is yet their chief pastor; and later, a congregation on the same principles was formed at Manchester. In the new grand temple at Paris, an organ and choir, and some slight changes in the ritual have been introduced, and also in the West Indies some congregations have adopted a certain reform. The rest of the Jews in Europe, Asia, and Africa, as well as a number of congregations in this country, still cling to their traditional practices and their ancient rituals.

JEWS IN AMERICA.

Shortly after the discovery of the New World, a few Jews sought a refuge there from the oppression of the Inquisition, which was then in full force in Spain and Portugal. We know that their first settlement was in Brazil, whither it is said, in 1548, a great number of New Christians were sent as a kind of banishment by the Portuguese Government. There they successfully cultivated the soil, and first planted the sugar-cane. Nothing more definitely is known about their names, numbers, or particular places of residence, and it is not until a good many years afterward that we have any better information about the Jews settling in America. In 1624, a number of French Jews came to Brazil, and together with others who had already lived on the continent for years, formed a new colony with David Cohen Nassi at their head. These were later joined by 600 emigrants from Amsterdam, under the leadership of two rabbis, Raphael Moses de Aguilar and Isaac Aboab. As this colony began to acquire a greater degree of influence than the Catholic Government of Portugal could well tolerate, measures were proposed to check the increase and power of the Brazilian Jews; but the conquest of the country by the Dutch brought about a complete change, entirely favorable to the Jewish population. The Dutch Government, and especially the new governor, John Maurice de Nassau, encouraged them by the entire toleration of their religion, and by every mark of distinction and courtesy. The States-General passed an ordinance, in 1645, in which "the persons, goods, and rights of the Jews in Brazil were taken under the special protection of the government, because of the fidelity and courage which that nation had, on every occasion, displayed towards the said government." The records of history bear witness how much the Jews distinguished themselves by their valor, both at the time of the conquest and in the defence of Brazil by the Dutch against the Spanish and Portuguese. One de Pinto was killed at his post while bravely defending one of the fortresses; and in the trying times of 1645 and 1654, great services were rendered by the family Cohen, who supplied the troops with provisions and ammunition. Out of this Brazilian colony grew another settlement, at Cayenne. The Dutch West India Company, by an edict dated 12th September, 1659, granted to David C. Nassi, above named, extensive rights and liberties at Cayenne for himself and companions. This congregation was increased by the arrival of several families from Leghorn, but its progress was hindered by the war, first with Portugal, and then with France, which took the country in 1664. Finding their position too uncomfortable, the Jews of Cayenne broke up *en masse* for Surinam, whither they were attracted by encouraging promises of Lord Willoughby who, in 1662, obtained from Charles II. a charter for the colonization of that country; and in three years the banks of the river in Surinam were adorned with forty or fifty plantations, and a Jewish population of about four thousand. They were on a footing of perfect equality with the English inhabitants; and when in 1666 the Dutch government made themselves masters of that colony, the rights of the Jews were entirely confirmed. At this time also a considerable number of Jewish families went to form a colony at Jamaica, where the cultivation of the sugar-cane was very much improved, owing to their settlement on the island. There are at present two congregations, one Portuguese and one German, at Kingston, and smaller Jewish communities at Spanishtown and Montego Bay. In 1652, the island of Curaçao, situated a few miles to the north of South America, was, as it is now again, under dominion of the Dutch government, and a large tract of land was granted to Joseph Nunes de Fonseca and others to found a colony of Jews in that island, but the attempt failed, there being no more than twelve settlers on the tract. Later, however, they became numerous and flourishing, and in the beginning of the eighteenth century they built the first synagogue, which was soon replaced by a larger and much better one. In 1863, a considerable number of families seceded from the old community to form a congregation on reform principles, and two years later erected a handsome temple, in which it is the privilege of the writer now to officiate as minister.

It is well-known that in 1614 the Dutch took possession of what was then called Manhattan Island, now New York. This was not done by the Dutch government, but under its sanction by an association of prominent merchants at Amsterdam who had formed a company under the name of The West India Company. We have already seen that the Spanish and Portuguese Jews, who had found an asylum in Holland, were wealthy and enterprising; and some of them were not only shareholders to a large amount, but also directors of the West India Company. The object of this company was ostensibly to promote the settlement of new countries, and for the general purposes of traffic; but in reality was organized to secure pecuniary gain by the capture of the richly laden Spanish vessels, and by the seizure of Spanish and Portuguese possessions in the West Indies and in South America. At one time this company had no less than seventy armed vessels in its service. In 1630, Bahia, or St. Salvador, then the capital of Brazil, was captured by its fleet, and for twelve successive years afterwards its conquests were frequent and important. About this time, however, a treaty of peace was concluded between the Dutch and the Portuguese governments; and when in 1654 Brazil was re-taken by the Portuguese, the Jews were ordered to leave the country, under protection, however, of the authorities, and with permission to take with them all their property; the viceroy granted them further time to arrange their affairs, and thirty vessels to convey them to Holland. Most of these emigrants returned to old Amsterdam, while a few of them set sail for New Amsterdam, now New York; and it appears that this was the first arrival of Jews within the limits of what is now called the United States. Only twenty-seven of them, men, women, and children, arrived here in the bark St. Catarina; and it seems that they were in a destitute condition, or that they had been obliged to leave in great haste, for upon their arrival their goods were sold at auction for the payment of their passage, and the amount realized being insufficient, two of their number were kept in custody; but as no further proceedings appear on the records, the matter seems to have been amicably arranged.*

Stuyvesant was then governor of New Amsterdam, and on many occasions showed his hostility to the Jews. He wrote to the home government, requesting "that none of the Jewish nation be permitted to infest New Netherland." The answer was worthy of Holland, "that his request was inconsistent with reason and justice." Still the Jews were frequently annoyed by the authorities and the people; and finding their new abode uncomfortable, a number of them

---

* From a lecture by Judge Daly, published in the *Jewish Times*, Vol. IV., Nos. 15–21.

went to Newport, Rhode Island, where religious freedom was made a fundamental principle of the commonwealth; and we find it recorded that, in 1657, a number of Jews from Curaçao also made Newport their home. Stuyvesant's letter, instead of having the effect he desired, had an opposite result, for it stirred up the Jewish members of the West India Company to ask for better protection and privileges for their brethren in the New World, and a special act was issued to that effect. In 1656, the first Jewish burial place in New Amsterdam was established on a piece of ground granted them for that purpose. In 1664, the city was taken by the English, and received the name of New York. As the Jews had to struggle with many difficulties, their number did not increase for some time, still they persevered in their efforts to establish their religious union as well as their worldly interests, and in 1695 a house on Beaver street, between Broadway and Broad street, was fitted up as a place of worship, with a congregation of twenty families. About the year 1728, a small stone structure was erected for a synagogue in the lower part of the town in Mill street, which street has since disappeared from the map. The congregation was called Sheërith Israel, and is the same Portuguese congregation well-known in that city. In the year 1733, a small number of Jewish families, about forty-five souls, immigrated from London and settled in Savannah, Georgia, where they landed on the 11th of July of that year. They were nearly all of Spanish or Portuguese descent, and soon formed themselves into a religious body or congregation. Later, some of these emigrants went to Charleston, South Carolina, and subsequently to other States, and from time to time many other families were induced to come to these shores from different parts of the world, and in this manner the number of Jews in this country increased, until they assumed the immense number and the high standing in which we now find them.

It would be an interesting study to trace the history of the Jews in the United States from the earliest date to the present time; but we have not now at hand the resources for such a compilation, nor would the limits of this SYNOPSIS permit us to expatiate; we will, therefore, content ourselves with giving a few interesting collateral facts.

It is a singular coincidence that the same year in which happened the terrible catastrophe of the expulsion of the Jews from the Spanish peninsula, was the year of the discovery of the New World; that the same power which brought on that misfortune, was also instrumental in finding an asylum for all who might be persecuted for the sake of their religion; and again that the same period which saw in Europe the important political changes tending to the emancipation of the Jews, was also the period in which the Federal Union shook off all foreign trammels, and finally declared all the inhabitants of the land as equal before the law. It was natural that the Jews of America, who now enjoyed perfect freedom, should commiserate their brethren who still groaned under the weight of oppression. Among the philanthropists who felt so inclined we notice particularly the benevolent Judge Mordecai M. Noah. In the early part of the present century, Mr. Noah had been United States consul at Tunis, and was eye-witness of the degradation and suffering to which the Jews under the crescent were yet subject. His kind heart yearned to do something for the alleviation of their misfortunes, and he devised the noble, though premature plan of an emigration of those eastern Jews on a large scale. The Judge was proprietor of a beautiful and fertile island called Grand Island, situated by the Niagara River and Falls, which land had been ceded to the Judge by the State of New York, in liquidation of a debt due to him. There he proposed to establish a Jewish colony under the governorship of a judge of their own nation, and in 1825 actually laid the foundation of a city which was to bear the name of Ararat, alluding to the mount where Noah's ark rested. He issued a proclamation to the chiefs of the principal Jewish communities in Europe, styling himself "by the grace of God, the first Judge in Israel," and asking his friends to promote the grand undertaking. In order to give more publicity to the project, he arranged for a grand and pompous procession, under the accompaniment of music and military parade; the principal personages being dressed in black with red velvet and ermine cloaks, and headed by himself as "The Judge." On account of the numerous attendance, the festivity was held, not on Grand Island, but in the city of Buffalo; they assembled in one of the churches, where divine service was held, after which the Judge ascended the pulpit and delivered a stirring address on the re-generation of Israel and the approach of the messianic time, to which he considered the present movement as preparatory. Had the well-meaning Judge been satisfied with a more modest beginning, the enterprise might have met with some success, while the very grandeur he wished to impart to it seems to have killed it in the bud. In 1843, the same gentleman projected a plan for the establishment of a Hebrew College in the United States, which plan, though apparently more feasible, was likewise premature and failed of success. The question has since been frequently discussed, and experiments to establish such a seminary have been made in New York and Philadelphia, but neither met with sufficient support. In 1873, however, the "Union of American Hebrew Congregations" has been inaugurated, and in connection therewith, as the principal object of the Union, a "Hebrew Theological College" has been opened. This institution is founded on a pretty solid basis and promises good results. The establishment of the "Union" and the "College" is due chiefly to the energetic labors of the Rev. Dr. Isaac M. Wise, who is now president of the Seminary and occupies one of the professor's chairs, without accepting any remuneration for his services. The "Board of Delegates of American Israelites," of which we made mention before, was called into existence at the time of the Mortara abduction, and had for its object the concentration of the American Jewish communities for the purpose of amelioration, protection, and education among the Jews wherever found. During the twenty years of its existence, it has done very good work abroad as well as at home, but being superseded by the establishment of the "Union" just mentioned, the "Board" has last year (1878), by mutual agreement, ceded its functions to that institution and dissolved. Among the numerous benevolent institutions formed in this country within the past forty or fifty years, the Bené Berith fraternity deserves particular mention. From a small beginning in the city of New York, in 1843, it has gradually increased, and now extends all over the United States, and counts its members by thousands. Its object was and is still, to promote union of feeling and union of action among American Jews, and it has accomplished much in that direction. It has borrowed something of the Masonic society in the manner of conducting its meetings and the mutual recognition of its members; but its outside workings in providing for the widows and orphans, not only of its own members, but of all needy Israelites, establishing hospitals, orphan asylums, and homes for the aged and infirm in different parts of the country, have been productive of unspeakable benefit.

These and similar institutions have contributed a great deal to establish concord among our people, and are an evidence to prove this fact—that while preserving the chief traits of our character, and adhering to the principles of our religion, we can yet mix in friendly intercourse with persons of a different creed; that we can be truly Jews and at the same time citizens of the world. This, indeed, appears to be the providential dispensation, that the Jew should be a true cosmopolitan; for the Jewish race, as if an exception to all other races, flourishes in every climate, and is as vigorous and as prolific in the frosty north or the American wilderness as it was in the genial climate of Spain, or on the hot plains of Mesopotamia. The expulsion from the Spanish peninsula, like the dispersion of the people from Palestine, seems to be intended to teach us that a perfect concentration, an entire exclusion of our race, is no part of the divine economy; that the command given to Abraham "Get thee out of thy country . . . and I will make of thee a great nation . . . and thou shalt be a blessing" is still applicable to his remotest offspring. And among the many lessons which a careful study of our history affords, this appears to be one, that the presence of Jews in the New World almost simultaneous with its discovery, is but another step in the long march of the wandering Jew, which is to continue until the time when Jehovah shall be Ruler over all the earth, and his Unity be universally acknowledged.

SECOND PART.

EXPLANATION OF

Some of the Mosaic Laws.

INDEX

TO EXPLANATION OF MOSAIC LAWS.

	PAGE
Introduction,	179
Distinction of clean and unclean animals.	182
Prohibition of eating blood and fat,	185
Not to seethe a kid in its mother's milk.	188
The manner of slaughtering cattle,	190
Heterogeneous mixtures,	192
Exchange of male and female apparel,	193
The manner of shaving the head and beard,	195
The Nazarite,	196
Divination, witchcraft, etc.,	198
Not to kindle fire on the Sabbath,	201
Sacrifices,	205
The making of fringes on the garments,	208
The phylacteries,	211
Writing on the door-posts,	213
Swearing. Taking an oath,	215
The right of primogeniture,	221
The levirate law,	223
Beheading the heifer,	226
The rebellious son,	228
Taking a bird's nest,	229
The Sabbatical Year and the Jubilee,	230
The leprosy,	233
Not to add to the law, nor diminish from it,	236

EXPLANATION

OF

SOME OF THE MOSAIC LAWS.

INTRODUCTION.

The great purpose of the Mosaic institution was to abolish all idolatrous worship, which in the early ages of the world was universal, and to train the Jewish people gradually to the service of the true God; that they might stand as a model of purity and rectitude, and be as an instrument in the hands of the Creator for the ultimate perfection of mankind generally. To accomplish this end, it was necessary, first of all, that Israel should be separated from the heathen nations among whom they lived, and that they should be different in their laws and customs, so as to lessen as much as possible their intercourse with other people. To this effect, Moses endeavored to make them an agricultural people, prohibiting them to make an absolute sale of their lands; he endeavored to discourage commerce with strangers by giving them rules of life which would render it inconvenient for them to live among other nations; he opposed emigration by making it the duty of all males to appear three times a year at the temple in Jerusalem; and he discouraged the spirit of conquest beyond Palestine by forbidding the king " to multiply to himself horses, silver, and gold," and by the absence of a standing army. These and many other civil and political regulations apparently had no connection with the religious sentiments of the people; yet in the Mosaic legislation politics and religion are so closely interwoven as to be virtually one and the same, since all the ordinances were delivered in the name of God, and a sense of man's obligation to obey God is religion. It is to be further observed that in the Mosaic Books—if we except the announcement of God's Unity—there are no articles of faith, nor is the observance of the precepts connected by the law-giver with a recompense in a future life; no relation established between the temporal and the eternal; no connection between man's present conduct and a spiritual reward. This, it would seem, was taken for granted, a necessary consequence. All mankind believed that their prosperity or adversity in life depended upon the observance or non-observance of certain religious duties; some believed also that the soul is immortal and that felicity or suffering in a future existence were dependent on man's good or bad actions in this life, and it is reasonable to think that the Israelites shared this belief. Moses declared simply that, if the Israelites obeyed the will of God, it should be well with them, and they should live happy, and if they failed to do so, they should feel the direct consequences of their misconduct, to show them that they were under the special supervision of their Creator, and to show the world a living example and positive proof that God rewards the good and punishes the evil.

The object of the Mosaic dispensation, then, being to purify the Hebrew people from idolatrous and immoral practices, the purpose of the following discussions is to explain in what manner the precepts could accomplish this object. The laws prescribed are quite numerous, and there are many for which we cannot find any apparent cause, unless we penetrate into the study of the condition and the circumstances of the Jewish people at the time those laws were prescribed to them. Some rabbis expressed the opinion that many laws were given without any particular purpose, except to try the obedience and fidelity of the people, and to the end that they should, at all times and in all their actions, how trifling soever, be reminded of the duties God imposed upon them. Some maintained even that it would be a depreciation of the divine commands to subject them to mere human reasoning, while their exalted divine origin is more apparent when the human mind cannot penetrate into their causes. The great and deeply learned Rabbi Moses Maimonides, however, took great pains to show that all the Mosaic precepts have their causes and their utility; and that none of them proceed from the mere arbitrary will of God. "The general intention of the law," says Maimonides, "is twofold, namely, to promote the soundness of the body, and the soundness of the mind; but the latter," says he, "is by far the most important." Now, as the human mind, generally, had been much perverted by superstition and by idolatrous practices, it was, as we said, the chief purpose of the Mosaic institutions to eradicate all ideas and all practices connected with idolatry or false worship, and to impress the Israelites with this great fundamental truth that *God is One*, that he is the sole Creator and supporter of all things existing; and that to him alone we owe reverence and obedience.

There is much difference of opinion among men of letters, whether the laws of Moses were quite original, or whether he borrowed them from the Egyptians and other nations by whom they were surrounded. But although the preponderance of argument is in favor of their originality, yet it is almost universally conceded that several of the Mosaic institutions were but modifications of more ancient established laws or usages, or improvements thereon, and that some such laws or customs were continued in accommodation to the sentiments and habits of mind of the people who had so long been attached to those customs that it would have been impossible at once to wean them therefrom, unless God would have, in a supernatural manner, changed their heart and mind. This was especially the case with regard to the institution of sacrifices, but it is apparent in various other instances, as we shall hereafter explain. On the whole, however, we cannot but admire the wisdom of the great legislator, and are forced to admit that, in laying before Israel this excellent code of laws, so admirably suitable for the time and country in which they lived, Moses must have been inspired with superior wisdom; though the modest teacher disclaims all credit for himself when he says, "Behold I have taught you statutes and judgments such as the Lord my God commanded me, that you should do so in the land whither ye go to possess it."

EXPLANATION OF MOSAIC LAWS.

"These are the animals which ye may eat among all the beasts that are on the earth."—Lev. xi. 2.

The eleventh chapter of Leviticus is almost entirely devoted to a statement of the distinguishing marks by which the clean and unclean animals, that is, those which are suitable or unsuitable for food, may be known; to an enumeration of those that might appear doubtful, and of the birds which are considered unfit to be eaten; as also of the fishes and reptiles, and some that pollute even by the touch. From this chapter, and from the repetition of it in Deut. xiv. it appears that quadrupeds are considered as clean or suitable when they have cloven hoofs and chew the cud; fishes having fins and scales are allowed for food; birds are not distinguished by any marks, but the carnivorous or the birds of prey are forbidden. Of serpents, worms, and insects, all that creep or have more than four feet are prohibited—locusts excepted. The reason for the prohibition of those animals named or designated has been the subject of much discussion among literary men, but the principal one, and the one on which all are agreed, is, that they are unwholesome for food. As we have nothing new or original to offer on this subject, the best information that can be had will be gained by culling some extracts of commentaries of the ablest writers, both Jews and Christians, on the matter. First of all, Maimonides* says briefly, "All those kinds of food which are forbidden in our law are unwholesome." R. Levi, of Barcelona, says, "As the body is the seat of the soul, God would have it a fit instrument for its companion, and therefore removes from his people all those obstructions which may hinder the soul in its operations; for which reason all such meats are forbidden which produce impure blood." A learned Christian commentator † observes, "While God keeps the eternal interests of man steadily in view, he does not forget his earthly comfort; he is at once solicitous both for the health of his body and his soul. He has not forbidden certain aliments because he is a sovereign, but because he knew they would be injurious to the health and morals of his people. Solid-footed animals, such as the horse, and many-toed animals, such as the cat, etc., are here prohibited. Beasts which have bifid or cloven hoofs, such the ox, are considered as proper for food, and therefore commended. The former are unclean, *i. e.*, unwholesome, affording a gross nutriment, often the parent of scorbutic and scrofulous disorders; the latter clean, *i. e.*, affording a copious and wholesome nutriment, and not laying the foundation of any disease. Ruminating animals, *i. e.*, those

---

* Moreh, Ch. 23. † Dr. Clark's Comment. on Lev. xi.

which chew the cud, concoct their food better than the others which swallow it with little mastication, and therefore the flesh contains more of the nutritious juices, and is more easy of digestion, and consequently, of assimilation to the solids and fluids of the human body. On this account they are termed clean, *i. e.*, peculiarly wholesome and fit for food. . . . On the same ground he forbade all fish that have not both fins and scales, such as the conger, eel, etc., which abound in gross juices and fat, which very few stomachs are able to digest. A very able French writer* says, "One of the most distinguishing traits in the character of Moses as a legislator, and one in which he was the most imitated by those who in after-ages gave laws to the eastern world, was his constant attention to the health of the people. He forbade the use of pork, of the hare, etc., of fish without scales, whose flesh is gross and oily, and all kinds of heavy meat as the fat (the suet) of the bullock, the kid, and the lamb; an inhibition supremely wise in a country where the excessive heat, relaxing the fibres of the stomach, rendered digestion peculiarly slow and difficult." "The flesh of the eel and some other fish," says Larcher, "thickened the blood, and by checking the perspiration, excited all those maladies connected with the leprosy;" and even goes on so far as to suppose that this was the reason why the Egyptian priests proscribed certain kinds of fish, and caused them to be accounted sacred, the better to keep the people from eating so unwholesome a kind of food. Plutarch gives a similar reason for swine being held in general abhorrence by them, notwithstanding they sacrificed them at the full moon to the Moon and to Bacchus. "The milk of the sow," he remarks, "occasioned leprosy, which was the reason why the Egyptians entertained so great an aversion for this animal."

---

* M. de Pastoret, Moïse considéré, etc., ch. vii., p. 528.

Several other non-Jewish as well as Jewish commentators express similar views regarding the Mosaic distinction between *clean* and *unclean* animals; among others, Michaelis observes, "That in so early an age of the world we should find a systematic division of quadrupeds, so excellent as never yet, after all the improvements in natural history, to have become obsolete, but, on the contrary, to be still considered as useful by the greatest masters of the science, cannot but be looked upon as truly wonderful."*

"It shall be an ordinance forever for your generations, in all your dwelling-places, that ye eat not any fat nor blood."—Levit. iii. 17.

The above is but one of the many passages in the books of Moses where the eating of fat and of blood is forbidden; and from the urgency and the frequent repetition of the command, we may judge that Moses desired to impress it strongly on the people's mind that a total abstinence from these things was necessary, as, on account of their strong propensity to use it, they were prone to recur to the error, and because the injuries resulting therefrom were manifold. This we shall find to be the case especially with regard to the use of blood, and therefore we shall treat of that first.

The reasons for the prohibition of eating blood may be divided into *moral* and *physical*. From a moral point of view it was interdicted: 1st, to prevent idolatrous practices. Blood used to be sacrificed to demons, and eaten by the offerers in order to seek association or communion with devils. Maimonides has stated at large the superstitions of the Zabii in offering blood as a sacrifice to the infernal objects of their worship, and R. Moses Bar Nachman† says, "They gathered up blood from the devils, their idol-gods; and then came to themselves and ate of that blood with

---

* Commentaries on the Laws of Moses, vol. iii., art. 204.
† Comment. on Deut. xii. 23.

them as being the devils' guests, and invited to eat at the table of demons, and so were joined in federal society with them; and by this kind of communion they were able to prophecy and foretell things to come." Horace* gives a satirical description of similar practices among his countrymen; and in the sacred books of the Hindoos there is a "sanguinary chapter," in which a minute description is given how blood is to be offered to the goddess Chandica, and the result produced by such oblations when the blood is drawn from certain animals, and even from persons. 2d. The use of blood was forbidden to prevent cruel practices, such as eating raw flesh, especially of living animals. Plutarch, in his *discourse of eating flesh*, informs us that it was customary in his time to run red-hot spit through the bodies of live swine, and to stamp upon the udders of sows ready to farrow, to make their flesh more delicious; and Herodotus† says that the Scythians, from drinking the blood of their cattle, proceeded to drink the blood of their enemies; and this is done even now among the New Zealand savages. We read also of a people east of Waday, in Africa, whose greatest luxury was feeding on raw meat cut from the animal while warm and full of blood; and the celebrated traveller Bruce relates with minuteness the scene which he witnessed near Axum, the ancient capital of Abyssinia, when some travellers he overtook seized the cow they were driving, threw it down, cutting steaks from it, ate them raw, and then drove on the poor sufferer before them. To oppose such horrible cruelties, it was wisely ordained by Moses that the Israelites should altogether abstain from blood.

But the use of this article was forbidden also from a physical point of view, and,

1st. Blood affords a very gross nutriment, and is very

---

* Sat. vii., Lib. 1.   † Lib. iv.

difficult of digestion, and if taken warm or in large quantities, may prove fatal, particularly bulls' blood; which was given, with this view, to criminals by the Greeks; and we read of Themistocles having purposely drunk a bowl of ox-blood during a sacrifice, which produced his death.

2d. Those nations which feed largely on flesh without a proper admixture of vegetable food are observed to be remarkably subject to scorbutic diseases; and if physicians are right in ascribing such tendency to animal food in general when too freely eaten, especially in hot climates, it must be acknowledged that the grosser and more indigestible juices of such food must have the greatest tendency to produce such injurious consequences; and blood, as the grossest of all, be the most inimical to health and soundness.

We now come to consider the other part of the text, the prohibition of fat. And here it is necessary to observe that the Hebrew word *Cheleb* cannot be understood to mean all fat, for it would be almost impossible to obtain meat from which every particle of fat were extracted, just as it would be impossible to extract all the blood, except it be done by a chemical process, and it cannot for a moment be supposed that this was the intention of the law. The prohibition has, therefore, been interpreted, and universally adopted to mean, that which is properly called *suet*, that is, the harder and less fusible fat about the kidneys and the loins, while that which is closely intermixed with the flesh, and forms, as it were, part of it, is allowed. And this appears clearly from Lev. iii., where the kind of fat which is to be offered on the altar is exactly described, while the other part was allowed to be eaten. The reason for the prohibition is simply, as Maimonides says, "that such fat is heavy, hard to digest, and generates thick and cold blood, and is, therefore, more fit to be burnt than to be eaten.

"The first fruits of thy land shalt thou bring to the house of the

Lord thy God. Thou shalt not seethe a kid in its mother's milk."
—Ex. xxiii. 19 and xxxiv. 26.

This text is repeated in its entirety as is seen above, and both times it occurs in connection with the observance of the three festivals, and the appearance of every male Israelite at the Temple. The second half of the text, relating to the seething of a kid, is again repeated in Deut. xiv. 21, and there it appears in connection with things forbidden to eat.

There is no regular division or classification in the Mosaic laws; they appear promiscuously throughout the Pentateuch; and the connection in which a certain command is found with preceding or following passages is, therefore, not always sufficient to determine its meaning. Still, we need not quite abandon the common rule of interpretation, that "the sense of a passage of Scripture is illustrated by the context," especially when we find passage and context exactly repeated; and we mean to apply the rule here. Few, if any, of the Mosaic laws have been more perverted and misunderstood, and carried to a further length than this one. The prohibition of seething a *kid* has been interpreted as meaning any kind of meat; its *mother's* milk, to mean the milk of any animal; from seething together we have gone to the prohibition of eating together; and from eating *together* to that of eating any meat and any milk within six hours of each other; and still further, even to keep utensils and dishes altogether separate for the use of the one and of the other. Now let us see what the commentators say. Our great Maimon, following, or rather averse to opposing, the rabbinical interpretation says,* "Meat eaten with milk appears to me to have been prohibited, not merely because it afforded gross nourishment, but also because it savored of idolatry; some idolaters probably

---
* Moreh, Ch. xxiii,

doing so in their worship or at their festivals. And I am *the more inclined* to this opinion from observing that the law, in noticing this practice, does it twice immediately after having spoken of the three solemn annual feasts; as if it had been said: When ye appear before me on your feasts, ye shall not cook your food after the manner of the idolaters who are accustomed to this practice. *This reason appears to me of great weight*, although I have not yet found it in the Zabian books. In another chapter* of his Moreh, when treating of superstitious practice, at planting and grafting trees, the same author says, " The ancient idolaters stated in their books that it was a practice among them to suffer certain things to putrefy or rot, and then, when the sun was in a certain position, to sprinkle, accompanied with particular magical rites, about the fruit-trees which had been planted, imagining that if this was done by the man who planted it, it would cause it to flower and bear fruit earlier than others usually do."

And that which Maimonides did not find in the Zabian books, another doctor has found in another book; and the information he gives us on the subject just forms the connecting link between the two explanations of Maimonides just quoted, and forms one whole for the elucidation of our point. This scholar† gives the following extract from an ancient Karaite comment on the Pentateuch, which at once illustrates these magical sprinklings and explains one of the Mosaic precepts. "It was a custom of the ancient heathen, when they had gathered in all their fruits, to take a kid and boil it in the dam's milk, and then in a magical way to go about and besprinkle with it all their trees, and fields, and gardens, and orchards; thinking by this means they should

---

* Chapter xii.
† Dr. Cudworth, quoted by Dr. Townley, " Researches," p. 365.

make them fructify and bring forth fruit again more abundantly the following year; wherefore God forbade His people, the Jews, at the time of their ingathering, to use any such superstitious or idolatrous rites."* The rabbis, who base upon this text the prohibition of eating meat and milk together, say that "*Kid* includes the young of the bovine kind, of sheep and of goats, unless it is specified as a kid of a goat." But Aben Ezra, a more reasonable and independent commentator, says, "This is not so, for nothing is called kid except the young of the goats, and in Arabic, the word has the same significance, and is never applied to any other species. . . . It is by tradition that the rabbis received that Israel should not eat meat with milk." From the foregoing we conclude that, as the first part of the text relating to the bringing of the first fruits to Jerusalem has ceased for us, so is the prohibition spoken of in the second part of the text not applicable to us, since idolatrous practices are virtually abolished from our midst, and the regulations of keeping meat and milk strictly separate are, therefore, without any proper foundation in the Mosaic code.

> "If the place which the Lord thy God may choose to put His name there, be too far from thee, then mayest thou slaughter of thy large and small cattle which the Lord has given thee, as I have commanded thee, and thou mayest eat in thy gates to the full desire of thy soul."—Deut. xii. 21.

The whole fabric of rabbinical ordinances concerning the manner of slaughtering cattle and fowls, on which volumes have been written, is based solely and entirely on two words (*in Hebrew*) of the text here quoted; but the fabric is so frail that it vanishes by the very touch. These *two words*, rendered in English, "as I have commanded thee," are taken as a basis, and the inference drawn therefrom is this: Since it says, "Thou shalt slaughter of thy cattle . . . as I com-

---

* See also Brande, art. Ambarvalia.

mand thee," we ask, Where do we find that the Lord commanded how to slaughter cattle? Answer—nowhere in the Scriptures: ergo, Moses must have received oral instructions concerning the manner of slaughtering. Now, this whole reasoning is founded on the presupposition that Moses received from God oral instructions besides the laws committed to writing; and that the words, "as I command thee," refer to the *manner* in which cattle are to be killed. But neither is true. That additional laws, not found in the Pentateuch, were revealed to Moses, (is a mere supposition assumed to give weight to all rabbinical institutions and consider them as divine;) and, "as I commanded thee," refers not to the manner of slaughtering, but to a passage in the preceding paragraph (verse 15 same chapter), where it is already stated that cattle not intended for offerings "thou *mayest* slaughter and eat in all thy gates" (not thou *shalt* slaughter), and need not be brought to the Temple. The quintessence of our text then, expressed in modern style, would be this: When you shall be settled in Palestine, where the Temple will not be near to you as is now the tabernacle, then you may slaughter and eat of your cattle in your own towns as you like, as I commanded you above (verse 15). And we find further support for our interpretation in the text following the one we are describing, viz., "As the gazelle and hart are eaten, so mayest thou eat them." This explanatory text is given chiefly to say that, even as the gazelle and the hart are never brought to the Temple, so your cattle for home consumption need not be brought there. At the same time we may draw the comparison in full, and learn from it that even as the gazelle and the hart are not killed by cutting the throat, but by shooting (see Lev. xvii. 15), so your cattle at home may be killed in any manner you choose. We do not at all dispute the propriety of the Jewish manner of slaughtering and examining the entrails, when considered as a sanitary regulation, and from the consideration of preventing cruelty to the animal by giving it as little pain as possible, but we maintain that there is no basis for it in the Mosaic laws.

> "Thou shalt not let thy cattle gender with a diverse kind; thou shalt not sow thy field with mingled seed; and a garment of mixed texture (of wool and linen) shall not come upon thee."—Lev. xix. 19.

The above contains three prohibitions, the second and third of which are repeated with some variation in Deut. xxii. 9-11.

We pass over the first of these three without any explanation because of the delicacy of the subject, and because what is to be said of the other two will serve at the same time to explain the first. But there is another kind of admixture yet to be mentioned, which, though not named in the text, is supposed to be included in the second, and that is, the grafting of trees.

Among the ancients, idolatry was much mixed up with agriculture, as Maimonides informs us, because they, in their ignorance of the relation of causes and effects, finding that the growth of plants depended much on the sun and moon, believed that these and other orbs were intelligent beings who, at pleasure, caused the fruitfulness or barrenness of the land, and therefore ought to be worshipped. From this ill-grounded belief resulted all sorts of superstitious practices, some most ridiculous and abominable, and for which it is often very difficult or impossible to account. One of these superstitious ideas was the mixture of seeds, of animals, and the materials for garments, in order thereby to represent the different conjunctions of the planets. In Deut. xxii. 9, a mixture of seed in planting a vineyard is especially forbidden, and we find that in the books of the Zabii it is stated that they were accustomed to sow barley and dried grapes together, and this was done at a particular time, when the planets were in a certain position, and, by so doing, they signified, it is said, that their vineyards were consecrated to Ceres and Bacchus, and were recommended to their protection. Smoke was also raised on such occasions, and certain circles made by the planter, according to the number of the planets whose influence was invoked. We read of such practices even in modern times, and a reliable author assures us that, even at the present day, in Yorkshire, England, it is customary to raise smoke in the fields when they finish ploughing ; and this is what they call "Burning out the witch." Similar ceremonies were performed at the grafting of trees, such as olives into citrons, and not only such idle ceremonies, but some very immoral and indecent practices were in use on such occasions. It was also required that those who were engaged in such worship, especially their priests, should wear garments made of a texture of wool and linen. Therefore Israel were forbidden to make any such heterogeneous mixtures or follow such practices, which would lessen their dependence and trust in God, or draw them into immorality and indecency.

"A woman shall not wear a man's apparel, neither shall a man put on a woman's garment ; for all who do so are an abomination to the Lord thy God."—Deut. xxii. 5.

This exchange of garments between male and female would seem an innocent and harmless thing, and unless we penetrate into its meaning and find the ground upon which it is based, it would be difficult to understand why it should be sinful to do so ; but an insight into the matter will soon convince us how suitable such a prohibition was at the time when it was announced, though it can be hardly of any weight or applicability to our time. Like the preceding command which we have explained, this also was ordained to prevent idolatrous practices; for, Maimonides informs us, that it was a custom among the ancient heathen, when a man presented himself before the star Venus, that he should wear the colored dress of a woman, and when a woman adored the planet Mars, she was to appear in armor. "Besides," says our author, "such exchanges would have a tendency to excite to licentiousness and unchastity. From another author* we make the following extracts, which will further elucidate the subject. "As the heathens made such a multiplicity of gods out of one and the same person, so, likewise, did they confound their sexes, making the same deity sometimes a god, sometimes a goddess, or rather all of them of both sexes. Hence it is that the Greeks used the word Theos for both gods and goddesses; and after the same manner was the word *Deus* used by the Romans. Hence it was that the Cyprians represented their Venus with a beard, having a sceptre in her hand, dressed as a woman, but masculine in her stature and name, *Aphroditos;* and the statue the Syrians worshipped in the temple of *Heliopolis*, was that of a woman clothed like a man. So at Rome they had a Fortuna Mascula and Virilis, and a Fortuna Barbata. The Gentiles, to signify this mystery of community of sexes in their deities, counterfeited themselves to be masculine-feminine in their worshipping them. They thought to please their gods by presenting themselves before them as like them as they could; and by wearing a habit different from their sex, to recommend themselves to such deities as they supposed of doubtful, or rather of both sexes. This was practised especially in the worship of Venus. Their women thought they could not appear more acceptable in the presence of the god of war than dressed in arms, and their men, in the presence of the goddess of love,

---

* Young, on Idolatrous Corruptions in Religion, vol. i., pp. 97–105.

than in the habit proper to the soft and tender sex; and so Philocorus, an old Greek author, tells us of the Asiatics, that when they sacrificed to their Venus, "the men were dressed in women's apparel, and the women in men's, to denote that she was esteemed by them both male and female." And we find that the same practices prevailed among the Assyrians, the Africans, the Phœnicians, and other nations.

"Ye shall not round the corners of your heads, nor mar (destroy) the corners of your beard."—Lev. xix. 27.

Of this prohibition Maimonides says simply that it was so ordained "because the priests among the idolaters were accustomed thus to poll and shave themselves." From other authors we cull the following information on this subject. "The Hebrew word which we translate corners signifies also the end or extremities of anything; and the meaning is, they were not to cut their hair equal behind and before, as the worshippers of the stars and the planets, particularly the Arabians did; for this made their head have the form of a hemisphere. Herodotus observes that the Arabs shave or cut their hair round in honor of Bacchus, who, they say, had his hair cut in this way. He says also that the Macians, a people of Lybia, cut their hair round, so as to leave a tuft on the top of the head. In this manner the Chinese cut their hair even to the present day. The hair was much used in divination among the Greeks; and particularly about the time of the giving of the Law, as this is supposed to have been the era of the Trojan war. We learn from Homer, "that it was customary for parents to dedicate the hair of their children to some god, which, when they came to manhood, they cut off and consecrated to the deity. Achilles, at the funeral of Patroclus, cut off his golden locks which his father had dedicated to the river-god Sperchius, and threw them into the flood." Pope, in his translation of "The Iliad," gives us the following interesting version.

> But great Achilles stands apart in prayer,
> And from his head divides the yellow hair,
> Those curling locks which from his youth he vow'd,
> And sacred grew to Sperchius' honored flood.
> Then sighing, to the deep his locks he cast,
> And roll'd his eyes around the watery waste.
> Sperchius! whose waves, in many errors lost,
> Delightful roll along my native coast!
> To whom we vainly vow'd at our return,
> These locks to fall and hecatombs to burn—
> So vow'd my father, but he vow'd in vain;
> No more Achilles sees his native plain;
> In that vain hope, these hairs no longer grow;
> Patroclus bears them to the shades below.

From Virgil we learn that the topmost lock of hair was dedicated to the infernal gods; and Dryden gives us the following lines in his translation of "The Æneid."

> The sisters had not cut the topmost hair,
> Which Proserpine and they can only know,
> Nor made her sacred to the shades below—
>
> .   .   .   .
>
> This offering to the infernal gods I bear,
> Thus while she spoke she cut the fatal hair.

This offering of the hair leads us naturally to the consideration of a similar offering required of the Nazarite at the expiration of his time of abstinence, and as prescribed in the following text.

"The Nazarite shall shave his consecrated head at the entrance of the tabernacle of the congregation; and he shall take the hair of his consecrated head, and put it on the fire which is under the peace offering."—Num. vi. 18.

A perusal of the chapter from which this text is quoted will show that a Nazarite was a person who by a voluntary vow bound him or herself to abstain for some time from strong drink and whatever comes from the vine. He was not allowed to shave or cut his hair, nor to touch a dead body, even of one of his nearest relations. When the time of his abstinence expired, he was to bring an offering to the Temple, and there cut off his hair, which he placed on the fire under the burnt-offering.

Maimonides, in commenting on this precept, leaves the ceremony to be performed with the hair entirely out of consideration; and looks upon the nazarean vow merely as a temperance pledge. The cause and reason of the precepts relating to the Nazarite, that is, of abstinence from wine, says he, is evident; for wine has in many instances been the occasion of death to multitudes, and many strong men have been slain by it. It was the peculiarity of the Nazarite to abstain from every kind of drink made from the vine, that he might be thereby advanced to greater honor, and learn to be content with the things that were necessary. He, therefore, who thus abstained, was accounted holy, and placed in equal dignity with the high-priest as to sanctity, not being allowed to pollute himself for his deceased father or mother. Another commentator* says: "The directions which God here gives about it (the hair), are manifestly opposite to the ways of the Gentiles. For the Nazarites are here directed to cut their hair at the door of the tabernacle, where it was also to be burnt; whereas the Gentiles hung their hair, when they had cut it, upon trees or consecrated it to rivers, or laid it up in their temples, there to be preserved. The Hebrew Nazarites also are required to offer various sorts of sacrifices when they cut their hair, of which we rarely read anything among the Gentiles, and all the time of their separation were to drink no wine,

---

* Spencer, De Leg. Heb.

nor eat grapes, etc., which was not known among the heathen. From whence it is, one may think, that they are so often put in mind of the Lord, in this law of the Nazarites, . . . to put them in mind, that, though they used which was common to other nations, yet it was in honor of the Lord only, whom they acknowledged to be the author of health, and strength, and growth." It is thus evident from this institution, as it is from various others, that they were retained in accommodation to the long acquired habits of the people; that the Israelites adhered to some of the practices of other nations, but were at the same time required in all their doings to acknowledge the Almighty as their God and Ruler.

"There shall not be found among you any one who causes his son or his daughter to pass through the fire, or who useth divination or an observer of times, or an enchanter, or a sorcerer, or a charmer, or a consulter with familiar spirits, or a wizard, or one who enquireth of the dead."—Deut. xviii. 10-11.

We have selected the above text from the many which contain similar prohibitions, because in this one we find nearly the whole nomenclature of the superstitious practices in which the heathen indulged. As we have already said so much in the preceding articles about these idolatrous habits, and, as every enlightened person must be convinced, not only of the folly, but also of the pernicious influence resulting from such frivolous and irrational acts, it might be thought superfluous to dwell here upon or to go into an explanation of the diverse practices mentioned in our text. Nor do we intend to treat of each of them separately, which would be a tedious discussion on account of the sameness which prevails in them, and because we could not devote sufficient space to it. But although idolatry is said to be exterminated from civilized society, in what is called our enlightened age, and that for this reason those Mosaic commands which have particular reference to idolatry have really lost their binding force on us, yet we find many traces of it still lingering even among intelligent and sensible people; and the superstitions of lucky days, of good and bad omens, of fortune-telling, spiritualism, and the like, have yet firm hold on the minds of many. And if we look into the *Shulchan Aruch*—which is still considered by many of our people as the guide of our religion—and we find there certain rules prescribed concerning the use of Amulets (Kemia) or herbs worn on the neck, some of which are said to be allowed, and others forbidden to be carried on the Sabbath outside of the city limits, according as they have been prepared by an accredited person, and have proved to possess the virtue of healing or not; and further, that it is allowed to wear as a remedy such charms as the egg of a locust, the tooth of a fox, or the nail on which a person has been hanged, and that the prohibition of "following the ways of the Amorites" is not applicable to these things, then we have indeed reason to say that all traces of idolatry are not yet banished from among us. Therefore, though it will be unnecessary to enter upon the *modus operandi* of these sorcerers, enchanters, necromancers, sooth-sayers, charmers, wizards, pythonists, and whatever else they may be called, it will not be amiss here to say a few words, not of explanation, but rather of exhortation, against these barbarous practices which still prevail among us, and which every sensible person ought to banish from his mind and oppose with all his power in the midst of those under his control or influence. We ought to oppose these things for two reasons: because they lessen our trust in God, and our submission to His providential decrees; and because they foster ignorance and superstition, which are the great drawbacks to civilization and the spread of true religion. When people were so enveloped in darkness that they could form no idea of an invisible God, they looked upon the planets as divinities, prayed to them and invoked their assistance, and practised many things which must now appear very foolish and ridiculous. These performances may all be classed under three heads, namely, acts done to avert evil, to procure favor of blessing, and to foretell events; and all what is done, not in a natural way, to accomplish either of these things, or what is done in the name of religion and for which we can give no valid reason why it should be done, is contrary to the spirit of our religion. And, therefore, such ideas as choosing a day as lucky for the undertaking of business, or of a voyage, observing the baying or yelping of a dog at night as the precursor of death; avoiding thirteen persons to sit down to table, and a thousand such unmentionable follies, should be strenuously opposed as unbecoming all who lay any claim to enlightenment. / So also the barbarous custom of tearing one's garments, and letting the hair and beard grow in case of death in the family; burning a lamp, called the perpetual light, in expectation that the soul of the departed may be affected by it, which may be a remnant of the vestal fires of the Romans, or the perpetual lamps placed in sepulchres, some of which are said to have been found burning after the lapse of several ages; all these and similar practices savor of idolatry, and should be disowned by all rational men. And, as a proof that no idea of true religion is connected with such acts, but that they proceed from weakmindedness, we may mention the fact that the illiterate, and those who show the greatest indifference for true religion, are generally very strict in the observance of these irreligious acts. Maimonides, in his Moreh, repeats again and again that the scope of the whole law, and the very hinge on which it turns, is this, that idolatry may be banished from among us, the very name of it be blotted out, and no power of assisting or injuring mankind be attributed to things supernatural.

"Ye shall kindle no fire in any of your habitations on the Sabbath-day."—Ex. xxxv. 3.

We proposed to discuss especially such commands as are open to different interpretations, and the one contained in the above text, free of all ambiguity though it may appear, has yet been the subject of much dispute among the rabbis, who seem to be almost agreed, however, on this point, that the text does not mean at all what its plain wording implies; that it has nothing to do with the real kindling of fire, but means something quite different. They set out by arguing in this way. In the Ten Commandments, and in several other portions of the Mosaic code, we find the prohibition of performing any labor on the Sabbath. But then, what is labor? What particular actions are to be regarded as such? Since the law is silent on the subject, and does not enlighten us by giving any definition as to what is to be considered as labor, nor to enumerate any particular acts, it is assumed that the Sabbath ordinance is repeated here, at the head of a chapter wherein the necessaries of the tabernacle are mentioned, to teach us that just such kind of work as was done in the erection of the tabernacle, these same occupations are to be looked upon as labor forbidden on the Sabbath. Still the question remains, What are exactly the manipulations forbidden? The orders for making the tabernacle are generally given in the words, "Thou shalt make" this and that; the particular names of actual labor mentioned scarcely exceed half a dozen, which are engraving, casting, filling, and setting of precious stones, spinning, weaving, and dyeing. Of the common occupations in building, nothing is said; still less is anything of field labor mentioned, and yet it could not be supposed that all such labor would be allowed. Therefore, the rabbis took upon themselves to say that all such occupations which were mediately or immediately necessary for the erection of the tabernacle are forbidden. Thus hunting and flaying, for instance, were necessary to procure skins for covering the tabernacle; and it was further necessary to *make fires* for preparing the colors for dyeing those skins; therefore, kindling a fire, like hunting and flaying is to be considered labor forbidden on the Sabbath. If so, then, that kindling fire is to be considered labor, and as such is included in the general list of forbidden occupations, why is this one specified more than any other? is the question asked. This interrogation is variously answered; but the final conclusion arrived at is, that the command of Ex. xxxv. 3 does not mean a prohibition of kindling, not the ignition of some combustible matter, but it implies a prohibition to the Sanhedrin against holding their tribunals on the Sabbath, and especially against executing capital punishments, one of which was burning. This exposition of the text is laid down in an ancient rabbinical work called Mechiltah; the same explanation is given in the Jerusalem Talmud; and appears as the adopted authoritative opinion.*

But we may be excused for deviating from the opinion given by the rabbis, and believing that, when the Law speaks of kindling fire, it means actual fire that burns, and not judicial debates and verdicts; and when it says "in all your habitations," it means wherever Israelites dwell, not only in the judicial courts. Assuming, then, that the Scripture means just what it says; and basing upon the principle that there must be a reason for every command laid down, we ask, Why should kindling fire on the Sabbath be forbidden? Why, when we feel cold and uncomfortable on the Sabbath, should it be criminal to start a fire; or, if we need light, should it be sinful to light a lamp? The solution to these questions may be easily found when we bear in mind

---

* See Sepher Hachinuch in its commentary on this command.

the repeated statement of our favorite author that, "the very foundation on which our whole law rests is, that it is designed to eradicate idolatry," and then find the relation between idolatrous worship and the making of fire. It is well known that among the many superstitious practices of the ancients was the worship of fire. This was especially the case among the Persians, and the Romans and Greeks followed the example. In the Mosaic laws we find a strict prohibition against passing children through the fire, and that the custom obtained among the early inhabitants of Palestine. And so deeply rooted seems this idea to have been in the people's minds, that it continued through many ages, and is not exterminated even at the present day. Solomon built a temple to Moloch upon the Mount of Olives, and Menasseh, long afterwards, imitated the impiety by making his son pass through a fire kindled in honor of this most abominable idol. Virgil, Horace, Theodoret, and other famous authors speak of it as existing in their time; and Maimonides informs us that in his day it was a custom for nurses to take new-born children and wave them to and fro in the smoke of certain herbs, which was, no doubt, says he, a relic of this passing through the fire. From other authors* we learn that it was a heathenish custom on new-moon days to make fire before the shops and houses and leap over them or between them, imagining that they who did so would thereby be purified and their evils burnt away, and that the Council of Trullo, held 692 C.E., condemned this practice; and that "on St. John Baptist's eve, the vulgar were wont to make fires for the whole night, and leap over them and draw lots, and divine about their good and evil fortune;" also "that there was a feast called *Amphidromia*, kept

---

* Young's Historical Dissertation on Idolatrous Corruptions in Religion, vol. i., p. 117, and Brand's Observations on Popular Antiquities, chap. xxvii.

by private families at Athens on the fifth day after the birth of a child, when it was the custom for the gossips to run round the fire with the infant in their arms; and then, having delivered it to the nurse, they were entertained with feasting and dancing." Dr. Moresin* states that he was an eye-witness of a remarkable custom which then existed in Scotland, to take a new-baptized infant and swing it three or four times over a flame, saying and repeating thrice: "Let the flame consume thee now or never." And finally, Mr. Borlase, in his account of Cornwall, says, "The Cornists make bonfires in every village on the eve of St. John Baptist's and St. Peter's days, which I take to be the remains of part of the Druid superstition." It appears, then, that the making of fires for idolatrous purposes has ever continued; that the origin of it is to be traced back to the earliest ages of history; that even some of Israel's kings yielded to this gross error, and it is supposed that, in reference to this false worship, the prophet said in the name of God, "Your new-moon days and your festivals my soul hateth."

The passage in Numb. xv. 32–36 may serve also to illustrate our subject, as it appears to stand in connection with the prohibition in our leading text.† A man was found gathering sticks on the Sabbath, and, on being brought to Moses for judgment, the severe punishment of stoning to death was pronounced upon him. The probability is, that he was punished, not for Sabbath-breaking, but because this gathering of sticks was a preparatory act to the building of a wood-pile for an idolatrous purpose. In Jeremiah vii. 18, the Israelites are reproached with "collecting wood and

---

* The Origin and Increase of Depravity in Religion.
† Herz Homberg in his comm. called Hacarem, in loco, takes the same view.

kindling fire, and making cakes for the queen of heaven." As all sorts of superstitious ideas were connected with idolatrous worship, it may be that the combustibles to be used for such bonfires were required to be gathered from abroad, not from the regular supply of wood for home-consumption, or it may be that a particular kind of wood, not always at hand, was desired for the purpose.

From the foregoing we conclude, then, that the command "Ye shall kindle no fire in any of your habitations on the Sabbath-day," was given with the same intention as most of the Mosaic laws were instituted, viz., to abolish idolatry; and that the lighting of fire, in our own houses or elsewhere, for comfort, for use, or for any enjoyment, is no transgression of this command.

> "The Lord called unto Moses and spoke to him from the tent of the congregation, saying: Speak to the children of Israel and say to them, if any person among you wish to bring to the Lord an offering of any of the beasts, ye shall bring your offerings of the large cattle or of the small cattle."—Lev. i. 1–2.

Thus begins the book of Leviticus, the first ten chapters of which are devoted to directions concerning sacrifices and Temple service. That the Mosaic laws were established for the great purpose of abolishing idolatry from among the Israelites, that many of the ancient practices to which the people were addicted were, with some modifications, retained for the sake of satisfying their cravings; and that it was the intention of the legislator to bring them gradually to a better and more rational worship, is apparent from none more than from the institution of sacrifices. In fact, this cannot be properly called a Mosaic institution, but a Mosaic modification of an institution which existed ever since man began to live on earth. That the Jewish sacrifices were not desired, but merely tolerated, is evident—

First: From the opening of the book of Leviticus, where

it says, "if any person wish to bring an offering."* It does not say, "Ye shall bring offerings," but in case one wished to bring a sacrifice, he is required to bring his offering to God's temple and nowhere else, and particular directions are given as to the manner of its manipulations.

Second: It appears more strongly from Lev. xvii. 1–7, where it is ordained that whosoever shall kill an ox or goat or lamb in or out of the camp, and not bring it to the tabernacle, shall be cut off from among his people. "To the end that the children of Israel may bring their sacrifices which they offer in the open field, that they may bring them to the Lord ... and they shall no more offer their sacrifices to the satyrs." Here it is plainly stated that they are required to bring their offerings to God, in order to keep them from offering to devils.

Third: We find various passages in the Prophets and in the Psalms, from which it appears that the sacrifices were not considered an important institution, nor a permanent one, but that moral worth in man was far more desirable than offerings. "Has the Lord as much delight in burnt-offerings and sacrifices as in obeying the voice of the Lord?" "Behold, to obey is better than sacrifice, and to hearken better than the fat of rams."† "To what purpose is the multitude of your sacrifices to me," says the Lord.‡ "I will not reprove thee for thy sacrifices, or thy burnt-offerings, to have been continually before me. I will take no bullock out of thy house, nor he-goats from thy folds."§ "Will the Lord be pleased with thousands of rams, or with ten thousand rivers of oil?" ‖ "I spoke not to your fathers, nor commanded them on the day that I brought them out of

---

* It is so interpreted by Kimchi, followed by Mendelssohn, and so commented upon by Hertz Wesseley.
† 1 Sam. xv. 23. § Ps. l. 7–8.
‡ Isa. i. ii. ‖ Micah iv. 7.

the land of Egypt, concerning burnt-offerings or sacrifices, but this thing I commanded them, saying, 'Obey my voice and I will be your God and ye shall be my people.' "* On these words of Jeremiah, Maimonides comments thus: "The meaning of his words is, as if he had said, 'The primary intention of every part of the law is, that ye should know me, and forsake the service of other gods; and the precepts which enjoin oblations, and command you to worship in my house, are given to instruct and assist you in this duty: for the reason why I have transferred this mode of worship to my own name is, to efface the remembrance of idolatry, and establish the doctrine of my unity.'" †

We might quote several pages from the Moreh in support of this opinion, that the offerings were merely allowed and not desired; but we will give only a few in addition to what has been said. "At that time the universal practice, and the mode of worship in which all were educated was, that various kinds of animals should be offered in the temples in which their idols were placed, and before which their worshippers were to burn incense and prostrate themselves; . . . therefore God did not ordain the abandonment or abolition of all such worship; for it is the well-known disposition of the human heart to cleave to that to which it has been habituated. . . . On these accounts the Creator retained those modes of worship, but transferred the veneration from created things and shadows to his own name.‡ It would be irrational to expect that those who have been trained up in the practice of those services and modes of worship should at once renounce them all, and adopt a contrary course of action. . . . So divine wisdom ordained that a kind of worship similar to that they had been accustomed to should be continued amongst them. . . . Although

---

* Jer. vii. 22-23. † Moreh Nebuchim, Ch. VII. ‡ Ibid.

God sometimes miraculously changes the nature of other things, he does not in the same way change the nature of man."*

From these premises we arrive at the conclusion that the ordinances concerning sacrifices, as prescribed in Leviticus, were intended for our ancestors only, and with the destruction of the second temple were forever abrogated. How can a reasonable and reasoning man entertain the idea that we should ever resort to the practice of disgracing a place of worship by turning it into a slaughter house, or believe that the burning of animals be acceptable to God? In an enlightened age, and among nations where idolatry is practically abolished, there can be no utility for such an institution, and therefore to continue to pray for a re-establishment of such rites is irrational and absurd, and the practice maintained can be looked upon only as a stubborn adherence to what is antiquated and obsolete.

"Speak to the children of Israel and say to them, that they make themselves fringes on the extremities of their garments, throughout their generations, and that they put on the fringes of the extremities a thread of blue."—Numb. xv. 38.

This is one of the few commands where the law gives us a reason for its observance. "That we may look upon it, and remember all the commands of the Lord," is added. Still we are much left in doubt as to how the looking upon the fringes would remind one of God's commands, and in entire ignorance about the way of making them; how many threads, how long, how to be twisted, of what material, etc. As to their effect in calling to mind God's commands, it may be said, simply: since the fringes were an unnecessary appendage to the garments, their very presence would put us in mind that they are placed there for some purpose;

---

* Ibid.

that purpose namely, that we should bear in mind that God is ever present, and sees us, and regards our actions, and even our thoughts. So said David, "I place the Lord constantly before me ; he is at my right hand, I shall not be moved." As to the peculiar adaptability of strings or fringes for this purpose, it appears that in ancient times, when writing was very little known, strings of various colors, peculiarly twisted, and with a certain number of knots in them, were used to denote certain facts. It is said, when South America was discovered, the early settlers of Peru found among the natives certain clusters of strings of various colors, with knots in them, carefully kept among the archives, which, upon inquiry, they were told were historical records.*

From Gen. xxxviii. 8 also it appears that it was customary for persons to carry with them a number of strings, though it is not stated what was their use ; but they must have been of some importance, since they were demanded as a pledge and placed on an equality with the man's signet and staff. The probability is, that Judah, who went to look after the interests of his farm and the shearing of his sheep, took those strings with him to mark thereon certain numbers or facts ; in short they served him for memoranda.†

---

* Mendelssohn's comment in loco (by Aaron Jaroslaw).

† The word פתיל employed here is the same as used in Deut. xv. 38, where it is rendered a *thread* of blue, and we understand it here also to mean a *thread* or *string*. In Gen. xxxviii. some commentators of the highest standing suppose it to mean a *loose cloth*, a *scarf* or a *girdle ;* others a string by which the signet was suspended. But with all respect due to these learned authors, we beg to differ with them, and we find our support in vs. 25, same chapter, where the identical articles are mentioned and there פתילים is used in the plural. It is not to be supposed that Judah wore more than one loose cloth, scarf, or girdle ; and as to the word meaning " a string by which the signet was suspended," this is also unlikely, for why should the woman be particular in asking

The next point for consideration is the *blue* thread, which the law requires to be placed on the fringe, and it may appear strange that this particular is not at all observed among those who still make use of the *Talet* and *Tsitsit;* surely the law requires this additional thread, and without it the fringe is incomplete. But, here again tradition steps in as usual to subvert the plain dictates of Scripture. The word here used for *blue* is תכלת. But that does not really mean *blue;* there is no known word in Hebrew to denote that color; and תכלת is the name of a mussel or scollop found in the Mediterranean Sea, with a blue shell, from which purple was made; and the additional thread on the fringe was to be of that color. But the Talmudical doctors insist that the thread was to be dyed with the blood of that shell-fish, and that it was to be found only once every seventy years formerly, and now, that is, for the last two thousand years perhaps, it is not to be found at all, and therefore the blue thread is to be dispensed with. Now are we to suppose that the great quantity of blue thread used for the curtains of the tabernacle and the priestly robes was dyed with the blood of a bivalve found only once in seventy years; and moreover that a thread which everybody was to wear on his garment, "throughout their generations," was to be dyed only with such blood? Would God give his people a command for daily observance which was so difficult, almost impossible to observe? That the insect which furnished this blue, as well as that from which the purple was obtained, and the scarlet insect, were very rare, is not to be disputed. But if the genuine blue for the fringe is not now

---

such a string, in itself of no value? This would naturally go with the signet. It is more reasonable to suppose that in the first instance (vs. 18) the second *yod* in פתילך has been omitted by one of the transcribers, that both should be read in the plural, and mean strings used for such purpose as we explained.

to be obtained, another blue might be substituted, or the wearing of the fringes should be altogether discarded, since without this the fringe is not complete.

"Thou shalt bind them as a sign upon thy hand, and they shall be as frontlets between thy eyes."—Deut. vi. 8.

It is well known that this text is taken as a basis for the construction and wearing of the so-called Phylacteries or Tephilin. The name *Phylacteries* is erroneously applied to these things, for that means a charm, an amulet, a thing for protection, and this was never intended as the object for which they were made. The name *Tephilin* is more appropriate, for this is derived from תפלה, prayer, and applied to these bandages intended to be worn during prayer-time. But the manner of constructing the Tephilin and the duty of wearing them, is altogether a rabbinical fabrication, void of any foundation in the Scriptures. In the first place, the very name of them is never once mentioned in the Bible, nor is prayer, of which the *tephilin* are to be the concomitants, as their name indicates, ever prescribed as a duty in the Mosaic books. How, then, is it to be supposed that Moses instituted some particular rites to be observed at prayer, of which he never spoke? But the most serious objection arises from the very passage which the Talmudists look to as the source of their authority. Let us examine the passage and the relation it bears to the context. "Bind *them* as a sign . . . and *they* shall be as frontlets." Bind what? *Them* and *they* are pronouns, and must refer to something previously named. And what is that previously named? "The things* which I command you this day." Consequently we are to bind the things commanded, and they must be frontlets. But how is this possible? How

---

* We prefer *things* to *words*, because things, not words, are commanded; and דבר expresses one as well as the other.

can we bind a command or make it into an ornament for the forehead? The rabbis, seeing this difficulty and yet believing that the verb *binding* is to be understood here in its literal sense, concluded that something was really to be bound on the hand, and built upon this their theory of the Tephilin. But the verb *to bind*, wherever it occurs in connection with things immaterial, such as command, kindness, truth, is always understood figuratively. Examples of such figures are numerous. When Solomon said, "Let kindness and truth not forsake thee; *bind* them about thy neck, *write* them on the tablet of thy heart," he surely did not mean that we should actually bind or write anything. When Isaiah, speaking of Israel's children, says "Thou shalt clothe thyself with them all as with an ornament, and bind them on thee as a bride does," who does not understand that he speaks figuratively? The same sense is to be given to the expression in the preceding text: "I have graven thee upon the palms of my hand;" all of which denote a cherishing, fostering, holding dear. And so is our text to be understood. The things which I command you shall be in your heart, teach them to your children, speak constantly of them, look upon them as upon a precious thing, such as a gem worn on the hand, and as a diadem on the forehead, so shall they be deeply and constantly impressed on your mind.

The objections against the rabbinical interpretation crowd themselves so fast upon each other and are all so weighty that we hardly know of which to take hold first. The command of teaching them to our children evidently refers to the same things as are to be bound on the hand and head and written on the posts. But if it be true that only those few portions the rabbis have selected are to be bound and written, then we are likewise to teach our children those portions only. Again, the portions selected for the

Tephilin and *Mezuzah*, or door-post, are not the same. Or, if the writing and binding on refer to all the commandments, then we should have to place a complete scroll of the law, or at least, a full list of the Mosaic commands, on our hand and head. Nor are the Tephilin ever placed on the hand, but on the arm. In Ex. xiii. 9, occurs a passage very similar to the one we are discussing: "It shall be as a sign on thy hand, and a remembrance between thy eyes." This refers to the exodus from Egypt; but no writing or binding are mentioned in connection with it, yet the rabbis apply it likewise to the Tephilin. More might be said on the subject in refutation of the adopted theory, but we think sufficient proof has been advanced to show clearly that the text in question is to be understood metaphorically, and that the making and wearing of Tephilin has no foundation whatever in the Mosaic code.

"Thou shalt write them on the door-posts of thy house, and on thy gates."—Deut. vi. 9.

The explanation of this command has been partly anticipated in that of the foregoing, but the meaning of it is not quite so easily determined. Some commentators understand this to be also figurative, like the words of Solomon quoted above, as, when speaking of kindness and truth, he says, "Bind them on thy neck, write them on the tablets of thy heart," so here it would imply, Let my commands be ever present to your mind, like a conspicuous thing placed on a post for remembrance. This interpretation is quoted by Aben Ezra, though not adopted by him. We said in the preceding article that the binding on of commands is impracticable, and, therefore, cannot be taken literally; but writing on a post, or affixing to it a schedule, is feasible; therefore, some commentators understand it to imply that something was really to be written on the door-posts after the manner of "the ancient Egyptians who had their lintels and imposts of doors and gates inscribed with sentences indicative of favorable omen, and this is still the case, for in Egypt and other Mohammedan countries—in Cairo, for instance—the front-doors of houses are painted red, white, and green, bearing conspicuously inscribed upon them such sentences from the Koran as *God is the Creator; God is one and Mohammed is His prophet.** And the Chinese likewise suspend on their door-posts slips of paper and pieces of cloth with certain inscriptions on them. But in the examples cited, something legible and intelligible is always placed in view of those who enter and go out, and the object of impressing an idea on the mind may be expected thereby to be accomplished. But the schedules placed at our doors are not understood, cannot be read even by the great majority of men, and are not visible to any one. If they were intended to act as a charm or a talisman, this would make no difference, as long as the writing were there, which needed to be legible only to the spirits for or against whom it was intended. By many non-Jewish writers this has indeed been supposed to be the object of the *Mezuzah* as well as the *Tephilin*—hence they called the latter Phylacteries—and even some Jewish authors entertained this view. But this idea must be entirely repudiated, for the Mosaic Law opposes all that has any affinity to sorcery or spell. Since, then, the *Tephilin* and *Mezuzah* are acknowledged to be used as mementos, they ought to be made so as to exhibit in legible characters the facts and ideas they are intended to call to mind. To what purpose can be this solicitude in having the scriptural portions they contain written with utmost correctness, that not one letter in them shall have the least defect, nor that any one shall

---

* Jamieson, Commentaries on the Scriptures.

touch upon another; that the vellum must be prepared just exactly so, that even the ink must be prepared in a peculiar manner, and all that for something which is never to meet the eye? Many and many a person puts on his *Tephilin* every morning, and continues the practice to the last days of his life, and dies in ignorance of what were their contents. And it is this ignorance which has led the multitude to look upon them as a mere charm; and hence many persons, void of all religious ideas, would not sleep a single night in a house not provided with a Mezuzah, not because they would miss this token of remembrance of God's command, but for fear lest some misfortune befall them.

The sum total of our argument is, that the text, taken in a figurative sense, may be still applicable to us, indicating that we should be ever mindful of God's commands, especially that we should duly consider their import and make it our study to penetrate into their meaning; but that the literal interpretation of it—if it ever was intended to be so understood—cannot be binding on us, because we Jews of the present day do not require texts or phrases on our doorposts; having ample opportunity to be reminded of our duties towards God and man by reading good books, by attending at our places of worship, and by seeking intercourse with good and enlightened men; the conclusive proof of which is found in the fact that the strict observers of the *Tsitsit*, *Tephilin* and *Mezuzah* are, as a rule, no better men than those who have discarded those observances.

"An oath of the Lord shall be between the two of them."—Ex. xxii. 10.

From the early records of the Bible it appears that oaths existed among mankind ever since they began to live in social communion; but that prior to the establishment of law or government, the fulfilment of engagements between man and man depended entirely upon their own veracity, with no responsibility to any authority.

As the sentiment of a superior Being who is cognizant of our doings is coeval with the existence of man, an appeal to the presence of that Being was made in all cases of solemn affirmation, but the manner of invoking that presence not being determined by law or common agreement, was left, it would seem, to the choice of those whom it concerned; hence we find different forms of swearing at different periods of time. The earliest form of an oath on record—and singular enough the same which is in vogue at the present day—is that of raising the hand up to heaven, in token of an appeal to God as witness to the fact to be affirmed. Thus Abraham said to the king of Sodom, "I have lifted up my hand to the Lord, the most high God, possessor of heaven and earth, that I will not take, etc." (Gen. xiv. 22). This mode of swearing seems to have been used when the obligation to be established was not a mutual one, but when one wished to take upon himself a voluntary vow in which either he alone was concerned, or that a promise was made in favor of some one else. Another manner of swearing was that the one who took the oath placed his hand under the thigh of him to whom he bound himself as to the performance of the deed promised; the latter, it is to be supposed, being at the time in a sitting posture. This was done only when a promise was made in favor of another; the person taking the oath, by placing his hand under the thigh of the one who administered it, declaring thereby that he placed himself at the disposition of the latter, and bound himself to obey his orders, or comply with his wishes. Examples of this we find in the instance of Abraham swearing his servant to go and seek a wife for his son (Gen. xxiv. 3), and Jacob adjuring Joseph to remove his bones to Canaan (Gen. xlvii. 29).

Still another mode of swearing was the custom of passing between the pieces of an animal or animals cut in halves, which was used in case of parties assuming a reciprocal obligation. This act seemed to imply that the contracting parties were thus united and jointly bound to their engagement. This appears from the covenant which God made with Abraham, Gen. xv. 10, and it is also alluded to in Jer. xxxiv. 19. Similar to this—that is, similar in its purpose of establishing a covenant—was the erection of a monument, or a pile of stones in commemoration of the agreement made, such as took place between Jacob and Laban on their parting (Gen. xxxi. 45), and such as the tribes of Reuben, Gad, and half of Menasseh erected on the border of Jordan, though this was done by one party, without the knowledge of the other, and afterwards agreed to; and this was done even in the case of one taking upon himself an obligation towards the Lord, as Jacob did at Beth-El (Gen. xxviii. 18). It should be borne in mind, however, that none of those ceremonies described constituted in themselves the act of taking the oath, but merely accompanied and preceded it; nor was it always necessary that any of the above ceremonies should take place, for we find also instances of swearing by the life of the king (Gen. xlii. 15–16). This custom, as well as the others described, was in vogue among various Oriental nations, and the last-named is still in use among the Persians, and rests upon the idea that the monarch represents, not only the power of the State, but also that of God. Of oaths confirming what had passed, we find no instances in the time of the patriarchs, though these may also have obtained. In the Mosaic laws, however, the affirmation by oath of things passed is clearly prescribed, as in the text heading this article, and the oath was to be taken in the name of Jehovah. "The Lord thy God shalt thou fear, Him shalt thou serve, and by His name shalt thou swear" (Deut. vi. 13). The prohibition of false swearing is strictly enjoined in the Decalogue and elsewhere, but perjury was not punishable by the civil law. God himself would punish the profanation of his name. The Greeks and Romans likewise considered perjury not a civil, but a religious offence. Though the Jews were required to swear by the name of God, the ceremony accompanying it is not prescribed; but that the raising of the hand was the most prevalent, appears from the frequent occurrence of the expression, "I lifted up my hand," when God would affirm what he had promised; and in the case of a suspected wife, we find that the oath was recited by the priest and answered by Amen, amen. So, also, was the pronouncing of a curse upon the head of him who should violate his pledge of conforming to the laws of God (Deut. xxvii. 15–26).

Having in the first part of this article considered voluntary vows as they existed prior to the proclamation of the law, we now come to consider them from the standpoint of Mosaic legislation. There is nothing in the Mosaic code to show that vows were desired or recommended, but once taken, they were held sacred and forever binding, even when made under an erroneous impression, or as the consequence of a false representation; no absolution appears to have been allowable under any consideration, except a daughter under the control of her father, or a wife restrained in her actions by her husband. When the Israelites had entered into a covenant with the Gibeonites, although they discovered afterwards that they had been imposed upon, they thought themselves still bound to their oath, and kept it. When Jephthah made a rash vow which afterwards proved to involve the life of his only child, he sought no absolution, but executed his promise even in violation of his parental feelings. The writer of Ecclesiastes (ch. v. 2–6) says, "Be not rash with thy mouth, and let not thy heart be hasty to utter anything before God; ... when thou vowest a vow to God, defer not to pay it, ... neither say to the messenger (angel) that it was an error." It is not necessary to say any more to show what great weight the Hebrews attached to a vow once pronounced. Yet the Talmudical doctors have taken the most unpardonable liberty in absolving persons of their most solemn engagements, even on the slightest pretences. It must appear incredible to those not acquainted with Talmudical lore, when learning to what extent they carried this license. On the subject of vows they undertake to clear a man of his conscience as if it had never been there. One may make ever so many vows, pledges, engagements, and break them on any pretence, "even if he vowed by the God of Israel," they say; and if he have no pretence to plead, the rabbi who absolves him may suggest one to him, to which he says, *Yes*, and he is free. One may say, "The vow I am about to make shall not be valid," or, "All or any vows I may make until such a time shall be void," and this relieves him from all engagement. They went even so far as to say, when one has made a vow, it is best to get absolved at once and be bound no more. The ordinary way of obtaining absolution was that one go before a rabbi, or before three laymen, and, after stating his case, say, "I regret," to which he received the answer, "Thou art absolved." Later, however, it was thought best to empower the person himself with the right to nullify his vows, either in advance or after they were made, for which purpose the known formula *Kol Nidre* was established, and which was later "smuggled into the synagogue service." That the recital of this formula should still be continued among the Jews of the present time, and the day which is considered the most holy in the Jewish calendar should be inaugurated by a public act of perfidy on the part of an entire congregation, is a matter both of regret and of shame. What on earth can be said in defense of a practice by which men allow themselves to break every honorable engagement entered into; to swear to their neighbors to do or not to do a certain thing and then go into the synagogue and say, "All oaths, bonds, pledges—and whatever synonyms they can find to express an engagement—shall be all null and void, for it was all a mistake"? Fortunately, it is but an empty form, for very few men are so depraved as to be in earnest when they say so, or when the minister says so for them, and it is to be hoped that the "Father will forgive them, for they know not what they do." But in the leaders of congregations who know what they do and what they say; those petrified men * who will forever adhere with stubborn tenacity to the established customs of their fathers, whether they be right or whether they be wrong; in them the fault is unpardonable. A great deal has been written against this unwarrantable practice by abler pens than the one which traces these lines, and the result hitherto produced has not been equal to the amount of learning and energy employed for checking the evil. The writer of this article, therefore, cannot hope that his efforts will at once effect a change among those who are determined never to

---

* We borrow this expression from a French author who says: "Lamartine, dans sa 'Critique de l'histoire des Girondins,' relève quelques erreurs d'appréciation et justifie ses changements de croyances en faisant la théorie, non pas de la versatilité, mais de l'amélioration et du progrès de l'intelligence. Il s'indigne contre ces hommes pétrifiés qui ne se dédisent jamais et 'veulent mourir, comme disait M. de Chateaubriand, non pas conformés à la vérité, mais conformés à eux mêmes.' En résumé, la vie est une leçon que la temps est chargé de donner à l'homme, en lui faisant épeler syllable par syllable les événements. Celui qui prétend avoir tout vu le premier jour est un homme qui n'avait ni raison de naître, ni raison de mourir, car il n'avait rien à apprendre en naissant."—*Le petit Journal.*

change, but it may open the eyes of some who are willing to see and appreciate the truth. And while writing an explanation on some of the Mosaic Laws, he deems it his duty to show also the force of the text. "If a man vow a vow to the Lord, or swear an oath to bind his soul with a bond, he shall not break his word, he shall do according to all that proceedeth from his mouth."—Numb. xxx. 3.

"Sanctify to me all the first-born ; the first offspring of every female among the children of Israel, of man and of beast, is mine."—Ex. xiii. 3.

The distinctions and privileges conferred upon the first-born were an institution peculiar to the Hebrews, and not in vogue among other nations. It existed among them even prior to the time of Moses. Thus we find the birth-right of Esau acknowledged in the family; when Zerah was born, the nurse was particular in noting his first appearance in the world; and so was the primogeniture of Reuben considered an inheritable right. We must remember that the Hebrew people, like their neighbors, in early ages consisted of independent families, whose affairs were directed by their chief or patriarch ; and this prerogative descended on the eldest son, who, from his birth, was distinguished as his father's successor, and privileged in the distribution of the estate. "The right of primogeniture in males," says Blackstone, "seems to have only obtained among the Jews, in whose constitution the eldest son had a double portion of the inheritance, in the same manner as with us, by the laws of King Henry the first, the eldest son had the capital fee or principal feud of his father's possessions." Before the time of Moses, the father had the right to dispose of this privilege and give it to another of his sons, as the instance of Jacob, who transferred it from Reuben to Joseph, the son of his most beloved Rachel, shows ; and it appears that the eldest son himself, when arrived at manhood, could dispose of it, as is seen in the case of Esau and Jacob. This power vested in the father to deprive his eldest son of the right of inheritance and give it to another, naturally caused much jealousy, especially in a family where polygamy took place; therefore, Moses instituted that none but the first son, if he were also the mother's first child, should enjoy the right of primogeniture, and be entitled to inherit a double portion of his father's estate. As this law interfered with the sentiments of parents who, notwithstanding its establishment, were likely to disregard it and still give the preference to a favorite son, a sacredness was attached to it, and the first-born declared holy to the Lord, so as to put a more powerful restraint upon its transgression, and the distinction extended even to brutes. Before the tribe of Levi was chosen for the Temple service, the first-born were honored with that preference. "The first-born of man and beast shall be consecrated to God," says the text, that is, the former were to be redeemed with five shekels of silver, which were given to the priest; the latter, namely the first issue of animals fit for sacrifice, were to be brought to the Temple, and the blood and fat offered on the altar, while the carcass was a gift for the priest. Why the ass was made an exception to this rule, and required to be redeemed with a lamb, or have its neck broken, we do not know; we conjecture that, as this was, besides the cattle, almost the only domestic animal in use (the horse being very rare, and the swine and dog held in aversion), the priest was to have his share of it, and, being an unclean animal, was to be redeemed. It is well known that, in the East, females always were, and are yet, looked upon as degraded beings, therefore, if the first-born was a female, the law of primogeniture did not apply at all. Daughters were excluded from all participation in the inheritance, except when there was no son, and, in that case, they were bound to marry none but one of their near relatives, so that the property might not be taken out of the family. Among the Greeks and Romans, and other nations, all inheritances, whether consisting of land or movables, were equally divided, in some cases, among all the male children, and, in others, among all the children alike ; but since the introduction of the feudal system, most European nations have, with some modifications, adopted the Jewish law of primogeniture with regard to the possession of estates and titles of honor. This ancient law, of course, has lost its binding force on us, as all temple-service and priestly gifts have ceased to exist; still, some Jews adhere to its observance by selecting some one who bears the name of Cohen, and presenting him with five pieces of silver coin as the ransom of their first-born son; and some go even so far, when they happen to have cattle, to separate the first-born and let it graze during its whole life-time until it die of itself ; not shearing its wool, if it be a sheep, nor applying the animal to any use whatsoever.

"If brothers dwell together, and one of them die and have no son, then shall the wife of the deceased not be married abroad to a stranger; her husband's brother shall come to her and take her for himself for a wife, and so perform the duty of a husband's brother towards her. And the first-born son which she may bear, shall succeed to the name of the deceased brother, that the name of the latter be not blotted out of Israel," and sequel.—Deut. xxv. 5-10.

This is what is called the *Levirate Law*. The term *Levirate*, is from the old Latin word *Levir*, signifying a husband's brother. It was an ancient custom among different nations of Asia that, if a man left a childless widow, and also one or more brothers, the eldest of the brothers should marry the widow. In Genesis xxxviii., we find an instance of it recorded in the case of the widow Tamar, which shows at the same time that, in case the second brother died, likewise without issue, the same obligation devolved upon the third; and we are informed that, "the Mongols, who inhabit quite a different region of Asia, and give themselves very little concern about their genealogies and descendants, have a law which, in like manner, enjoins the marriage of a brother's widow. From the history of Ruth and Boaz it appears further that, among the Hebrews, not only the brothers, but the nearest of kin were expected to marry the widow who was left without a son, so as to keep up the name of their kinsman. This ancient custom was retained and established as a law in the Mosaic code. It is somewhat analogous to the law of primogeniture treated above, inasmuch as both rested upon the idea of perpetuating the name and estate of the family. To die childless, especially without leaving any male issue, was considered a disgrace and a curse; it was especially pronounced against certain crimes mentioned in Lev. xx. 20–21. The object of the Levirate law, then, was to perpetuate the name of the deceased, as the first son proceeding from the second marriage was to inherit the estate of the departed uncle, and thus keep up his name. Should, however, the brother decline to marry the widow, then she was to go before the judges and complain of his unwillingness. He was then summoned to appear before the magistrates, and, if persisting in his refusal, was to submit to a public insult, according to the custom of the times. This insult was, that the widow take off the shoe from his foot, spit out before him, and say, "So shall be done to the man who refuses to keep up the name of his brother." This ceremony is called in Hebrew *Chalitsa*, which means *Loosening*.

The *Levir*, it is seen, was not compelled by law to marry the widow, it was optional with him. If he did marry her, the first son she would give him was to bear the name of the deceased man, and, as this son would be also his own natural heir, the estates of the two brothers would be blended and the whole go by the name of the late brother, while the name of the living one would be forgotten. This was actually a sacrifice of the man's own and his family interest for the sake of perpetuating the memory of his relative. Hence it would frequently happen that brothers or other near relatives refused an alliance with the relicts of their kinsmen; and upon this ground the nameless person who, in the regular order of succession, came in first to take Ruth for his wife, declined the marriage, and said, " I cannot perform the duty of a kinsman, lest I destroy the name of my own inheritance." We learn also from Ruth iv. 7, that in the transaction of some important business, such as the transfer of an estate, "a man take off his shoe and give it to his neighbor, and this was a testimony in Israel." It signified that he yielded up his title, his hold, his footing, we may say, to that which he might justly claim as his own. It is yet a common saying among the Dutch, when a son succeeds his father in any office or position, that "he enters, or treads into his father's shoes." So we say in English, "waiting for a man's shoes," and the French say, "être sur un grand pied dans le monde," which originated at a time when a man's rank was known by his shoe,* all of which shows that anciently as well as in modern times the *shoe* was used figuratively to express a man's standing in the world. Now, it appears to me that the loosening or pulling off of the shoe by the widow, as prescribed in Deut. xxv. 9, was to indicate

---

* This custom of wearing immensely large shoes arose in the eleventh century, under Philip I. They were made with long points turned up at the toes, and extended heels assuming sometimes the shape of a bird or the tale of a scorpion. Those of a prince measured two feet and a half, while those of plain citizens were allowed to be only twelve inches. The fashion was invented by the earl of Anjou; was immediately adopted in France; and the Normans brought it over to England. See Markham's Hist. of France, p. 100.

that she took disdainfully from her brother-in-law that which she thought him unworthy to hold; she wrested from from him his claim to her person and his *foothold* to her husband's property, and, as a mark of contempt for his want of affection and generosity, spit out before him, upon which the bond which held them together was entirely dissolved, and she was free to marry any other, which she was not allowed to do until this ceremony was performed. This ceremony of *Chalitsa*, or loosening of the shoe, and the foundation upon which it rests, it will be clearly perceived, has its origin in the idea which anciently prevailed of preserving the identity of families, and preventing the transfer or absolute sale of land from one tribe to another. Need it be said that such distinctions are not and cannot be preserved among Jews of the present day, when we know that the identity of families was lost already in the later days of the first Temple?* The ceremony in question, therefore, has long since become an antiquated statute; notwithstanding which some of our people still observe it with utmost rigor and with the usual rabbinical appendages.

"If, in the land which the Lord thy God gives thee to possess it, a slain person be found lying in the field, and it is not known who has slain him, then shall thy elders and thy judges go and measure (the distances of) the cities around the slain person," and sequel.—Deut. xxi. 1–9.

By this precept it was ordained that, if the body of a murdered person was found somewhere in an open place, at a distance from the population, and after diligent search the murderer could not be found, the elders of the town nearest to the spot where the corpse lay, should take a heifer that had never been worked, lead it to a valley which was not cultivated, and there strike off the head of the heifer. The elders were then to wash their hands on the spot and declare

---

* See Jost, Gesch. d. J. u. s. S., p. 30.

before God that they were ignorant of the crime, that is, that they had done all they could to discover the criminal, and they prayed God that the innocent might not be made to suffer for the guilty.

We have no explanation of our own to offer for this peculiar ordinance, but give here the commentary of Maimonides on the subject: "The utility of the precept respecting the beheading of the heifer," says he, "is also evident; for the city bringing the heifer is that which is nearest to the body of the man who had been murdered; and it most frequently happens that the murderer is from that place. Then the elders of the city call God to witness that they have neglected nothing that was necessary for the security and guarding of the ways, and had diligently examined and searched all travellers, saying, as our rabbis expressed it, 'This man was not killed through our negligence or forgetfulness of any of our common or public regulations; nor do we know who killed him.' Now by this investigation into the deed, by the going forth and protestation of the elders, and by taking the heifer and striking off its head, a great deal of conversation took place about the affair, and gave publicity to it, by which means the murderer was probably found directly, or was discovered by some one who had been accessory to the murder, or had overheard something respecting it; or it might become known by certain signs and indications that such a one was the murderer. But if any man or woman rose and said such a one committed the deed, the heifer was not beheaded; and, as it was well known that, if any one knew the author and concealed the fact, calling upon God as witness and as an avenger that he knew him not, such would be the greatest folly and sin, it was rendered highly probable that if any one knew the murderer he would be detected, and the detection would be important; for if the house of judgment did not put him to death, the king had the power to order his execution on evidence being given against him, and if the king did not cause him to suffer, the avenger of blood might do it by lying in wait for him. It must, therefore, be acknowledged that the beheading of the heifer was of use in the disclosure and discovery of murder. This was also promoted by the circumstance that the place where the heifer was beheaded might never again be ploughed or sowed, which was done that the owner of the land might use every effort and neglect nothing to detect and apprehend the murderer, that the heifer might not be slain and the land be polluted forever."

"If a man have a refractory and rebellious son, who will not hearken to the voice of his father and mother, and they chasten him and he will not listen to them; then shall his father and mother lay hold of him and bring him out to the elders of the city and to the gate of his place" . . . see sequel.—Deut. xxi. 18–21.

We are naturally struck with the apparent severity of the law which ordains the stoning to death of what we might call a bad boy. But we observe, in the first place, that the age of the son is not mentioned. The law cannot well be supposed to refer to a mere boy or child to whom the expressions rebellious, a glutton, and a drunkard cannot well be applied; nor can it be applicable to one grown up to manhood and beyond the control of his parents, since it says, "his father and mother shall take hold of him and bring him out to the elders of his city." It is, therefore, reasonable to think that it refers to a lad, say between fifteen and twenty years of age, and that it means, that if a boy or young man were found so incorrigible that no admonition or remonstrance of his parents could affect him; that he, notwithstanding the corrections of his parents, would indulge in drunkenness and profligacy, they were to bring him before the elders or judges of the town and declare that their son was incorrigible and rebellious, a glutton and a drunkard, and he was then stoned to death; for it was thought better to check the evil in the beginning, and even root it out by killing so stubborn a sinner than to let him grow up a worthless man, a bad example, and a corrupter of society. And, indeed, our experience shows even now, in many cases, where the disposition is so determinately inclined to evil that no amount of correction or good example can ever be expected to reform the criminal, that it would have been better for the public welfare had the person been early removed from society than to let him continue his wicked pursuit during a long life; and the case proposed in the text could be only such an extreme one, when the very parents were to be the accusers. And, although the punishment of death, and that a public execution, must appear even then too severe, it was necessary in those early ages when no milder forms of correction were established, and when the people were not sufficiently civilized to be governed by gentle means; and it is therefore that we find in many instances the penalty of death prescribed even for apparently small offences.

"If thou meet on the road, either on a tree or on the ground, a bird's nest, in which are young birds or eggs, and the dam sitting upon them, thou shalt not take the dam with the young; thou shalt send away the dam, and then mayest take the young."—Deut. xxii. 6–7.

There are many of the Mosaic commands which are much involved in obscurity, and we are left to conjecture the object and frequently also the meaning of the command. The precept regarding a bird's nest is one of those for which it is difficult to assign a reason. Michaelis thinks that it was forbidden to take the hen and young in order to prevent the destruction of birds which were useful in destroying injurious insects; but then it would have been better to order the nest to be left altogether untouched. A more reasonable cause for the precept is assigned by Maimonides, who thinks the object was to prevent cruelty to animals, as it would pain the old bird to see her young ones carried away. If, therefore, the finder wished to make use of the eggs or of the young birds, he should despatch the dam, so as to give her as little grief as possible. On the same ground it was forbidden to harness an ox and an ass together to the plough, as they are generally of unequal strength and this would overexert the weaker one. For this reason also it was forbidden to muzzle an ox while threshing, and other similar commands of kindness to man and beast are based on the ground of humanity and beneficence.

"Speak to the children of Israel and say to them: When ye come into the land which I give you, then shall the land rest, a sabbath to the Lord. Six years shalt thou sow thy field, and prune thy vineyard, and gather the produce thereof, but the seventh year shall be one of strict rest to the land . . . And thou shalt number seven sabbatical years, seven times seven years. . . . and ye shall sanctify the fiftieth year, and proclaim liberty throughout the land to all its inhabitants," and sequel.—Lev. xxv.

The whole of this chapter is devoted to the institution of the Sabbatical year and the Jubilee, and the various ordinances connected therewith.

As the seventh day of the week was instituted as a Sabbath-day, so every seventh year was appointed a year of rest for man, and beast, and land. Hebrew slaves were set free; all debts and claims among Israelites were cancelled; and the whole of the book of the law was read publicly before the multitude. This institution was of great benefit to the people: they were taught thereby the principle of freedom and equality among men; all persons, like children of one family, had free and indiscriminate use of what the land spontaneously produced; and the land itself, by being left fallow for a year, was thereby much improved. It served also—as Calmet observes—to inspire the people with sentiments of humanity, by making it their duty to give rest, proper and sufficient nourishment to the poor, the slave and the stranger, and even to the cattle; and to accustom the people to submit to and depend on divine Providence which would by an extraordinary provision, support them even while they were not occupied in agriculture. It served further to detach their affections from earthly things, and make them disinterested and heavenly-minded, and to show them God's dominion over the country, that He, not they, was Lord of the soil; and further to recall to mind the work of creation by the week of years as well as by the weekly Sabbath.

The Jubilee was celebrated every fiftieth year, and was characterized by the same observances as the ordinary or Sabbatical years, and was moreover distinguished (1st) by a general sounding of trumpets on the day of atonement, "to proclaim liberty throughout the land to all its inhabitants;" (2d) by a release of all slaves, even those who had voluntarily relinquished their freedom, at the end of six years, and had their ears pierced in token of their continual servitude; and (3d) by the returning of all landed property to its primitive owners, or to his inheritors in the family and tribe to which it originally belonged; so that no family was allowed to accumulate too great riches, nor the poor and unfortunate be forever deprived of their patrimonial inheritance. An attentive consideration of the subject will show the utility of this law, and the wisdom and benevolecne which prompted its enactment. Palestine was originally divided by lot amongst the tribes and families of Israel, and the inheritance of each family was, by the previous directions of the law of Moses, made inalienable, thus establishing a commonwealth on truly democratic principles without incurring the disadvantages and dangers of communism. Doubts have been entertained by biblical critics as to whether the land of Canaan was so fruitful as to produce corn and other necessaries of life in sufficient abundance for three years, since the sixth year was to produce a supply for its own consumption, for the seventh in which there was no sowing or reaping, and for the eighth of which a course of seasons was requisite to bring the crops to perfection. But as it is explicitly stated (Lev. xxv. 21): "I will command my blessing upon you in the sixth year, and it shall bring forth fruit for three years," it is needless here to argue upon the possibility of such a thing. Independent, however, of the miraculous divine intervention necessarily connected with this law, and without which it must have been impracticable, we cannot but admire the excellence of an institution which, while establishing periodical public festivals for the recreation and enjoyment of the people, had at the same time the tendency to impress them with such sublime ideas as equality, liberty, benevolence, and dependence on a superior Being. We find that in later ages the Greeks established their Olympiads, the Romans their Lustra, and the Christians their Indictions, which were probably derived from the Jewish Sabbatical year and Jubilee. But how far superior were the latter to the former which were devoted only to debasing performances and tended to demoralize and corrupt those who partook in them! Nor need it be supposed that the whole of the Sabbatical year was given to festivity or revelry, for although agricultural labor was interdicted, they could fish, hunt, take care of their bees and flocks, repair their buildings and furniture, manufacture cloths of wool, linen, and of the hair of goats and camels, and carry on commerce. Yet, favorable and excellent as this institution may appear, and suitable also to the taste of the people as it would seem, it was much neglected even in the most flourishing time of the Jewish monarchy, so that in the five centuries succeeding the reign of Solomon not two Sabbatical years were properly observed, though after the Babylonian captivity they were regularly and properly celebrated.

"This shall be the law of the leper."—Lev. xiv. 2.

The laws concerning the leprous and the disease itself are described in the 13th and 14th chapters of Leviticus. This disease is, thanks be to Heaven, hardly known among us even by name; and as the ordinances concerning the same can have no applicability to us, a discussion of them in this book might appear superfluous. Still, as none of the Mosaic precepts, even those that have become obsolete, can be looked upon as entirely void of interest to us; and as the chapters just named are among the weekly portions read to us from the pulpit for our instruction or edification, it is proper that we should be enlightened on these scriptural lessons we are to listen to, especially when we hear of leprosy in clothes and in houses, which must appear quite unintelligible. The law gives but a superficial description of the appearance of the disease; to obtain a better idea of it we must consult the opinions of physicians who have made this malady a subject of special study.

That kind of leprosy which is spoken of by Moses appears to be what is called the White Leprosy, and is nearly thus described by Mr. Robinson, a medical practitioner of India: "One or two circumscribed patches appear upon the skin, neither raised nor depressed, shining and wrinkled, the furrows not coinciding with the lines of the skin. That part of the skin affected with the disease is so entirely insensible that you may with a hot iron burn to the muscle before the patient feels any pain. These patches spread slowly until the skin of the whole of the legs, arms, and gradually often the whole body becomes alike devoid of sense; wherever it is so affected, there is no perspiration, no itching, no pain, and very seldom any swelling. Until this singular apathy has occupied the greater part of the skin, it may rather be considered a blemish than a disease; nevertheless, it is most important to mark well these appearances, for they are the invariable commencement of the most gigantic and incurable of diseases. Next, the pulse becomes very slow, the toes and fingers numbed as with frost, glazed and rather swelled and nearly inflexible. The mind is at this time sluggish and slow in apprehension, and the patient appears always half asleep. The soles of the feet and the palms of the hand then crack into fissures, dry and hard as the parched soil of the country; the extremities of the toes and fingers under the nails are incrusted, and the nails gradually lifted up. Still, there is little or no pain. The legs and forearms swell; ulcers now appear on the inside of the fingers and toes; a discharge of reddish matter comes on; the muscles become flabby and powerless; and the joint being penetrated as with an auger, the extremity droops, and at length falls a victim to this cruel, tardy, but certain poison. Thus are the limbs deprived, one by one, of their extremities, till at last they become altogether useless. Even now death comes not to the relief of, nor is it desired by, the patient, who, dying by inches, and a spectacle of horror to all besides, still cherishes fondly the spark of life remaining, and eats voraciously all he can procure. He will often crawl about with little but his trunk remaining, until old age comes on, and at last he is carried off by diarrhœa or dysentery, which the enfeebled constitution has no stamina to resist." Among the properties of this terrible malady are (1) that it is hereditary, (2) that it is infectious, and (3) that it is incurable; at least, no means of cure have hitherto been discovered. The disease is peculiar to Asia and to hot climates generally. It was much more prevalent in olden times than it is now, but it is still a common disease throughout all Syria, and in Egypt it is said to be more frequent and virulent. Cutaneous diseases generally are ascribed by medical men to want of cleanliness, unwholesome food, dampness in dwellings, and want of fresh air, to all of which poor persons are often exposed; and the Israelites in Egypt undoubtedly suffered much from these causes. They were poor, degraded slaves, lived sometimes in marshy parts of the country along the Nile; their families increased rapidly in their crowded dwellings; and these things all tend to promote scorbutic diseases. Besides, the frequent use of fish which they obtained in Egypt for nothing,* tends to spread the infection. Therefore, on the entering of Israel into Palestine, the preventives against the spread of leprosy were a necessary and wise institution.

The infection of houses and clothes, spoken of in Leviticus, is called leprosy merely by analogy. In Bern, for instance, says Michaelis, they speak of the *cancer of buildings*, which is with equal propriety a Swiss, as the *leprosy of buildings* is a Hebrew expression. The house-leprosy, then, appears to be a kind of distemper which affects the walls of houses much exposed to dampness and foul air, and which produces an efflorescence we commonly but incorrectly call saltpetre. If this corrosion is allowed to spread further and further, it may cause the destruction of the whole wall, and ultimately of the entire building. Things that are placed near such a wall are spoiled, and persons sleeping close to it may be injured in their health. The consideration of these circumstances, says the preceding author, will render the Mosaic ordinances on this subject easily intelligible. Their object was to check the evil in

---

* Numb. xi. 5.

the very bud; to extirpate it while it was yet extirpatible, by making every one, from the loss to which it would subject him, careful to prevent his house becoming affected with leprosy.

The leprosy in clothes is believed to be occasioned by a species of animalcule, such as breed in wool shorn from a sheep that died of disease, or such as are the cause of the itch, or it may be the infection which is called mildew and dry-rot. Michaelis states that, according to the information he received from an eminent woolen manufacturer, the wool of sheep which die by disease, and which is technically called *dead wool*, is apt to breed vermin, especially when worn close to the body and warmed by it; he, therefore, conceived that it was an additional proof of the consummate legislative policy of the Mosaic institutes to bring into discredit and disuse stuffs already become threadbare and fretted, and particularly in climates which must have been so favorable to the rapid multiplication of vermin.

"Ye shall not add to the thing which I command you, neither shall ye diminish aught from it, but observe the commands of the Lord your God which I command you."—Deut. iv. 2.

From the manner in which we treated the preceding subjects, it will be sufficiently evident that we entirely reject all rabbinical authority in the interpretation of the Mosaic commands, and we would here say a few words in vindication of our position. We reject both rabbinical authority and their interpretation, because as to the first, the authority exercised by the rabbis is self-assumed, usurped, not conferred by any power we are bound to recognize, but tacitly submitted to by the multitude, and as to the second, theological doctors of the present age are by their researches, and the general progress of science, better qualified to determine the meaning of ancient laws and customs; they are better able to divest themselves of that strong partiality which fettered the minds of the talmudical doctors and their successors. It is further evident to every impartial critic that the rabbis have in very many instances perverted the plain, even the most unequivocal sense of scriptural precepts, have said many things that are false, and things that are foolish; and the system of interpretation adopted by them is often contrary to the rules of logic and to sound reasoning. But not only have the rabbis misinterpreted Scripture, they have set their authority above that of the divine law, and have, in open violation of the text above quoted, added to and diminished from the Mosaic commands. We will give only a few instances in addition to what has been said, fully to illustrate and confirm our statement. The observing of two holidays instead of one is an addition to the Mosaic Law, and in violation of it. When Israel dwelt in Palestine, when they had no calendar, and the beginning of each month could be determined only by the appearance of the first phases of the moon,* and those living at a great distance could not receive timely informa- as to which day had been fixed upon by the Sanhedrin as the first of the month, those people were justified in observing two days, so as to make sure of keeping the right day; but since the Jewish calendar has been accurately computed for all future time, the necessity of keeping more than one day has been obviated, and to prescribe the observance of an additional festival is contrary to the dictates of the Mosaic code.

Another instance where the rabbis assumed authority above that of the written Law, is in the use of the *Lulab*

---

* The Turks even now reckon their year by lunar months, and watch the first appearance of the moon for the celebration of their great fast of *Ramadan*, which they observe much in the same way as we keep the Day of Atonement.

and *Shophar*. We are commanded in the Scriptures to make use on the first day of the Tabernacles of the four species of plants mentioned in Leviticus xxiii. 40. There is no exception made in the text to dispense with the use of them in case this first day of the feast should happen on the Sabbath. Yet the rabbis have taken upon themselves to ordain that no use should be made of these emblems on the Saturday. And why not? By a rabbinical ordinance, which has no foundation in the Scriptures, it is forbidden to carry any article on the Sabbath beyond the city-limits, or from without into it. For fear now that any one who may have neglected to provide himself with the four specimens alluded to, might go outside of the city to fetch them, they forbade the use of them on the Sabbath altogether; thus practically verifying what they said, "The rabbis have fortified or enforced the observance of their own institutions more than than those of the Law." The same is the case with the blowing of the *Shophar*, which is ordained without exception to take place on the first day of the seventh month; and the rabbis again contradicted the order in case that day should happen on a Saturday, for the reason just mentioned, that it might not be at hand, and would have to be brought from without the city-limits. On the other hand, they required us to make use of the four specimens during six additional days of the Tabernacles; and to blow the *Shophar* on the second day of the seventh month, neither of which is Scriptural, and while performing the ceremonies to say, "Blessed art thou, O Lord! who has commanded us to do so." This shows clearly that the rabbis both added to and diminished from the word of God, though we are repeatedly warned against doing so.

Besides the instances now given of *Shophar* and *Lulab*, which are Scriptural ordinances, and extended by the rabbis upon their own authority to a time not prescribed in the

Law, there are other observances of which not a word nor the slightest intimation appears in the Mosaic books, such as the washing of hands in the morning and before meals, the lighting of the Sabbath-lamp, and the Hannucah lamp, the reading of the Hallel, and several others, with which they have connected a blessing in which we are to say that God commanded us to do these things, which, however, is quite contrary to truth.

But the rabbis have gone still further in the assumption of their authority, solemnly declaring that he who denies the truth of their interpretation of Scripture and the oral law generally, is equal to one who denies the truth of divine revelation, and shall be excluded from enjoying the rewards and blessings of eternal life. Thus even the enlightened Maimonides, in his work *Yad Hachasacah*, declares, "These are they who have no part in the world to come, but are cut off and perish, and are condemned on account of the greatness of their wickedness and sin forever and ever—the heretics, and the deniers of the law," and goes on to specify among the latter, "he who denies the interpretation of the law, that is, the oral law."* This is indeed the highest degree of arrogance which any religious expounders ever dared to assume, to say, if you do not accept our interpretations, you are everlastingly condemned.

The idea that the rabbinical decisions rest upon divine authority, in consequence of a chain of traditions brought down to us from the time of Moses, is long since exploded and a hundred times disproved. During the whole period of the first Temple, there were no rabbis nor traditions. The system originated about the time of the Maccabees. To establish the claim of divine authority, or even of divine

---

* We are strongly inclined to believe that the author held different views when, later, he wrote the Moreh Nebuchim.

sanction, for the Talmud and its collateral productions, two things would be essentially necessary. In the first place, a perfect unanimity of opinion among the rabbis, both with regard to the exposition of the written laws, and on the oral laws said to have descended traditionally from the divine Author; and second, a perfect agreement between these and the plain words of Scripture would be required. But instead of agreement, there is great diversity of opinion in the interpretation of the Law, and some of the oral laws are in downright contradiction with the written, as we have shown.

We are quite willing to give the rabbis all the credit due to their honesty of purpose, and readily admit that their motives were pure, and that they labored with the best intention of upholding the sacredness of our religion, and render it invulnerable by even the smallest violation. But zeal will often rise to enthusiasm and to fanaticism, and our rabbinical teachers have exhibited these qualities in a very high degree. While admitting their honesty of purpose, it must at the same time be borne in mind that the sphere of their thoughts and views was very narrowly limited. The state of almost total exclusion in which they lived, and preferred to live, rather than mix with those who entertained different views, and the cruel oppression and hatred which they suffered on the part of those under whose dominion they lived, contributed largely to those false opinions being rooted deeper and deeper into their minds, until they became settled maxims and principles not to be doubted. This is about the best apology we can find for men of intelligence, of learning, and of good motives, establishing rules and principles which must appear inconsistent and repugnant to reason and common sense, and overloading us with a multitude of observances preposterous, puerile, and often ridiculous.

As to ourselves, Jews of the present age, the words of the law, as expounded by our modern teachers, are all-sufficient for our moral and religious edification; we need no "hedges to the law," hedges, too, so closely twisted and so thorny as to place the law itself beyond one's reach. Our great aim is to preserve the Scriptures in their purity, to penetrate into the spirit of our law and our religion, and though remaining a distinct tribe among the nations of the earth, to proceed on the path of progression with the rest of the world, to advance with their advancement, and improve with their improvement.